Britain's Railways in Wartime

The Nation's Lifeline

LOCOS

BRING THEM THE GOODS

MINISTRY OF SUPPLY

Britain's Railways in Wartime

The Nation's Lifeline

Anthony Lambert

Published by Historic England, The Engine House, Fire Fly Avenue, Swindon SN2 2EH
www.HistoricEngland.org.uk

Historic England is a Government service championing England's heritage and giving
expert, constructive advice.

First published 2018

ISBN 978 1 84802 482 3

British Library Cataloguing in Publication data
A CIP catalogue record for this book is available from the British Library.

Brought to publication by Jess Ward, Publishing, Historic England.

Typeset in Georgia Pro Light 9/11pt
Edited by Merle Read
Picture research by Susannah Stone
Proof read by Kim Bishop
Indexed by Osprey Indexing
Page layout by Pauline Hull Design
Printed in Czech Republic via Akcent Media Limited.

Frontispiece
Some wartime posters lacked artistic merit, but the message is clear: the Eighth Army in
North Africa is able to function thanks to railway logistics.

Pxii
A tank leaves a Midlands factory bound for the Eastern Front, in October 1941.

Contents

Dedication   vi

Foreword   vii

Acknowledgements   viii

Introduction   ix

Abbreviations   xi

1   Before the First World War   1

2   First World War home front   7

3   First World War theatres   77

4   Second World War home front   99

5   Second World War theatres   165

6   In memoriam   170

Memorial gazetteer   187

Notes   196

Picture credits   202

Bibliography   203

Index   205

Dedication

This book is dedicated to the Rt Hon Sir William McAlpine Bt 1936–2018.

Sir William chaired the Railway Heritage Trust from its formation in 1985 until his death early in 2018. He chaired the board meeting when this book was first discussed, and took a great interest in its progress and development. Sadly he is not able to see the finished work, of which he would have been very proud.

Foreword

The railway has long been the forgotten weapon of war. It was first deployed by Bismarck against Austria and France, when the ability to move men and matériel at speed was crucial in set-piece battles such as Sadowa and Sedan. The Great War was the first that required the mobilisation of entire states, and thus of their transport systems. What horses had long supplied for Europe's battles, was now provided by steam engines on rails.

The scale of operation was transformed. Railways required new skills and commitments. The energy required near the front was replicated as national economies had to be converted to a war footing. The bombing of civilian areas further increased the importance of the railways, as rail links were vital arteries for supplies across the country. In Britain the crucial role of railways was recognised in both world wars by the necessity of grouping private companies under one national command.

Railways generated a strong esprit de corps, which was reflected in the prominence given to the memorials erected to those who died in their service. Fine memorials survive at Paddington, Waterloo, Liverpool Street, Manchester Victoria and at many other stations, some such as Jagger's at Paddington are great works of public art. They all merit our attention and care.

Anthony Lambert's book reviews the whole range of railway activities in times of war, and looks particularly at the role of the railwaymen and, increasingly, women who were involved in supporting the war effort, both at home and abroad.

Simon Jenkins

Acknowledgements

The author would like to thank the following for their kind help and for sharing their knowledge: Simon Colbeck, Michael Dunn, Lord Faulkner, Bob Meanley, David Morgan, David Postle, Ted Talbot, David Thompson, Steve Tull, Michael Whitehouse, Michael Williams and Michael Wrottesley.

The author is grateful to Virgin Trains East Coast (now LNER) for assistance with travel facilities and to the staff at the London Library, The National Archives, the National Railway Museum and the University of Warwick for their help in accessing books and records.

Finally, many thanks to Susannah Stone, who has done a marvellous job of finding suitable illustrations, and to Andy Savage of the Railway Heritage Trust, who has been a constant source of invaluable help, especially with the location and care of war memorials. The Railway Heritage Trust has sponsored the book, and any royalties arising to the Railway Heritage Trust will be used to fund the restoration of the recently discovered Lancashire & Yorkshire Railway Carriage & Wagon department memorial.

Introduction

In the long and absorbing history of Britain's railways and the men and women who have worked on them, the most challenging years were those of the two world wars. Quite simply, neither could have been won without the railways. There was no question of relying on any other mode of transport than the railways in the First World War; and it is no exaggeration to say that a major factor behind eventual victory in the Second was that the railway network and its capacity had not been reduced since 1918. Though road transport had become common by 1939, reliance on it would have been both impossible and fatal, given the rationing of fuel through shortages. As General Ludendorff concluded in 1918: 'There comes a time when locomotives are more important than guns.'[1]

Yet the contribution of the railways has often been overlooked in books about the wars. One of the most analytical and engaging books devoted to the later conflict compares the combatants' productive capacity and its contribution to the outcome, but makes not a single mention of the transport requirements for war industries, and the only reference to the supply of their output to battle zones is the astonishing fact that Hitler's invasion force of Russia in June 1941 comprised 3,350 tanks but still relied on 650,000 horses.[2]

As the London & North Eastern Railway's official historian of its role in the Second World War put it, 'everything that was grown, made or mined, had to be carried, and soldiers, sailors, airmen, and civilians also had to be carried. This was largely the task of the railways.'[3]

This book is not about the way railways became part of the strategy or tactics of military campaigns; that has been ably covered by others.[4] Rather it pays tribute to the way the railways and railway men and women responded to the demand that they do more with fewer resources, which, in the case of the Second World War, were being depleted by aerial attack. The book inevitably includes many statistics as well as dates, but it is impossible to comprehend the magnitude of the railways' contribution to the wars without them. The focus is largely on the railways of Britain, but sketches of the overseas theatres – inevitably much less well documented – give some idea of the work of railway construction and operating companies, which were largely made up of railwaymen.

The voices of the railway men and women who endured the greatest stresses imposed on them have largely fallen silent, with few personal reminiscences of their day-to-day experiences and feelings. It therefore requires an imaginative response to the story of what they were called upon to do – to cope with the extraordinary change in the character and volume of passenger and goods traffic, to endure the dangerously long hours, to overcome fear. Small wayside stations, which for decades had slumbered in a rural idyll of dispatching seasonal agricultural traffic and receiving a dozen wagonloads a week of general merchandise, could be transformed into a frenzy of activity by the location of a camp or supply depot on its doorstep. Disruption through bomb damage could turn the shift of locomotive crew or guard into an indefinite wait for relief – abandoning one's train was unthinkable.

The railways in both conflicts embraced a far larger number of occupations than we now associate with them, because the railways were then among the largest public companies in the world. Besides their primary function, they operated hotels, docks, ships, warehouses, bus services, delivery services, farms, even aircraft. During the First World War, Britain's railways were operated by about 120 railway companies, ranging in size from the London & North Western Railway – once the largest joint-stock company in the world – to the 2½-mile Easingwold Railway. The operating efficiencies of unified management during the First World War were a major reason for the Railways Act of 1921, creating the 'Big Four' companies – the Great Western, London Midland & Scottish, London & North Eastern and Southern railways – which owned the railways through the Second World War. By 1939 London's Underground railways, trams and buses within a 30-mile radius were under the control of the London Passenger Transport Board, which had been set up in 1933.

Railway company names have usually been abbreviated after the full name is first given, except where companies share the same abbreviation (Caledonian/ Cambrian, Mersey/Metropolitan/Midland or Festiniog/Furness). Railway, station and place/county names have been rendered as they were at the time; for example, Portmadoc during both world wars, Poperinghe not Poperinge, Festiniog rather than Ffestiniog, and so on. By tradition, 'up' lines are those taken by trains to London, irrespective of the compass, while 'down' lines take trains away from London; hence 'down' trains on the West Coast main line are, counter-intuitively, heading north. For the most part no attempt has been made to provide contemporary values to figures of wages, nor to decimalise shillings and pence, shown as 6s (or 6/- if that is how it is given in a quote) and 3d. Measurements have been given in whatever form was current at the time and place. Track gauges have been given in both imperial and metric because of their international character and usage. The principal primary sources have been those in The National Archives at Kew.

Abbreviations

AGM	annual general meeting	LT	London Transport
ALCO	American Locomotive Company	LYR	Lancashire & Yorkshire Railway
ARP	air-raid precautions	M&GNJR	Midland & Great Northern Joint Railway
ASLEF	Associated Society of Locomotive Engineers and Firemen	MSWJR	Midland & South Western Junction Railway
BEF	British Expeditionary Force	NBR	North British Railway
CME	chief mechanical engineer	NCO	non-commissioned officer
CPR	Canadian Pacific Railway	NER	North Eastern Railway
DSO	Distinguished Service Order	NLR	North London Railway
EEF	Egyptian Expeditionary Force	NRM	National Railway Museum
GCR	Great Central Railway	NSR	North Staffordshire Railway
GER	Great Eastern Railway	NUR	National Union of Railwaymen
GNR	Great Northern Railway	POW	prisoner of war
GNSR	Great North of Scotland Railway	RCH	Railway Clearing House
GSWR	Glasgow & South Western Railway	RE	Royal Engineers
GWR	Great Western Railway	REC	Railway Executive Committee
HBR	Hull & Barnsley Railway	RHT	Railway Heritage Trust
HR	Highland Railway	ROD	Railway Operating Division
LBSCR	London Brighton & South Coast Railway	SECR	South Eastern & Chatham Railway
LMR	Longmoor Military Railway	SMJR	Stratford-upon-Avon & Midland Junction Railway
LMS	London Midland & Scottish Railway	SR	Southern Railway
LNER	London & North Eastern Railway	TNA	The National Archives (Kew)
LNWR	London & North Western Railway	UW	University of Warwick
LSWR	London & South Western Railway	WD	War Department

1 | Before the First World War

The value of railways when military force had to be used became evident from the first modern railway: as early as 1830 the Liverpool & Manchester Railway was pressed into carrying troops to the docks at Liverpool on their way to suppress trouble in Ireland. What took very much longer was for military authorities and governments to understand not only the tactical and logistical potential of railways, but also the administrative relationship that would produce the best outcomes.

The first British law requiring the railway to give preferential treatment to the Army was passed in 1842. At a House of Commons committee hearing on railways in 1844, the Quartermaster General, Sir James Willoughby Gordon, reported that 118,000 troops and 12,000 women and children had been moved by train during the preceding two years, and that a battalion of 1,000 men could now be taken from London to Manchester in 9 hours rather than marching in 17 days.[1]

Appreciation of the role railways could play in war was reflected in opinions about proposed and desirable routes of new lines. Even the Duke of Wellington – generally opposed to a development that allowed 'the lower orders to go uselessly wandering about the country'[2] – wanted a railway that paralleled the coast between Dover and Plymouth. As soon as the prospect of a national railway network became a likelihood, the Admiralty and War Department (WD) expressed concern over the handicap of a change of gauge on the way to embarkation ports such as Southampton. (The Department became the War Office in 1857, but the old name persisted for military transport services.)

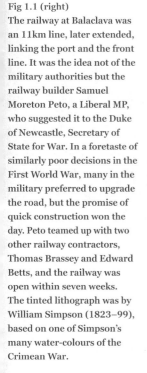

Fig 1.1 (right)
The railway at Balaclava was an 11km line, later extended, linking the port and the front line. It was the idea not of the military authorities but the railway builder Samuel Moreton Peto, a Liberal MP, who suggested it to the Duke of Newcastle, Secretary of State for War. In a foretaste of similarly poor decisions in the First World War, many in the military preferred to upgrade the road, but the promise of quick construction won the day. Peto teamed up with two other railway contractors, Thomas Brassey and Edward Betts, and the railway was open within seven weeks. The tinted lithograph was by William Simpson (1823–99), based on one of Simpson's many water-colours of the Crimean War.

With so many land borders, the Continent was even more fertile ground for creative thinking about the role railways might play when conflict arose. The first published treatise appeared in 1833 in Westphalia, though the speed with which ideas were translated into rails on the ground varied from the prescience of German states to the initial lethargic complacency of France.

Troop movements by rail to put down continental rebellions became common from the 1840s, but it was the British use of a railway in the Crimea in 1855 that would significantly influence future thinking. The line built to link Balaclava harbour with the front line before Sebastopol was intended to address a shambolic supply situation rather than ferry troops.

The French learned lessons from their successful use of railways, both logistically and tactically, in the help they gave the Italians to evict the Austrians from their country in 1859. The Austrians' destruction of track and bridges as they retreated added a new tactic to warfare and a factor for railway engineers to prepare for in war. One of the unfortunate results of military considerations was the decision by some countries to adopt a different gauge from their neighbour(s) to hamper invading forces; though this certainly worked when Germany invaded Russia in 1941, breaks of gauge have bedevilled the economics of peacetime railways.

With each major war, notably the American Civil War, the Second Schleswig War, the Austro-Prussian War and the Franco-Prussian War, efforts were made to learn from the use or misuse of railways. The Prussian Chief of

Fig 1.2
The American Civil War was the first war to provide lessons in the various ways that railways could be used to win, or lose, a war. It also revealed the devastation that artillery could cause, as demonstrated by this view of the damaged roundhouse at Atlanta, Georgia, in 1864.

Fig 1.3
Percy Girouard (1867–1932)
graduated first in his class
from the Royal Military
College of Canada at Kingston,
Ontario, and developed so
promising a reputation on
railways in Maine that he
was headhunted to run the
Woolwich Arsenal Railway in
London from 1890 to 1895.
After his work on railways
in the Sudan and South
Africa, he was made high
commissioner in Northern
Nigeria by Winston Churchill
when under-secretary of
state at the Colonial Office.
After serving as governor
of the British East Africa
Protectorate (Kenya),
Girouard became managing
director of the Elswick Works
of Armstrong Whitworth.

Staff, Helmuth von Moltke, was in the forefront of structural reorganisation to combine military and civilian minds in planning mobilisation and campaigns. His country's victory over Austria in 1866 was in part ascribed to a superior mobilisation plan and its execution, as well as more and better railways, but the supply side still left much to be desired. It was only thanks to a quick victory that near-paralysis on the railway did not lead to serious trouble.

The Franco-Prussian War of 1870–1 was fought on a much larger scale and has been called 'the first and only major railway war of nineteenth-century Europe'.[3] The swiftness of the Prussian deployment allowed von Moltke's forces to fight on French soil, whereas the use of the railways by the French military seemed to reinforce the flaws of its system. The war made clear the value of rapid movement and therefore the crucial role of the railway.

The necessity of communication and awareness of practicalities between railway and military authorities was well understood by one of the key officers in the Boer War (1899–1902), Lieutenant Eduoard Percy Cranwill Girouard. His training combined service on the Canadian Pacific Railway (CPR) with a commission in the Royal Canadian Engineers, and his skills were demonstrated in the way he overcame daunting challenges to build the first part of the Sudan Military Railway in 1896. His organisational abilities were praised at length by Winston Churchill in his 1899 book about the Sudan campaign, *The River War*, and on the eve of the Boer War he was President of Egyptian State Railways, charged with clearing congestion at the port of Alexandria.

When the conflict erupted in South Africa in 1899, Girouard was made Director of Military Railways and created a liaison structure that protected the railway from arbitrary and ill-conceived demands from military commanders. Lord Kitchener described Girouard as his 'principal adviser in all the numerous and intricate questions pertaining to railway administration in South Africa'.[4]

For Britain, the Boer War was something of a dress rehearsal for the First World War. The railways retained control of operations, working with the War Office and Admiralty, and successfully embarked 528,000 troops with their horses and equipment through Southampton. The smoothness with which the London & South Western Railway (LSWR) made possible the dispatch of 5,000 men in a day owed much to the railways' experience of moving troops on manoeuvres at summer camp, as well as huge numbers of civilians during wakes weeks and to sporting events and exhibitions.

The only possible conclusion of any study of 19th-century conflicts made on the eve of the First World War was that what we would now term 'logistics' could win or lose a war. The architect of the 1905–6 eponymous plan for the invasion of France, Alfred, Graf von Schlieffen, wrote:

> The railways have become an instrument of war without which the great modern armies are not able to be assembled or moved forwards. Today you no longer ask how many battalions your enemy has but how many railway lines: you no longer compare only the valour and armaments of opposing forces, but the capacity for action of their railways. Since 1866, and especially since 1870, we have entered through this a new phase in the conduct of war.[5]

This would prove even more true in that conflict, involving the movement of men and matériel on a previously unimaginable scale.

Embarking on a perilous journey. (armoured train destroyed at Chieveley.) Horace W Nicholls.

Fig 1.4
The caption records that this armoured train was destroyed at Chieveley, so it is almost certain to have included Winston Churchill, who was aboard the train derailed at Chieveley on 15 November 1899 and captured by the Boers. The troops on that day entrained at Estcourt. The photograph was taken by Horace W Nicholls, who was working for the London-based periodical *South Africa*, having served his apprenticeship under his photographer father in the Isle of Wight and Huddersfield. He went on to become the first chief photographer of the Imperial War Museum.

Legislative and volunteer preparations in Britain

Volunteers formed a substantial part of the armed forces throughout the Victorian and Edwardian period. In 1861, a decade before the Cardwell reforms placed the militia and reserves under the War Office, volunteers numbered 134,000 riflemen in 200 battalions, 24,000 artillery gunners and 2,900 engineers.[6] The last category attracted growing numbers of railwaymen as the contribution railways could make in time of war became better understood.

There have been military engineers in Britain since William the Conqueror brought some over to construct castles, the most able becoming the King's Engineer. This title was not necessarily held by one person until Charles II created that of Chief Engineer of England with Sir Charles Lloyd in the post. Technological advances of the early 18th century led to the formation in 1716 of a Corps of Engineers, which was granted the Royal prefix before the century was out.

A volunteer railway corps was suggested in 1860 at the Institution of Civil Engineers by its secretary, Charles Manby.[7] Five years later the Engineer and Railway Volunteer Staff Corps was formed by the Institution to provide technical advice to the Royal Engineers (RE). It was made up of officer ranks only, with 30 lieutenant colonels and 28 majors drawn from dock and civil engineers, as well as railway managers and engineers. Its principal objective was to facilitate 'the combined action among all the railways when the country is in danger', and one of the main duties was 'the preparation, during peace, of schemes for drawing troops from given distant parts and for concentrating them within given areas in the shortest possible time'.[8] It created the concept of standard routes and point-to-point timings across a Britain divided into nine sectors based on military commands. Though it was anticipated that the Government would issue instructions and the railways would continue to manage operations, full state control was authorised by the Regulation of the Forces Act 1871. Section 16 of the Act stated:

> When Her Majesty, by order in Council, declares that an emergency has arisen in which it is expedient for the public service that Her Majesty's Government should have control over the railroads of the United Kingdom, or any of them, the Secretary of State may, by warrant under his hand, empower any person or persons named in such warrant to take possession in the name or on behalf of Her Majesty of any railroad in the United Kingdom ... and the directors, officers, and servants of any such railroad shall obey the direction of the Secretary of State as to the user of such railroad ... for Her Majesty's service.[9]

Its ham-fisted wording led to protest from railway companies until they were reassured that it implied superintendence rather than operation or even confiscation. The National Defence Act of 1888 was seen as another can of worms in its prescription that naval and military requirements should take precedence over every other form of traffic on the railways whenever an order for the embodiment of the militia was in force. It did not say how this was to be done.

An early example of battalions created by a single railway company was the 2nd Cheshire Engineers (Railway) Volunteers. This battalion was formed in January 1887 and recruited entirely from London & North Western Railway (LNWR) employees – firemen, cleaners, boilermakers and riveters, fitters, smiths, platelayers, shunters and pointsmen. It comprised six companies of 100 men each, of whom 245 enlisted in the RE and were placed in the First Class Army Reserve for six years, forming the Royal Engineer Railway reserve. During the Boer War, 285 officers and men saw service at the front. Under Lord Haldane's reforms, the Volunteers and Yeomanry were combined into a Territorial Force in 1908, and the battalion became part of the Cheshire Royal Engineers (Railway Battalion).

Fortunately no one took up the suggestion made by the LNWR's general manager, Sir George Findlay, at a lecture given to the School of Military Engineering at Chatham and incorporated in his 1889 book on railway management,[10] that the Corps should take over control and operation of the railways in time of war. Senior railway officials would don uniform and become civil servants. (When Sir Sam Fay, general manager of the Great Central Railway [GCR], became director of movements at the War Office in 1917, with the rank of general, he refused to wear uniform.)

In 1896 an Army (later War, following Admiralty objections) Railway Council was created by the Secretary of State for War composed of six railway managers and two members of the Engineer and Railway Volunteer Staff Corps.

The success of the arrangements for sending troops to South Africa was put down to the independence and authority of the railway transport officer based at Southampton. His decisions could not be overturned even by a general. In contrast, the Boer War revealed Britain's ill-preparedness for overseas conflict, when men with railway experience had to be extracted from fighting units to operate the railways. Even worse was the contrast between Britain and its allies in the Chinese Boxer uprising in 1900: a puny British force of 40 men

Fig 1.5
Sir Herbert Ashcombe
Walker (1868–1949) became
one of Britain's most brilliant
railway managers, rising
from his first position as
a clerk on the LNWR at
Euston to be the longest-
serving general manager of
the Southern Railway. He
chaired the REC throughout
the First World War.

under a subaltern contrasted with an entire railway battalion with appropriate equipment fielded by both Germany and Russia. To augment the total full-time British railway units of 200 men and another 345 railwaymen in a Special Railway Reserve, in 1905 the War Office proposed establishing a Railway Corps from serving railwaymen who would be available for overseas service, but no agreement could be reached over the financial terms.

Though the War Railway Council met only four times in its 16 years, it coordinated the production of mobilisation timetables, collated by the LNWR in 1904, reflecting its ownership of the prime Anglo-Scottish route. The timetables were so radically revised by the War Office in 1912–13 that the LNWR had to create a special department to cope with its 'secretarial' responsibilities. At the end of July 1914, for example, the LNWR sent the railway's plans under private cover to each of its district superintendents, and working sheets and timetables were prepared for issue the moment the order to mobilise was given.[11]

In 1912 the Railway Executive Committee (REC) was formed in the wake of the Agadir crisis of 1911 which heightened tension and had the effect of making the defence of France against Germany a tenet of British foreign policy. The REC superseded the War Railway Council. Herbert Walker became REC chairman in 1914 and it operated from a few rooms at 35 Parliament Street, Westminster, with about 18 clerks. The REC was given 21 months to be in a position to implement the provisions of the Regulation of the Forces Act and take over control of the railways. It succeeded by the skin of its teeth, the last telephone connections being completed a week before war was declared.

Manoeuvres

Moving large quantities of men, horses and guns was a familiar task for many railways which served regimental headquarters and training grounds. Foremost among them was the LSWR, which had carried significant military traffic to the Aldershot area since the 1870s. For manoeuvres in September 1910 it had transported 25,080 troops, 6,722 horses and 1,174 guns within 48 hours at a time of heavy holiday traffic. Army camps were generally connected to the railway. For example, in 1905 the 4¼-mile Bordon Light Railway was built from a junction at Bentley in Hampshire to serve the camp laid out in 1899 at Bordon with accommodation for 5,000 men. A connection was made there with Woolmer Instructional Military Railway – the Longmoor Military Railway (LMR) from 1935 (*see* p 50).[12]

During the summer months, many railways had been involved in the movement of Territorial Army units to training camps. The War Office had chosen the Aberystwyth area as the venue for so many of them that the Cambrian had had to double single-line sections and install additional passing loops. On a single Sunday in 1912, 4 August, Bow Street station handled 45 specials carrying 13,000 Territorials and 800 horses.

Though the outbreak of the First World War was sparked by a wholly unforeseeable single shot, the railways were not ill-prepared.

2 | First World War home front

At midnight on 4 August 1914 a letter was sent from the War Office to railway companies stating that the King had signed an Order in Council under the provisions of the Regulation of the Forces Act of 1871 and that the railways had been taken over by the Government under that Act. Excluded were 46 minor railways with a combined mileage of 499. Railway companies should 'carry on as usual' subject to instructions from the REC, of which the President of the Board of Trade was titular chairman.

Control of the railways was vested in the REC, which comprised the general managers of initially 10 companies under the nominal chairmanship of the President of the Board of Trade, but effectively under Herbert Walker:

Caledonian Railway Donald A Matheson

Great Central Railway Sir Sam Fay

Great Northern Railway Charles Dent

Great Western Railway Frank Potter

Lancashire & Yorkshire Railway John A F Aspinall (knighted 1917)

London & North Western Railway Sir Robert Turnbull

London & South Western Railway Herbert Walker (knighted 1915)

Midland Railway Sir Guy Granet

North Eastern Railway Sir Alexander Butterworth

South Eastern & Chatham Railway Francis H Dent

As Walker succinctly put it, 'The control of the railways has been taken over by the Government for the purpose of ensuring that the railways, locomotives, rolling stock and staff shall be used as one complete unit in the best interests of the State for the movement of troops, stores and food supplies.'[1] The REC would confine its functions 'to co-ordinating the work of the railways, and to dealing with those general problems which were common to all the systems and which, even in peace times, would have been solved by conference amongst railway directors and managers.'[2]

There was no question of changing the management structure, the statement being accepted of the General Manager of the LSWR, Sir Charles Owen, when he said before the war that the railways would be able to meet the demands of the nation in the event of war, providing 'the arrangements are left in the hands of the railway officers concerned'.[3]

The wisdom of this was later endorsed by the 1919 Select Committee on Transport on the working of the railways under war conditions:

The changes which have been introduced and the high efficiency which has been witnessed in the working of the traffic by the railways during the war, have been due far more to a patriotic determination on the part of all concerned to do their utmost to assist the country in the time of national emergency, regardless of corporate or personal interests, than to the direct imposition by the Government of its will upon the railway companies.[4]

The REC operated from a London office of the LNWR at 35 Parliament Street, though the London offices of the Midland and Lancashire & Yorkshire railways and the Railway Clearing House (RCH) also did much work. On 6 August 1914 it was agreed that the REC would meet every day at 10 am, 2 pm, 6 pm and 9.15 pm, when all questions of policy should be discussed, and 'The Chairman was further authorised to call Meetings on emergency matters at any hour of the day or night.' This punishing schedule appears to have been moderated to a daily or even weekly meeting except during crises. The REC was supplemented by a Communications Board presided over by the Quartermaster General of the Forces and formed by representatives of various state departments and members of the REC.[5]

The financial terms for compensating the railways were discussed in August:

To ascertain the compensation payable the aggregate net receipts of all the railways taken over during the period for which they are taken over shall be compared with a similar aggregate for the corresponding period of the previous year. The ascertained deficiency shall be the amount of compensation due. Provided that if the aggregate net receipts for the first half of the year 1914 are less than the aggregate net receipts for the first half of the year 1913, the ascertained deficiency shall be reduced in the like proportion. Any question as to the amount of the deficiency, in default of agreement, [will] be determined by the Railway and Canal Commission.[6]

Compensation would be paid for abnormal wear and tear and for deferred maintenance.

Probably the first war-related trains were those conveying from London the ambassadors of enemy nations to the ports of embarkation. The British Government was anxious they should receive the utmost courtesy, in contrast to the dispatch of the British and French ambassadors from Berlin; a crowd broke the windows of the British Embassy, eliciting an apology from the Kaiser, but the French ambassador was offered no facilities for his return. The German ambassador to Britain, his wife and suite, and some German subjects left a closed-off Platform 9 at Liverpool Street at 8.20 am on 6 August for Parkeston Quay. A restaurant car was provided for breakfast on their way to board a Great Eastern Railway (GER) ship, *St Petersburg*, which returned with Sir Edward Goschen, the British ambassador to Germany.

The Austrian ambassador, Count Mensdorff, and many eminent Austrians left on 16 August, departing from Paddington at midnight to travel to Falmouth in a train of 12 coaches en route to Genoa, hauled by Star class 4-6-0 *Princess Mary*, seen off by the GWR's Superintendent of the Line, Charles Aldington. The Turkish ambassador and his suite left Charing Cross on 5 November in special cars attached to the Folkestone boat express.[7]

Mobilising the British Expeditionary Force

Years before the war, the Aberystwyth area had been chosen by the War Office as the most suitable for the large summer Territorial Army camps; a halt for a Territorial camp was even opened on the narrow-gauge Vale of Rheidol Railway at Lovegrove in 1910, and the Cambrian Railways had to carry out many improvements to cope with the traffic. New passing loops were installed and single-line sections doubled.

When war was declared, Territorial units were in summer camp, so the first task was to return them to their bases. The LNWR ran 76 trains for units in North Wales, and the Cambrian was so hard-pressed that every coach on the railway, even those in works but serviceable, was deployed. The 16th Brigade of 2,000 men was encamped with 200 tons of equipment at Llanidloes, while further south at Rhayader was an artillery camp of 500 men, guns and horses. Both had to be disbanded and the units transferred to the east coast and Plymouth respectively. A few days later two Welsh Territorial Army units in camp at Aberystwyth and Portmadoc had to be returned by the Cambrian in 26 special trains carrying the 5,000 and 4,000 men (respectively) to their home stations.

The railways were justly proud of the speed and efficiency with which the British Expeditionary Force (BEF) was dispatched to France through

Fig 2.1
Troops arriving at the LNWR side of Birmingham New Street station, at the west end of Queens Drive. The tram from/for Kings Heath is standing in Hill Street.

Southampton, and all kept precise records of what they moved, though many of the trains ran over the lines of at least two companies. Because the LSWR served both Southampton and 176 camps, many of them around Aldershot and Salisbury Plain, it was at the forefront of these moves and had become known as the military line even before the war.

Embarkation of the leading five divisions of the BEF commenced on 10 August 1914. Between 9 and 26 August, the railways operated 689 special trains to transport 126,496 troops, 354 guns, 42,294 horses, 6,151 vehicles and 2,007 bicycles.[8] The trains averaged 30 vehicles for the transport of complete units: 3–4 bogie coaches, 10–15 horseboxes (cattle and even open wagons were used) and 15–20 flat, open or miscellaneous wagons for guns, stores, camp equipment and ammunition. Details have survived of the moves that month of the Central Field Force:

> 13th: 16 trains of Cavalry from Warwick to Bury St Edmunds via Rugby and Peterborough.

> 14th: 16 trains of Cavalry from Winchester Cheese Hill station to Colchester via Newbury and Acton.

> 15th: 16 trains of Cavalry from Reading to Bury St Edmunds via Acton and Victoria Park. 32 trains for the North Midland Division from Burton to Luton and 47 trains from Derby to Luton.

> 16th: For the Highland Mounted Brigade 16 trains of cavalry, 13 from Blairgowrie and 3 from Beauly (8am, 10am and noon) to Huntingdon. For the Highland Infantry Division 87 trains to Bedford. 2 from Auchterarder via Carlisle and the Midland, 12 from Stirling via Carlisle and the Midland, 15 from Inverness via the Great North of Scotland Railway [GNSR] and East Coast to be handed over to the Midland at Hitchin, and 58 from Perth, to be divided between the Caledonian Railway and North British Railway [NBR] as between Perth and Carlisle where all handed over to the Midland. 78 trains for the South Midland Infantry Division from Swindon to Leighton and Bletchley via Oxford. [70 troop trains passed through Edinburgh Waverley on the 16th.]

> 17th: 16 trains of Cavalry from Grantham to Bishop's Stortford via Peterborough.

> Railway Transport Officers being sent to Perth, Derby and Swindon. Elsewhere local Railway Officials to contact Commanding Officers.[9]

Some idea of the scale of additional workings is given by the number of loaded trains (so excluding empty-stock workings) operated by the LNWR between 4 August and 30 September 1914: 1,465 naval and military trains; 751 trains of government stores; 165 trains of coal for the Admiralty; and 84 miscellaneous, such as refugee and ambulance trains. These trains carried 361,798 officers and men, 63,551 horses and 8,169 guns and transport vehicles. The pressure on paths was so great that the normal timetable had to be suspended.[10] In one 14-hour period, Southampton handled 73 trains, arriving at 12-minute intervals. The LSWR acted as Secretary Company for all movements and organised the timetable by giving a required arrival time at the handover point on its system. Each of the companies involved would work back in the same way, so a train from York would have handover times calculated at Basingstoke (GWR to LSWR), Banbury (GCR to GWR) and Mexborough (NER to GCR).

Normally sleepy railways such as the Midland & South Western Junction Railway (MSWJR) became feverishly busy because of the various military sites it served. Between 5 August and 31 December 1914 it operated 566 special troop trains, plus 53 special ambulance trains, and delivered 10,000 trucks of government stores to the ordnance depot at Tidworth, as well as supplying the hutments at Ludgershall and Chiseldon from which station a 2-mile connection was built to new cavalry barracks at Draycott.[11] Even at large stations, additional resources were needed; extra staff were needed at Rhyl station to cope with supplies required for the nearby camp at Kinmel Park, which had accommodation for 25,000 men.

The LSWR and GWR transported the first Canadian troops who arrived at Plymouth on 14 October 1914, requiring 92 special trains to ferry them to camps on Salisbury Plain. By 31 January 1915 the GWR had moved a total of 32,835 officers, 926,260 men, 87,825 horses, and 669 guns and limbers.[12] Troop trains were standardised as far as possible: each company formed trains to carry 20 officers and 620 men. When nurses required transport in sufficient numbers to warrant a whole train, they were made up of first-class lavatory or corridor coaches. A troop train was involved in the worst railway disaster on Britain's railways, at Quintinshill near Gretna Green on 22 May 1915, though its causes cannot be attributed to the war. Despite arriving on a local passenger train which was shunted to allow an express to overtake it, the relieving signalman forgot all about it and accepted a southbound troop train, which resulted in a head-on collision. A northbound sleeping-car express ploughed into the wreckage, adding to the conflagration induced by escaping gas from the troop train's lighting system. Officially the death toll was 227, of whom 215 were soldiers, 9 passengers and 3 railway employees, though the Army later reduced its total by 1.

The early months were but the start of four years of troop movements to the Continent and to hospitals, on exercises and on leave, all of which required liaison between the forces and the railways and unprecedented cooperation between the companies. This is illustrated by the way locomotives and trains operated across company borders, exemplified by a few minutes at the LSWR's Swaythling station near Southampton in April 1915, when an observer recorded two complete GER trains, a GWR 4-4-0 on a LNWR train and a SECR L class 4-4-0 No. 772.

It was common for the military to send letters of appreciation to the railways, if rather stiffly expressed. In May 1916 Lieutenant Colonel Malcolm of 60th (London) Division thanked the GWR for moving the Division in 88 special trains from Warminster to Codford en route to France: 'The work entailed upon the Railway Staffs at week-ends and other times has, the General Officer Commanding is aware, been at times difficult, but he is glad to feel that the result has been such as reflects credit both upon the Officers of the Railway Company, the Railway Employees and the Troops.'[13]

Sometimes unfamiliarity with railway travel and practice produced a tragedy. On 24 September 1917 a contingent of New Zealand troops arrived at Plymouth Millbay and boarded a LSWR special train for Bulford Camp near

Salisbury. The men had been told that a meal would be provided at the first stop, but when the train halted for signals at Bere Ferrers, many of them jumped out and 10 were run down and killed by the 2.12 pm Exeter–Plymouth.[14]

Despite the exceptional activity in the early days of the war, it was expected that normal traffic would decline to such an extent that on 15 August 1914 the REC discussed 'whether the Companies anticipated there would be any difficulty in keeping their men fully occupied'. By that day the number of men called up as Reservists or Territorials or who had volunteered was already about 27,600. Sharing the expectation that there would be a significant fall in traffic, the Government had expressed the wish 'that no large body of regular men should be dispensed with prior to August 15th' – in other words, made redundant. It was hoped this would not be necessary, but the REC laid down some principles for the companies which must be adopted: the number of casuals should be severely limited; if men in locomotive, carriage and wagon shops had insufficient work for want of materials or because locomotives and stock could not be released for repairs, they should be put on short time to share the work; companies would be open to take necessary steps if there was insufficient work for 'men engaged in the manipulation of traffic', but it was undesirable that they should be dismissed.[15] Two days later the REC received a deputation from the National Union of Railwaymen (NUR) to discuss possible redundancies, and the NUR was invited to set out its views.

There had been vague discussion about curtailing unnecessary services, especially those put on for summer holiday traffic, but the first instruction to companies to discontinue a type of traffic came on 18 August, when the carriage of homing and racing pigeons was stopped at the written suggestion of the Chief Constable of East Suffolk.[16] The same day the Hull & Barnsley Railway (HBR) helpfully reported that it had found full work for its men by utilising them for patrolling and watching vulnerable points on the railway, but three days later the War Office decided that the number of men protecting and watching vulnerable locations could be reduced, and a list of those that should still be protected would be drawn up.[17]

By September the NUR had become concerned about the continuity of employment. Men at some companies – GNR, LYR, HBR and NBR – had agreed provisionally to a suspension of the guaranteed week should it be necessary to avoid dismissals. The NUR argued that if the Government had guaranteed net receipts, it should also guarantee wages and proposed that it be assured that no suspension of the guaranteed week would take place without a further meeting of the Railway Conciliation Board (see p 55). The East & West Yorkshire Union Railway had broken this agreement in September by booking off three signalmen, two shunters and three guards, and officials and clerks who 'assisted in the working of the trains'.

At the time the BEF was being sent across the Channel, a reverse movement posed another challenge for the ports. Over 75,000 refugees arrived at Dover and Folkestone between August 1914 and May 1915, most of whom were taken by train to London and other cities. In just one day, 15 October 1914, the SECR dispatched 4,144 refugees in eight trains, five for London and one each to Liverpool, Manchester and Glasgow.[18] The exodus from Belgian cities had been so great that, for example, there were only a few hundred people left in Antwerp when the city surrendered on 9 October. Thousands of the arriving refugees were Belgian railway workers, and the SECR general manager, Francis Dent, who

Fig 2.2
Belgian refugees in a Rhyl &
Potteries Motors charabanc
being welcomed at Rhyl
station on 6 October 1914.
It is estimated that roughly
250,000 Belgians were
refugees in Britain, and a
great effort was made at a
local level to find them
homes. In November 1914,
for instance, a group of
Willesden railwaymen and
their wives obtained
permission to use the old
police station at Harlesden
to house refugees and even
found a Belgian priest to
provide for their spiritual
needs. Over 90 per cent of
Belgian refugees had returned
home within a year of the
armistice.

chaired the Belgian Railways Refugees Sub-committee, tried to find employment
for them. About 750 were taken on by the railways as fitters, platelayers and
loaders, while many others were found work in munitions factories. A house
bought by the GWR in Eastbourne Terrace, Paddington, was suggested as
accommodation for some of them,[19] while 43 families were accommodated in
railway hotels, some for up to four years. By the end of the war, over 120,000
refugees had come through Folkestone alone.

The early months of the war were a portent of things to come in the
way that service quality declined. At a meeting of the REC Committee of
Superintendents on 18 December 1914, blame for delays and congestion
was directed at the number of special trains, closure of certain sections of line
for the transportation of troops, shortage of cartage because of government
impressments of horses and vehicles, shortage of staff due to enlistment, transfer
to rail of previously seaborne traffic, darkening of depots and bad weather.[20]

Nonetheless the first test of the railways was passed with flying colours,
as attested by Lord Kitchener in *The Times*: 'The railway companies in the
all-important matter of railway transport facilities have more than justified the
complete confidence reposed in them by the War Office, all grades of railway
services having laboured with untiring energy and patience.'[21]

Protecting the railway and home defence

There was an almost febrile anxiety at the beginning of the war about the
likelihood of sabotage or spies on the railway, and even invasion. The idea that
invasion was part of German strategy was never dispelled; even in July 1916,
when Captain Fryatt was shot as a *franc-tireur* (*see* p 65), there was discussion
as to whether the driver and fireman of the armoured trains patrolling the coast
should be in uniform to avoid Fryatt's fate in the event of invasion.

Fig 2.3
An obviously posed photo-
graph that suggests a level
of protection which was
short-lived. The location is
the south-eastern portal of
Strood Tunnel in Kent, and
its rather curious profile is
explained by its having been
a canal tunnel until the SER
bought it in 1846 and laid
two lines through it.

The Army Council in August 1914 identified various lines that should
be protected, such as Immingham–Barnetby (Admiralty coal) and Salisbury
Plain–Southampton, and certain structures close to a possible invasion area were
guarded; close to Norwich in vulnerable East Anglia the River Wensum Swing
Bridge and the viaducts at Flordon, Lakenham and Forncett were protected.
Track workers were often assigned to these duties, and the NUR's *The Railway
Review* records Dorking gangers saying they 'would be glad to receive help owing
to their men being taken away for watching bridges and tunnels', and that gang
men in the Penrith district were guarding bridges for 96 hours a week.[22]

GWR platelayers were assigned to the protection of vulnerable bridges, and
military guards were posted to protect the Severn, Bincombe and Dorchester
tunnels and the Saltash Bridge. Some of the most heavily guarded lines were
those in the Highlands. Guards protected 37 Highland Railway (HR) bridges
and tunnels in 1915, the number being reduced to 23 the following year.

Early arrangements were rather ad hoc, with many points being protected
by such locally organised bodies as cadet corps and boy scouts. The REC
recommended that such protection should be discouraged, and that police, though
made aware which lines/structures were important, should not be used. Guard
duties were soon handed over to the National Reserve under Brigadier General
Edward Grove. A REC subcommittee had come up with five categories of line:

A   Lines of primary importance. To be protected throughout by troops
    controlled directly by the War Office as at present.

B   Lines of secondary importance. Only vulnerable points to be guarded,
    by National Reservists.

C   Lines which may require guarding from time to time. Unarmed
    watchmen currently guarding certain points should cease and armed
    National Reservists be employed instead.

D Lines requiring protection of certain points for Military or Naval reasons – route of coal trains. Left to Commands. Guards should be National Reservists.

E Lines with vital points whose replacement would be costly. National Reservists under REC.[23]

By November only exceptional strategic structures were being watched, though there was an invasion scare that month which generated an order for 840 trains to counter a threat to the Norfolk coast. It is unlikely that anything like that number was reached, but 177 troop trains passed over London's North & South Western Junction line.[24]

By January 1915 all the platelayers occupied in 'watching duties' on War Office scheduled routes had been withdrawn. Using men unfamiliar with railway operations had had unfortunate consequences, as Frank Potter, general manager of the GWR, reported: 'Special steps were taken to instruct the soldiers where they might stand with safety, but I regret to say that 14 men have been fatally injured by the trains, while two have been inadvertently shot by sentries.'[25] In reporting the death of two soldiers while guarding the railway at Slough and Vauxhall, *The Railway Review* said that 'this dangerous work was rendered necessary owing to a large number of alien enemies being allowed in the country'.[26] During 1915, 44 soldiers were killed and 41 injured while guarding railway lines.[27]

The GER issued identification cards 'to men whose duties require them to walk upon certain sections of the line'.[28] An instruction was issued by the REC that companies should report any tenants of arches who arouse suspicion of being 'evilly-disposed',[29] and the GNR told its employees that 'Great caution must be exercised in answering enquiries in connection with military business, particularly over the telephone.'[30] On the GWR, troops engaged in protecting the railway were housed in old carriage bodies,[31] while the LNWR also used old carriage bodies to create about 120 sentry boxes, supplementing platelayers' cabins and station waiting rooms.[32]

The need for blackout in the First World War was minimal in comparison with the Second, but an increase in bombings in 1916 prompted the LSWR to instruct that 'blinds in long distance trains should be drawn at the last stopping place before sunset, and in all other trains timed to reach their destination after sunset the blinds must be drawn at the starting point, and, as far as possible, passengers should be warned not to interfere in any way with the blinds whilst the train is running'.[33] The Defence of the Realm Act prohibited various activities, which included travelling alone in a railway carriage over the Forth Bridge.[34]

To counter a raid or full invasion, the country was divided into commands, each of which was given a 'Secretary Railway Company':

Scottish Command NBR
Northern NER
Western LNWR
Eastern and London District LNWR
Southern LSWR
Aldershot LSWR

The function of the Secretary Railway Company was 'to keep in close touch with the Headquarters of the Commands and to co-ordinate and give effect to the requirements of their Commands as regards local moves, both normal and emergency, which concern more than one company's railway system'.[35] They also acted as local agents for the REC.

Reinforcement of the commands would begin after 12 hours' notice, except for 'the reinforcement of the forces in the Scottish, Northern or Eastern Command areas with machine-gun companies from Grantham or Clipstone', which would start after 8 hours' notice. Grantham had 'Motor Machine-Gun Batteries', and road movements would be used for distances under 40 miles.

Railway arrangements for all the reinforcing schemes were either incorporated in printed schemes or issued separately, using standard routes and timings, published by the REC. For example, in the Eastern Command rolling stock was held permanently in readiness at Parkeston. Trains of five standard types with varying compositions of compartments, cattle trucks, vehicle trucks and brake vehicles would be assembled at Ipswich (two trains), Norwich (four trains) and Colchester (one train), and Norwich, Ipswich and Tonbridge each had four trains for shuttle movements from the detraining point to nearer the coast.

For the Northern Command, arrangements were planned according to the location of a 'raid'. Detraining points were:

North of the Tyne Killingworth, Newcastle and Newcastle Forth
South of the Tyne Blaydon, Low Fell and Durham
On the Tees Middlesbrough and Stockton
North of the Humber Hull Paragon and Hull Southcoates
South of the Humber/
Lincolnshire coast   Healing, Brigg, Louth and Willoughby

Supply regulating stations would receive supplies, ammunition and so on. They had a supply of ammunition based on a maximum of one day's requirement for the number of troops likely to be based there. Daily trains would run from the supply depot concerned, pick up trucks of ammunition at the supply regulating stations and continue to the railhead allocated for the formation.

The War Office would issue the executive orders to the commands once the Secretary Railway Companies had ascertained when all railway companies affected by the moves would be ready to receive or dispatch troops. To expedite information about emergency troop movements, communication circuits were improved; in East Anglia, for example, they were upgraded from single-needle to telephone.

If an area had to be evacuated, locomotives were to be entirely withdrawn from within 20 miles of the coast or rendered useless. Between the Humber and Dungeness, stock was only be to cleared from routes, sidings and stations if required for military purposes. Hospitals would also be evacuated.

Schemes to deny the enemy use of the railway were to be worked out between local commanders and the railway companies. Arrangements were made for destruction of telegraph lines, and telegraph superintendents of railway companies had lists of men willing to serve in an emergency. They would be enrolled in the Special Railway Volunteer Companies of the Volunteer Force and provided with military uniforms. Railwaymen were attached to defensive armoured trains (*see* p 53).

Supplying the fronts

An issue of the *Railway Magazine* early in the war was prescient in stating that 'it is manifest that the conduct of the war is almost as much dependent upon the efficiency and sufficiency of the railway communications as it is upon the direct war equipment'.[36] The LSWR bore the brunt of the movement of men and matériel to France because of its ownership of Southampton Docks, which had become the principal ocean passenger port in Britain thanks to completion of Ocean Dock in 1911. Through Southampton passed 20,223,954 men in 58,859 special trains and 1.5 million horses, 11,208 guns, 114,278 vehicles, 481,357 wagons of stores, 37,418 bicycles and 2,166 tanks, which were conveyed by ships (or train ferry from Southampton until Richborough was ready; *see* p 82) to Dieppe or Cherbourg. The ports of Newhaven and to a lesser extent Littlehampton helped to relieve Southampton as conduits for supplies to France.

Though the movement of servicemen in troop trains and leave specials was on a colossal scale, it was keeping them provisioned, the supply of raw materials to war factories and the movement of their products to where they were needed that occupied most of the railways' resources. Probably the greatest tonnage moved by the railways from factories was munitions, as the artillery barrage or mines became the only way to try to open up opportunities for the infantry

Fig 2.4
The LYR's Horwich Works was one of many railway workshops turned over partially to munitions manufacture. Here shell cases are being repaired before refilling; artillery shells were designed to be recycled. From June 1915 the works turned out 2,200 shells a week. The photograph was taken on 23 March 1917.

to advance against barbed-wire entanglements and trench fortifications. The Ministry of Munitions addressed the shortage and malfunctioning of shells in 1915 by building new factories and co-opting existing engineering works, such as those of the railway. Over 200 government factories were built, many devoted to producing munitions, and by 1917 about 2 million workers were engaged in this unpleasant and risky work. Some of the largest were located in Wales and Scotland, which decreased their risk to population centres and their vulnerability to the limited bombing of the First World War, but increased the distance the railways had to carry their products to southern ports.

One of the largest of the new plants was the cordite factory at Gretna/Eastriggs, which stretched for 12 miles across the border between England and Scotland. Besides standard-gauge sidings, it was served by an internal 2ft (610mm) gauge network with 125 miles of track and 34 locomotives. In response to the shell crisis of 1915, the Glasgow & South Western Railway (GSWR) was providing 20 trains a day to convey workers, numbering 11,576 women and 5,066 men by 1917.[37] Whole trains of Gretna cordite paste took the Settle & Carlisle line for Brent en route to the explosives factories near Faversham, which were served by the metre-gauge Davington Light Railway. One of the Kent factories was the scene of the worst explosion in the industry, in 1916, which killed 116 people.

Large quantities of cordite paste (cordite at the next stage of processing) were also produced at the Nobel Explosives factory among the sand dunes at Ardeer on the Ayrshire coast, served by the Caledonian and GSWR. Between December 1915 and February 1918, 1 or 2 trains a day, normally of 12 vans, were dispatched to the Royal Naval Cordite Factory near Wareham in Dorset or to other explosive plants.[38]

The NER itself became responsible for a munitions factory built on railway land off Westmoreland Street, Darlington, to make high-explosive 18-pounder shell cylinders. Originally built in 1915 by contractors Armstrong Whitworth,

Fig 2.5
This photograph of the 2ft (610mm) gauge rail-connected Examination Bag House on 26 July 1916 gives no idea of the scale of the cordite factory at Gretna in Dumfriesshire where over 11,000 women worked. It required the first town planned and built by the Government in Britain. The building was probably used for checking the quality of cordite bags. Cordite used by the Navy for charges was placed in silk bags, and it was imperative to keep it at a stable temperature, avoiding both cold and heat.

Fig 2.6
The Minister of Munitions,
Eric Campbell Geddes
(1875–1937), had a distinctly
unorthodox background for
the only non-royal to hold
simultaneously the ranks of
general and admiral. Born in
India, he was educated in
Scotland and drifted around
the US as a lumberjack and
steelworker before becoming
a stationmaster on the
Baltimore & Ohio Railroad.
After an older sister gave him
a stern talking-to, he went to
India to build light railways
and become superintendent
of one. Geddes was one of
the 17 figures depicted in
the monumental canvas,
Statesmen of World War I,
by Sir James Guthrie in the
National Portrait Galley.
The trustees of the NPG
had a hand in choosing
who should be depicted in
a series of three paintings
of key British figures in the
conflict commissioned
and given to the gallery by
Sir Abraham Bailey.

the factory provides some insight into the challenges of wartime planning. The original intention was that the NER would transfer labour from its workshops for training in the use of machinery supplied by Armstrong Whitworth, and that it would take over the factory at valuation when the war ended.

Right from the start, there were communication difficulties. In September 1915 the NER's general manager, Sir Kaye Butterworth, wrote to the Minister of Munitions, Eric Geddes, who was the former NER deputy general manager, asking him to advise 'with whom to communicate in the Munitions Department, so that I may get something settled with somebody. You will readily understand that I am getting a little tired of being driven from pillar to post.' Matters did not improve.

The following year the factory manager, Arthur C Stamer, wrote to Vincent Raven, yet another former NER man, who had become chief superintendent of ordnance factories at the Royal Arsenal, Woolwich, asking if he could help with supplies of raw materials. He ended with the observation: 'I see Mr. Lloyd George has been asking Munition Workers to take no holidays, or to curtail them as much as possible at Whitsuntide!! Perhaps you might inform him that so far from taking holidays, our Munition Workers are forced to take them by the action of his Department.'[39]

It was decided that the NER should take over full responsibility for the factory from 1 July 1916, but the previous month Butterworth had again had to write to Geddes:

> ... a fortnight ago, at six hours' notice, our work was suddenly stopped, and we were told to stop making H.E. shells, and to get ready for starting on shrapnel. This promise, however, has not been fulfilled, and we are just working from hand to mouth. We have had to dismiss 400 girls, and we only have three days' work next week for the remainder, and after that it is uncertain whether we shall have any work at all for them.[40]

Butterworth complained that no one was giving clear directions, Armstrong Whitworth had been blaming the Ministry of Munitions, and vice versa:

> One trouble in communicating with the Ministry of Munitions is that one generally finds one self in correspondence with a fresh individual every time one writes – hence my troubling you on this occasion. ... It is quite impossible that we should go on indefinitely as we are doing now. It is neither fair to Stamer, nor his staff, nor to the unfortunate girls who have been brought to Darlington in a belief that their work would be continuous, and it is bringing credit neither to the Company, nor to anyone else concerned in it.[41]

After the matter was resolved, the works went on to turn out 1,064,665 18-pounder shrapnel shells.[42]

The labour-intensiveness of munitions production required special trains for workers. To deliver the workforce to the largest wartime factories, the GWR alone ran 360 extra trains a day to factories such as those in Hayes, Avonmouth and Henbury near Bristol, Pembrey in South Wales and Queensferry near Chester. The numbers involved were huge: the factory at Pembrey between Carmarthen and Llanelly was staffed by people as far afield as Swansea and required seven additional trains daily in July 1916.

The Midland Railway alone served 258 munitions factories, and one of the largest – National Shell Filling Factory No 6 at Chilwell, near Attenborough in Nottinghamshire – turned out over 1 million tonnes of shells a year, requiring up to 539 wagons and 11 trains a day.[43] The GWR served 47 ammunition works and storage depots. One of the most remarkable for its underground tunnels, and one that would play a similar role in the Second World War (*see* p 152), was Ridge Quarry near Corsham. It was taken over in 1915 to store TNT and cordite. Another on the GWR was the Ordnance Depot at Didcot, which had over 30 miles of sidings. The GER served 203 munitions works, 16 government factories, 9 government depots and 31 aeroplane depots.[44]

The carriage of munitions was naturally fraught with danger and governed by elaborate precautions. An incident which nearly became a precursor of the 1944 Soham catastrophe (*see* p 153) occurred in 1917, when the 1.45 pm Gloucester to Salisbury goods train was nearing Charfield in Gloucestershire. GWR goods guard Kilmister saw that one of the wagons was on fire and succeeded in attracting the attention of the driver, who stopped the train. It was discovered that the wagon contained explosives, so Kilmister uncoupled the wagon and the crew drew it beside a water column and extinguished the fire.[45] There is no record of any recognition of their bravery.

Potentially the most disastrous accident involving ammunition occurred on 18 April 1918, when three ammunition trains collided inside the 502-yard Redhill Tunnel on the London Brighton & South Coast Railway (LBSCR) 'Quarry Line' in Surrey, filling a 40ft length with debris from rail to crown. The rear part of an up goods train had broken away and come to a stand when another up goods ran into the wagons, derailing them. Before a warning could be given, a down goods ran into the wreckage and nearly all wagons of that train were derailed. All three trains were carrying ammunition, including cordite, but astonishingly no explosion occurred, and the line reopened two days later. On this occasion the gang foreman who cleared the tunnel was appointed to the Order of the British Empire.

One of the most dangerous movements was the carriage of cordite paste for the Admiralty. It was carried in specially constructed zinc-lined vans fitted with steam heating, which would be applied if the outside temperature fell below 40°F (4.4°C). No other vehicle could be used, and the bespoke vans were not to be used for any other traffic. Accompanied by a competent inspector in a passenger train brake van carrying fire appliances, the trains ran at 'fish train' speeds (the fastest goods train speed, for perishables) and had to arrive early to allow daylight unloading. If the van was stopped, it had to be placed in a safe position, with minimal shunting and no risk of another vehicle being shunted against it, and guarded by a watchman.[46]

The volume of traffic to factories turned over to war work increased dramatically. Vickers' traffic at Barrow doubled in the first year of the war and was five times what it had been in 1905. On 26 December 1915 there were 1,447 wagons of traffic consigned to Vickers waiting in Barrow sidings and docks to be unloaded; by the next summer, improved traffic handling had reduced the number to 419.[47]

The war created many new and peculiar traffics. Most obvious was the carriage of guns and tanks. The Furness Railway carried many out-of-gauge loads such as 14in naval guns made by Vickers, mounted on 28 wheels with a total weight of 130 tons. They were tested at Eskmeals along the Cumbrian coast.[48] The GNR conveyed the first tank from the Lincoln Works of William

Foster, best known for traction engines and agricultural equipment, to Hatfield Park for trial and demonstration under great secrecy – they were euphemistically described as 'water carriers for Mesopotamia'. The tank was demonstrated to a 'Landship Committee' in January 1916, and the first order for Mark I tanks was placed the following month, divided between Foster and the Metropolitan Carriage, Wagon, and Finance Company, of Birmingham.

The LNWR carried 3,288 tanks between April 1917 and the end of May 1919, 2,202 of them from Spon Lane between Birmingham and Wolverhampton. The nearby Metropolitan Railway Carriage & Wagon Co was the largest manufacturer of the Mark IV tank used en masse at the Battle of Cambrai in November 1917. Most tanks were sent to southern ports, but others went to 'tankodromes' set up at Wool and Newbury.[49]

In July 1918 the HBR noted that: 'Arrangements are being made for Fruit Stones and Nut Shells to be collected throughout the Country, and as the traffic is urgently required all reasonable efforts must be made to ensure prompt despatch.'[50] These were required to produce fillings for gas masks: it had been found that charcoal produced from natural fibres from fruit and nut seeds/ stones reduced the potency of chlorine gas.

Besides its responsibility for traffic on the West Coast main line, the LNWR seemed to have had a disproportionate number of war factories. The Queensferry munitions factory near Chester dealt with up to 300 wagon movements a day and alone accounted for 1,513,000 tons of traffic during the war.[51] The chemical works around Runcorn and Widnes generated over 1 million cylinders of poison gas, tear gas, hydrogen and sulphur chloride. Also dispatched by the LNWR were 10¾ million hand grenades, filled at a factory at Fenay Bridge and Lepton on the Kirkburton branch near Huddersfield. Warrington factories sent out 325,000 miles of wire in various forms. From Northampton 12 million pairs of boots were sent to the Army – the weight of those carried by the LNWR alone amounted to 36,381 tons.[52]

Liverpool became the principal port for receiving food supplies. In the second half of 1913 the LNWR worked a monthly average of 36 trains of empty wagons to Liverpool to handle the traffic; in 1917 it was 276 trains a month, and in 1918 the LNWR alone carried 60,570,000 tons of freight.[53] The railways carried some wartime food traffics free of charge: 'Christmas Puddings from the British and Foreign Sailors Society for men serving in Trawlers and Drifters at various Auxiliary Patrol Bases would be conveyed free of charge.'[54]

Though the railways lost staff, locomotives and wagons to the war, they gained some new capacity through the construction of new passing loops, sidings and connecting chords, often between different railway companies. An example of a new chord built purely for government traffic was the link between the GCR and LNWR between Whetstone Junction and Blaby Junction at Leicester; it was closed by 1919. On the NER alone, new lines were built into 3 quarries, 7 shipbuilding yards and 13 factories, as well as extensions at others. Platforms were lengthened, and some sections of line quadrupled, such as Wrawby Junction–Brocklesby in Lincolnshire and Doncaster–Thorne.

Though the British Army was one of the most mechanised in 1914, horses and mules were still required in huge numbers, and efforts were made to secure them before war was declared. For example, an agreement was made on 18 April 1913 between Herbert Walker on behalf of the LSWR and the Assistant Director of Remounts for the purchase at 48 hours' notice of 'serviceably sound and suitable' horses. The agreement was to be invoked if the Secretary of State was of the opinion that the country was in national danger. The horses were to be aged between 6 and 10 years, and the LSWR was to supply 100 heavy draught horses and 100 light draught horses from Nine Elms Stable Yard in Miles Street, South Lambeth Road, London.[55] A similar arrangement must have been made with the GWR, which in August 1914 handed over 221 horses registered for Army purposes, plus an additional 40.[56]

There was no prospect of securing sufficient horses within Britain, so experts were sent abroad to buy them for the Army Remount Service. The radical MP and first president of the Scottish Nationalist Party, R B Cunninghame Graham, was sent to Argentina because of his knowledge of the country and horses, and others went to North America. Avonmouth and Liverpool were chosen as the ports through which horses would be imported, to be forwarded to four principal remount depots, at Ormskirk in Lancashire, Shirehampton near Bristol, and Romsey and Swaythling in Hampshire, the last extensive enough to warrant a narrow-gauge rail network around the two camps. Swaythling was the largest and received trains from all over the country; for example, the NBR sent horses from depots at St Boswells, Gorgie, Cupar and Maryhill.[57]

These new depots supplemented pre-war remount facilities at Woolwich, Melton Mowbray, Arborfield in Berkshire and Chiddingfold near Godalming. Horses arriving at Liverpool were entrained at Riverside station and taken by

Fig 2.7
Horses being unloaded at Ormskirk on 11 December 1914, destined for the Lathom Park Remount Centre. The number of horses being transported during the war quickly exceeded the supply of bespoke horseboxes so cattle vans were impressed, as here.

the LYR the 15 miles to the Remount Depot at Lathom Park, which had been made available for horse training by the trustees of Lord Lathom, free of charge. Between August 1914 and 1 November 1917, 215,300 horses and mules were brought to Lathom via Ormskirk or Burscough Junction stations. Railway staff were responsible for feeding and watering horses every six hours if the animals were unaccompanied.

Ships carrying the thousand horses a week arriving at Avonmouth used the King Edward Dock, which had been opened in 1908. The horses were taken to Shirehampton Remount Depot for two or three weeks' quarantine and training, often by Canadians from the Legion of Frontiersmen. Mules were sent on to Bratton Court near Minehead, often 500 at a time, for three weeks' training.

As a measure of the rail traffic that remount depots generated, forage for Army horses required a total of 2,555 wagonloads a week, and during the war about 434,000 horses and over 280,000 mules were imported from the Americas, Spain and Portugal. Not all movements required rail transport; both Swaythling and Romsey depots were close enough to Southampton Docks for the horses to be ridden or led to the ship bound for France.

Theft of goods in transit does not seem to have been as great a problem in the First World War as it became in the Second. Ten LYR employees were imprisoned for a month for pilfering goods transhipped at Thornhill, Yorkshire. The articles found in their possession included tea, tinned food, hair oil, matches, margarine, sugar, boots, boot nails, sheets, belts and purses.[58] A case was reported in the *GWR Magazine* in November 1916 when three GWR carmen and a foreman at Paddington Goods were convicted of theft and dismissed. It resulted in short industrial action. A more general comment in the January 1918 edition suggested that by this stage in the war, it had become a more serious problem:

> It is a regrettable fact that a considerable number of Great Western men of long service, who were formerly held in the highest confidence, have lately lost their characters and positions through pilfering goods in transit or receiving articles stolen by others; and the ugly truth has to be told, that the service is far from purged of those who are guilty of similar doings.

Stationmasters often developed a close working relationship with neighbouring camps and facilities through the extra traffic. Canadian troops occupied a camp at Seaford in Sussex from October 1916 to July 1919, and the stationmaster, Harold Hollingdale, was a given a canteen of cutlery with an engraved plate for his 'unvarying courtesy and helpfulness'.[59]

Haemorrhaging staff

The remarkable response of railwaymen to the call for volunteers produced an almost immediate problem for the railway companies, once they had realised that 'normal' traffic had not declined in the way initially anticipated. They could ill afford to lose experienced men, whose skills and knowledge had been developed over many years, at a time when far more was being demanded of them.

A commitment was given that railwaymen volunteering would be re-employed in a position similar to the one vacated, and service with the colours would count for an increment of salary or wages. The superannuation or pension

Fig 2.8
GWR war recruits headed by
a Scottish regimental band in
the cab road beside Platform 1
at Paddington station.

Fig 2.9
Stations were scenes of
strong emotions as recruits
and troops were entrained.
The Argyll and Sutherland
Highlanders are reviewed by
Provost Raffan in the main
ticket hall of Stirling station.

Fig 2.10
Families seeing off soldiers at
Stirling station.

fund would be maintained, and the GWR promised that 'the circumstances of the wives and families of married men and dependants of unmarried men [would be] kept under observation'.[60]

It was not envisaged that honouring the promise to re-employ enlisted men would be a problem, providing demobilisation was done gradually. The GWR supplemented the Government's separation allowances to the wives and families of non-commissioned officers (NCOs) so that they received four-fifths of the man's wages when in GWR employ. For officers, their wives would be given an amount which, with an allocation of one-third Army pay, would make up approximately four-fifths of the man's salary when with the company. Companies agreed that occupants of the companies' houses would not be disturbed, and concessionary coal rates would be maintained. Most importantly the companies also agreed to continue at their own expense membership of the pension and widows' and orphans' funds, and of provident societies.

With such reassurances and a prevailing optimism that the war might all be over before one even got to the front line and saw some action, staff losses were immediate and substantial. So concerned was the REC that a circular letter was sent to railway companies on 8 September 1914:

> The attention of the Executive Committee has been drawn to the fact that such a large number of railwaymen are enlisting in His Majesty's Forces as would tend to impair the efficient working of the railways. It is felt that some action should be taken to prevent so many men leaving the railway service as would render it difficult to find means to carry out, not only the requirements of the public, but also the requirements of the Army and Navy Authorities in case of emergency. It is not the wish of any of us to discourage men to enlist, but, at the same time, it is felt that a man who is required for the working of the railway service is rendering as good service to the State by remaining at his employment as he could possibly be if he enlisted with the Forces.

> The War Office have been asked to give an instruction to all their recruiting Officers and Agencies that no railwayman is to be allowed to enlist unless he presents a written statement from the Railway Company who employ him to the effect that he has approached the head of his Department and has obtained the necessary permission to enlist.

> It is felt that if after his warning any man enlists without having obtained permission he should be treated as having left the Company's service and that no special steps should be taken to keep his position open for him on his return from the War.[61]

The GCR's general manager, Sir Sam Fay, endorsed this view. Even by August 1914 he was saying that 'the number of Reservists and Territorials being called up from the Railways is very great indeed, and we have no more men for the working of the traffic than are needed'.[62] A letter was sent by the REC to the War Office on 4 September expressing concern that the number of railwaymen responding to the recruitment drive called for steps to control it, 'otherwise we are afraid the efficient working of the railways will be seriously impaired'.[63] The REC wanted the War Office to issue an instruction to recruiting officers not to accept any railwayman without that certificate. The War Office agreed.

Yet paradoxically many railwaymen were downgraded or put on shorter hours at the outset of the war, creating considerable ill feeling. Midland goods guards on 30/- a week were having to work as goods porters at 24/- a week, and Midland locomotive men at Swansea were working 2–3 days a week with no guaranteed week, whereas the GWR men at Swansea were also working fewer days but being paid for a week. Hours and days were being reduced across the board by many railway companies: HBR goods guards were working 8 hours instead of 9, LSWR coach painters 42 hours instead of 54, and at the GNR locomotive and carriage workshops at Doncaster the hours were down to 39 instead of 54.[64] These reduced hours were short-lived.

By 9 October 1914, 7,952 GWR men representing 10.12 per cent of the total staff had enlisted, and at first there was a reluctance to take on new permanent staff in order to save expenditure. In that time the GWR had taken on only 2,012 temporary employees to fill the gaps, though it realised that supernumerary labour 'is always much less satisfactory than that of appointed staff'.[65] The policy had to change because some posts, such as signalmen, guards, shunters and ticket collectors, could be occupied only by appointed staff. By January 1915, out of 3,657 new staff, 1,219 were appointed. Similar percentages had volunteered at other companies.

It took little time for the first complaints about long hours to be voiced. On 31 January 1915 a mass meeting of all grades of railwaymen at Crewe expressed 'great dissatisfaction' at the long hours, of up to 14½ hours in the locomotive department.[66] In Eastleigh the Revd B W Keymer told a meeting:

> It is only right that people should realise what a strain this war has involved on the railway workers. I have already visited railwaymen who are absolutely broken down as a result of the strain ... One was a driver who went straight to his bed and died, after having been 48 hours on the footplate. Some have had even longer stretches than that.[67]

The tussle between the War Office's insatiable demand for men and the REC's deepening concern over the loss of skilled staff and its effect on services was a recurrent theme of the war. A letter from B B Cubitt of the War Office dated 18 December 1914 reported that it had been brought to the Army Council's attention that 'there are still many men employed by Railway Companies on unskilled labour who are eligible for fit service in the Army'. The War Office wanted steps taken to induce such men to enlist. The REC replied that everything in their power had already been done, and over 55,000 men previously in railway employ were now in the forces. Steps had had to be taken to prevent losing men to the detriment of train services: 'Many of the Departments are now under-staffed and very great difficulties have been experienced in replacing the men who have left the railway service for the purpose of joining the Army and Navy.'[68]

The maladroit activities of the Order of the White Feather in shaming men into enlisting by giving men not in uniform a white feather led to the distribution in February 1915 of a badge for 'all railwaymen of military age who cannot be spared from their duties, to signify that they are already performing a service to their country. ... the use of the Royal Crown has been sanctioned by His Majesty the King and indicates that the employment followed by the wearer is a national service'.[69] Despite this, two months later the general secretary of the Associated

Society of Locomotive Engineers and Firemen (ASLEF) could still complain to the War Office that 'our members are jeered at and even molested in the streets by dockyard workers and soldiers, because they have not enlisted'.[70] Ignorance of the railways' vital role and the necessity of employing men in certain occupations was still being displayed in letters to the press in 1917 complaining about the employment of men of military age on the railways. The GER's chairman, Lord Claud Hamilton, made a robust justification of their role at the company's annual general meeting (AGM).[71]

Kitchener's demand for more recruits prompted a study in March 1915 to see how many men aged between 18 and 45 could be replaced by youths under 18, by men over 45 or by women. On behalf of the REC Sir Herbert Walker, knighted that month, issued a notice on 22 March expressing the view that:

> ... the present circumstances render it undesirable that men of military age should be accepted for service by the Railway Companies, and it is requested that you will give instructions that no applicant between the ages of 18 and 40 is to be given employment unless it is possible to be satisfied that such applicant is unsuitable for enlistment in His Majesty's Forces.[72]

By 25 March, Walker had received a return detailing railway employees of military age. He wrote to the railway companies:

> ... it is found that there are still employed on the railways of the country over 250,000 men of military age and it may be taken that pressure will be brought to bear upon the Companies to release a proportion of this number. In these circumstances, it is considered that you should carefully review every case in which permission to allow an employee to enlist has been refused by your Company in order to determine whether it would now be possible to withdraw such refusal. It is also desired that you should investigate the position in all Departments and in respect of all grades in order to decide whether by abolishing or suspending work, or by the diminishment of services, or further co-operation between Departments or with other railways the business could be efficiently carried on with a still smaller number of men than you at the present employ.[73]

Some in Government spoke up for the work of railwaymen. The Rt Hon Earl of Selborne asked on 26 August 1915:

> Have you thought what the railwaymen are doing? An immense number of men have been taken from the railways. The railways are carrying now a volume of trade such as has never been carried on our railways before, and the strain on those men is very great. That is nothing but silent heroism; as necessary and as great a contribution to victory as the work of the seaman or the work of the soldier.[74]

The loss of skilled men was also being felt in the railway workshops: the LNWR was informed by Cunard in September 1915 that it had carried some 600 mechanics of British nationality from Canada and the US for several engineering firms and that more were available, 'especially in the Turning and Fitting branches, if such inducements as a return passage after 6 or 12 months were offered coupled with third class return fare'.[75] Skilled Belgian railway refugees started work in February 1915 at Doncaster Works where only a small number of the 5,000 staff had been released for the front and great difficulty was found in replacing them: 'The Belgian refugees and Britishers are reported to be working with perfect harmony at Doncaster, and no friction has been experienced.'[76]

In May 1916 the GWR was experiencing such difficulties in handling the large amount of goods traffic because of staff shortages that salaried staff were helping out. They were 'paid at the rate for time and a quarter calculated on the rate of the grade in which they are working and a refreshment allowance of 1/- per night'.[77] What made matters worse was the loss of higher skills. On the GWR the highest rate of enlistment was in the Loco Department; by January 1916 it had lost 7,009 employees to the forces (23.8 per cent) yet had taken on no appointed staff and just 1,197 temporary staff. The inevitable consequence, and one which would last the duration of the war, was long hours worked and consequent overtime payments.

By the autumn of 1915 it was unclear whether Army recruitment could remain voluntary or whether conscription would be necessary. To test the position, Kitchener's Director General of Recruiting, the 17th Earl of Derby, initiated what became known as the Derby Scheme, under which eligible men aged 18–41 who were not in a 'starred' (reserved) occupation had to attest whether or not they were willing to enlist. Those who agreed were placed in a group according to marital status and age, to be called up in a defined order if required. Nationally 38 per cent of single men and 54 per cent of married men publicly refused to enlist, so conscription became inevitable. On the railway, 30 grades were 'starred' under the scheme, which meant that they were placed in the reserve and provisionally exempted from actual service. A railwayman would

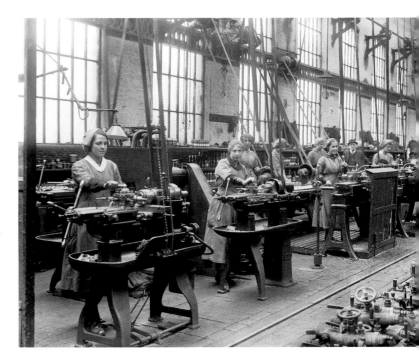

Fig 2.11
The loss of skilled men in the railway workshops was partially addressed by employing women on machine tools, as here at the LYR's Horwich Works in May 1917.

not be called up unless it was decided that he should no longer be provisionally exempted. The railway companies could also claim that men not starred were still essential for the operating efficiency of the railway.

Following passage in March 1916 of the Military Services Act, which introduced conscription for able-bodied men between 18 and 41, two general managers, Frank Potter of the GWR and Guy Calthrop of the LNWR, met the War Office Director of Recruiting appointed in May, Brigadier General Auckland Geddes (Eric Geddes's brother). They reached an agreement that only those who could be spared by the railway companies would be called for military service. The War Office would issue a card to railway employees as evidence that the holder was not to be called for service without reference to the company concerned.[78] There was 'some agitation among [GWR] drivers and firemen' who 'objected to younger firemen being retained and contended that older men should not be released until all the younger men had joined the Colours'.[79]

The huge number of casualties on the Somme – 57,470 on the first day, 1 July 1916, alone – increased pressure on the railways to release more men. As the battle neared its end in November, the GWR tried to release men under 26 'other than those working as shunters, firemen, signalmen, etc.'[80] Train services would have to be reduced still further to allow this, and passengers would have to reduce the weight of luggage so that it could be dealt with by women. All parcels traffic would have to be prepaid. It was proposed to extend the employment of women in wages grades – as platform and parcels porters, van drivers and goods workers – and to dilute skilled labour at Swindon Works. 'These steps are to an extent being opposed by the men, and in the case of the mechanics it has been found necessary to arrange a meeting with the Trade Union representatives in order to come to an understanding on the subject.'[81] It was expected that these measures would allow the release of 2,500 men by March 1917.

By 17 October 1916 the railways had released 119,600 men for naval or military service, leaving 523,337 in post supplemented by 18,936 casuals and 22,037 women who had replaced men, plus another 14,082 in other capacities.[82]

To assist the process, a Committee on Recruiting and Substitution of Railwaymen was formed, comprising Frank Potter (GWR), C H Dent (GNR), F Tatlow (Midland Railway), Colonel W A White (Recruiting Directorate, War Office) and Major A Redman (Movement Directorate, War Office), with Guy Calthrop (LNWR) as chairman. Its first meeting was held at the REC Parliament Street offices on 17 November 1916 and was also attended by Felix Pole (GWR) and George Stocks (REC). The function of the committee was:

> ... to discuss the various questions that arise in connection with the recruiting of railwaymen for service in the Army and cognate questions, and to agree upon the steps that should be taken to increase the number of men to be made available for the Army, and at the same time to ensure that due consideration is given to the technical requirements of the Railways.[83]

Men were classed A, B or C according to their fitness for front-line service. The military commands had been assessing enlisted railwaymen who were unlikely to be fit for general service and proposed that they should be offered the chance to return to railway duties. In return, the railways should 'liberate' an equal number of Class A men, in addition to 12,000 single railwaymen between 18 years 7 months and 25 who could be released by the end of March 1917.

Some grades were not to be released, such as shunters, guards and signalmen, and there was recognition that too many critical staff had already been lost: the Caledonian and HR were 'in a serious position with regard to the repair of their engines', and the recruitment of any more telegraph linesmen from the smaller railways would make it impossible to carry out work.[84]

The employment of women

Besides calling railwaymen out of retirement, an obvious solution to the shortage of men was the employment of more women. With rare candour, the *GWR Magazine* in May 1915 conceded that Britain had lagged behind other countries: 'hitherto the work in booking offices has been outside their sphere of activity, although in other countries this has been regarded as an occupation for which women are entirely suitable'. Herbert Walker later reflected on this cautious, even sceptical, outlook: 'It has to be admitted that the subject was approached with a considerable amount of trepidation. The companies had little or no experience as to the suitability of women for the work, and it was questionable whether their strength and endurance would not be too severely tested.'[85]

By early 1915, waitresses were serving on GCR and GWR restaurant-car services, and in April, Miss Lidster, the daughter of a GWR chief inspector, became the first station-mistress in South Wales, at Troedyrhiw Halt on the GW & Rhymney Railway Joint, and another woman was appointed to Trelewis Halt. The GCR was employing 'strong, healthy women as carriage cleaners' in Manchester, pioneering female porters at Kilnhurst near Doncaster and at Gainsborough, and employing women engine-cleaners at Sheffield, who earned £1 for a 53-hour week. The engine cleaners were supplied with working suits of trouser overalls, coat and cap in dark blue 'galatea', and they had their own spacious mess-room with whitewashed walls. They had a hot wash before leaving work at 5 pm, and the men had 'accepted their presence with a good grace'.[86] Women were employed as booking clerks on the LNWR at Willesden Junction, and the new station at Maida Vale on the Bakerloo extension was staffed entirely by women,[87] as was Irlam o' the Heights station in Salford under the first LYR station-mistress.[88]

Training schemes were set up for women. The LBSCR received 250 applications in a week to attend its large classroom at East Croydon under Miss Strevett, who had become a booking clerk at Hailsham station, where her father was stationmaster and therefore well qualified to instruct girls for telegraph, booking-clerk duties and general office work.[89] But the principal occupation for women was clerical duties: at the outbreak of war the GCR employed 70 women as clerks; by October 1916 it had 1,526 on the payroll, far exceeding the next largest category of porter at 454.

The Australian widow of Grimsby MP Sir George Doughty, Eugenia Stone, wrote a series of articles in the *Grimsby Telegraph* on 'Woman at Work'. Her article on 15 July 1916 was about 'Great Central Railway Clerks and Barrow-women' and rather over-egged the likely enthusiasm of the women for the work they were doing: 'She pursues her invoice-making or her summarizing or her abstracting or her tracing with the utmost relish. ... All her work interests and grips her. ...The girls and women are proving themselves not only capable of doing men's work, but in many instances – naturally not all – are doing better than those they are substituting.' It provoked a series of letters accusing her of 'window-dressing': 'a feeling of disgust went round amongst the male clerks at our station, not caused by prejudice, but because her statement was very misleading.'[90]

The first REC letter encouraging companies to employ women clerks through the labour exchanges was sent in March 1915. The possible implications of this solution were not welcomed by the unions, and in June the trades unions 'asked for an assurance that the [employment of women] was an emergency provision for the period of the War and that after the War the status quo will be reverted to'. The GWR agreed that men would get their jobs back, but there was 'an obvious objection to giving an undertaking that women will be dispensed with at the end of the war'.[91] The agreement reached between the REC and the NUR in April 1915 simply accepted that the war work undertaken by women would not be taken as a precedent for peacetime.

Official encouragement of more women in the workforce led to a flood of applications. In Sheffield, 100 women signed up as engine cleaners in a fortnight, and by August 1916 there were 2,000 women passenger and goods porters. Many were wives or daughters of railwaymen serving in the forces. The introduction of conscription in January 1916 accelerated the process; by the end of the year 34,000 positions previously regarded as suitable only for men were occupied by women.[92]

Fig 2.12
Women cleaning windows and using a vortex vacuum cleaner at the SECR's London Bridge station in 1918. Water is being pumped into the roof tank above the lavatory. Note the advert for French money exchange for officers in uniform.

The attitude of the NUR towards the influx of female labour was at best wary; ASLEF's members were less affected, as drivers' and firemen's roles remained male. Many were concerned that women posed a threat to their jobs, or those of returning servicemen. A writer in the NUR's *The Railway Review* for 18 June 1915 expressed this anxiety: 'It would be pure affectation to deny that the advent of girls on our railways has not created a profound uneasiness that tends to upset the smooth and harmonious relationship between the men and the companies' headquarters. Not one man in ten thousand believes their presence is of temporary duration.'

Others pointed out that opening NUR membership to women had been on the agenda for the 1914 annual conference, recognising that they had been employed by railways long before the war and should be welcomed into the union. The Bromley branch protested that the decision might endanger the expectations of 'our boys in France' that their positions would be open on their return: 'How are we to do this and act honourably towards our female members? ... The condition of [female] membership should embody that the privileges enjoyed while in the union shall cease when their services are dispensed with for the purpose of reinstating the men.'[93]

In recognition of the growing number of women employed on the railways, the June 1915 AGM of the NUR altered the union's rules to allow women to become members for the first time. The 1914–18 membership registers of the NUR provide a clear illustration that women railway workers were seen as only a temporary, emergency measure – entries for women workers were written in red ink, rather than the standard black.

The general secretary of the NUR, J E Williams, received a communication from the GCR's general manager, Sir Sam Fay, in August 1915, stating that:

> An assurance was asked for and given that the employment of women in capacities in which they had not formerly been employed was an emergency provision arising out of the circumstances created by the war and would not prejudice in any way any undertaking given by the companies as to the re-employment of men who had joined the Colours at the conclusion of the war.[94]

At first the unions wanted women to be paid the minimum rate of wages applicable to men, and the GWR pointed out that 'the general practice is to pay women 3/- less per week than the commencing rate for men, this being justifiable by the general experience that women are not as efficient as men'.[95] They also received the minimum rate for the grade in which they worked. A conference held under the auspices of the NUR London District Council in September 1916, 'to consider the many phases of the question relative to the employment of women upon the railways', was attended by 66 delegates, representing 33 branches, including 'a large number of lady members who very soon made their presence both known and felt'. Among the concerns expressed about women working on the railways was their impact on the promotion of men, which was regarded as slow enough without them, despite the loss of men to the forces.

Issues of propriety were also debated. In October 1916 the NUR reported that:

> ... fierce indignation has been aroused amongst the female staff at the Central Station, Newcastle, by an intimation that they are going to be supplied with trousers. Whoever is responsible, they say, for the proposed innovation

can have little idea of the insult they are offering to that most valued asset of the pure mind, modesty; and they are asking if the officials responsible would like to see their own wives or daughters turned into objects of ridicule and jest.

The women were determined to refuse to wear trousers even if it meant giving up work. The writer acknowledged that 'there are various classes of work, such as window cleaning, engine cleaning, etc., which entail climbing about, where the bifurcated garment may be advantageous, but in the case of those who are brought so much in contact with the public, and more especially with trainloads of both soldiers and sailors, women in trousers would be subject to great criticism and ridicule'.[96]

At a meeting of carmen at Nine Elms goods depot on the LSWR, 'the question of female labour was hotly discussed from all points of view, especially that employed as vanguards. Are they to take the place of Carmen? What is the opinion of the wife of a young carman who is accompanied by a young, single girl as vanguard?' A resolution was passed that unless the female vanguards were withdrawn, 'we don't do another stroke of work, therefore we must go into the Army'.[97] A similar objection was made about women taking over signal boxes: they would be exposed to being alone with a man when the fireman of a train waiting signals was obliged to carry out Rule 55 and enter the signal box. The Chalk Farm branch of the NUR strongly opposed 'the employment of women on the [Marylebone] goods banks and in the stables, as we believed that arrangements could be arrived at that would save women from tasks so unwomanly'.[98] NER guards in the Hull and Sunderland districts protested 'strongly ... against women being appointed to the position of passenger guards on the NE as they consider them a danger to themselves, other railway employees, and the general public, and ask for their immediate withdrawal'.[99] Despite such opposition, women guards were employed on the Caledonian Railway, GNSR, GWR, LNWR, LSWR, NBR and NER.

Some contemporary comparisons between the efficiency and aptitudes of the sexes now make embarrassing reading. The HBR found 'that Women clerks can be safely employed in Accounts work, provided that the supervision is by senior men clerks. It has been found that girls of about 16, or who have just finished their education more quickly adapt themselves to their duties than older women who have not kept up their School work.'[100] Over 100 women were employed at the SECR's Bricklayers Arms goods depot, where 'there is scarcely anything they can't do, and if they get into difficulties there is keen competition between the male staff and the Carmen to help them out'.[101] The GWR is thought to have employed the first woman special constable, Miss Annie Eva Martin, who was sworn in on 5 March 1917. She had been on probation for three months and 'had shown exceptional ability'.[102] The GER had six policewomen at Liverpool Street, one of whom became a sergeant.

At a conference in Lincoln in September 1917, signalmen in the Eastern District of the GCR rejected the idea that women were suited to signal-box work: 'Sex disabilities, failure to realise the full responsibility attached to signal-box duties, their general excitability and nervous temperament, together with the liability to distraction and periodical ill-health, are all against them.'[103] A few women took to the occupation, such as Madeline Parker, who joined the GCR Signalling Department at 20 and worked in Ardwick No 2 signal box from May 1917 to December 1918 and again during the Second World War.

Fig 2.13

Particular resentment was expressed by railwaymen about the employment of women in signal boxes. Under blackout conditions, this woman is working an unidentified GER box on a double-track line.

But an anonymous railwayman praised their contribution in a letter to
The Railway Review:

> Whatever duties the ladies have taken over, they do them with all their
> might. They go through the toil and turmoil of the railway day with a
> sublime patience and self-abnegation, and with a degree of success thought
> to be unattainable. They have undertaken railway work, not as a means of
> livelihood, but as a voluntary service, because all the human help procurable
> was needed to bring victory to the Allies' cause.[104]

In December 1917 the *Railway Magazine* gave the view that 'women have been
found such efficient railway servants that they are certain to be retained'.

Photographers were fond of recording women cleaning locomotives,
usually in specially devised clothes. Women employed as cleaners at the NER's
Middlesbrough and Neville Hill sheds wore trousers and knee-length overalls
since 'skirts would have embarrassed their movements'.[105]

One of the largest employers of women before the war was the LNWR,
which counted 2,123 women and girls on its staff, and this rose to a maximum
at any point in the war of 9,154. An indication of the types of employment taken
by women and the ratios between them is given by this undated snapshot of the
LNWR's female staff:

Clerks 2,871

Carriage cleaners 591

Engine cleaners 257

Goods checkers 69

Goods porters 865

Labourers 213

Messengers 80

Munition workers (Wolverton) 150

Porters (platform, parcels) 399

Miscellaneous others 567[106]

The peak employment of women came in September 1918, when 68,801
women were at work on the railways, representing about 16 per cent of the
workforce, but neither the substitution nor enlistment percentages reached
the levels of urban tramways. Research carried out for the American Electric
Railway Association after the US entered the war showed that, between July
1914 and April 1918, 48.8 per cent of British male municipal tramway workers
and 50 per cent of non-municipal tramway workers had enlisted. Women
employed on municipal tramways had risen from 1,200 in July 1914 to 18,800
by April 1918 and from 200 to 5,600 on non-municipal tramways. They were
chiefly employed as conductors and in smaller numbers as car cleaners, ticket
inspectors and drivers. 'Women [drivers] are only employed in a few towns, but
these in some cases have them in very considerable numbers.'[107]

Not all welcomed this. In early 1917 the Coventry Trades Council passed
'a resolution viewing with alarm the introduction of female tram drivers on the
Corporation tramways in the city on the grounds of the danger to the health of

Fig 2.14
Women cleaning a GCR 4-4-0
at an unidentified locomotive
shed.

the women so employed, and the danger to traffic'.[108] A Board of Trade paper of 1918 suggested that substitution of females for males had practically reached its limit, and vacancies were being given to discharged soldiers and sailors.[109]

Despite the influx of women workers, the hours worked by railwaymen remained excessive. The NUR's general secretary and MP for Derby, J H Thomas, told Parliament that signalmen were 'being retained on duty 7 days a week of nearly 90 hours, with only a very occasional day off'. He asked the President of the Board of Trade, Walter Runciman, whether he was aware that so many railwaymen had been released that boys were now acting as firemen on goods trains. A boy of 15, Henry Watt, acting as fireman had been involved in an accident on 11 September 1916 at Wallneuk Junction on the Glasgow & Paisley Joint Railway in which 28 passengers were injured. Runciman replied that employment of boys as firemen was not to his knowledge a general practice, but he had drawn the attention of the railway to the remarks of the inspecting officer.[110] On the Isle of Wight Central Railway, stationmasters were reported in February 1916 to be working an average of 100 hours a week, and were compelled to work four out of every five Sundays instead of every other Sunday.[111]

Meetings with the unions in May 1917 indicate the strain under which railwaymen were working. NUR representatives met Sir Herbert Walker of the REC, Francis Dent of the SECR and the GWR general manager, Frank Potter, and strongly opposed the release of more men, citing the long and consequent strain. Resentment among railwaymen at the depletion of staff had reached the point where the NUR wanted a say in who could be released. At another meeting ASLEF objected to all railwaymen being given a medical examination when only a small proportion of them could be released without impairment of services. At the June 1917 NUR AGM in London, the Congress entered:

> ... an emphatic protest against the release of more railwaymen for military service on the ground that (1) ... an undue strain is already being placed on the men, and (2) ... substituted labour has already proved to be inefficient and a serious menace to the railwaymen and to the travelling public; and that should the release of men be continued this Congress empowers the Executive Committee to use every means to secure the safe working of the railways.[112]

The dissolution of the Russian Army during the summer of 1917 and subsequent October Revolution increased demands from the War Office for more men, despite having agreed in the spring that no more railwaymen would be called up. The release of German divisions from the Russian front led to an initial demand for 100,000 railwaymen; this was reduced to 41,000, and an agreement was eventually reached at 21,000.[113] A letter from a shunter in Sheffield opined that 'the continued drafting of railwaymen of practical experience into line regiments and at the same time passing clerks into the ROD [Railway Operating Division] is causing a great deal of discontent throughout the country'.[114]

During the summer of 1917 pressure was building for strike action in support of the demand for an eight-hour day, though ASLEF and the NUR were divided over its appropriateness during hostilities. That August's ASLEF *Locomotive Journal* lamented that:

> The hours worked on the Highland Railway are the most excessive in Britain – 12 hours per day – and it has been no uncommon thing for some

men to lift 3, 4, 5 to 6 days extra a fortnight, and even for Sunday time they only get ordinary time. I remember the time when the Highland Engine Drivers were the associates of Dukes and Earls, and the pay was as high then as it is now, and in many cases these men used to carry a gun, and had permission to use it on the journey to have a try at a grouse or pheasant. These old days are changed on the Highland.

On 17 August ASLEF decided on strike action, complaining that 'N.U.R. jealousy did its best to discredit the movement, and to console the Government.' For its part, the NUR newspaper thought 'the action of [ASLEF] can fairly be described as a policy of frightfulness, and the adoption of the doctrine that in things paramount might is right'. J H Thomas spoke of the truce agreement, that while the war lasted 'every effort would be made to adjust differences by means of conciliation and arbitration'.[115] He noted that despite being head of the largest trades union in the world, with 370,000 members, including a majority of organised locomotive men, he had not had one word from ASLEF.

The Government applied Part 1 of the Munitions Act (1915), which prohibited any stoppage of work and put the matter to arbitration after the differences between the REC and ASLEF had been provided. Sir Albert Stanley, President of the Board of Trade, committed the Government to a shorter working day after the war and a 5s increase in War Wages was awarded to drivers, firemen, motormen and cleaners.

On 22 August 1917 ASLEF's General Secretary John Bromley sent a telegram to [?] Holme in Hull: 'Members must not strike Government guarantees given on eight hours day negotiations proceeding on outstanding matters advising branches accordingly.'[116]

By December 1917 the GWR reported difficulty handling the traffic due to a more pronounced shortage of engines and men and to the 'recent unsettled feeling of the men. Whether the matter will be relieved by the recent increase of war wages remains to be seen, but it is doubtful whether contentment is in any way induced by concessions made in such rapid succession as has been the case in connection with the war bonus and war wages.'[117] The general shortage of mechanics, boilermakers and wagon repairers was so severe by March 1918 that the Committee on Recruiting and Substitution of Railwaymen heard calls from companies for the return of such skilled men from the forces, and suggested that recruiting in railway workshops should cease unless substitutes were provided.

In June the committee had to reprimand the Knott End Railway for failing to release anyone since 1 January 1917, even though 27 of its 37 staff were of military age. The general manager refused to countenance the idea of employing women or for one stationmaster to look after two stations, even though the entire railway's passenger numbers in April 1918 averaged 167 a day. It took a letter from the railway's chairman to arrange the release of nine men.

Such rural idylls were the exception. At the beginning of 1918 ASLEF sent the Board of Trade a dossier with thousands of cases of excessive hours at almost 200 locomotive depots. It showed that:

... our members are working turns of duty of anything from 12 hours up to 30 hours, with the majority of cases ranging between 15 and 20 hours on duty, while a very large number are over the latter figure. Our members

Fig 2.15
Sir Guy Granet (1867–1943) was one of the most capable railway managers to be taken into Government service. Trained as a barrister, Granet became general manager of the Midland Railway and revolutionised the handling of freight traffic. Among his appointments during the war were Deputy Director of Railways and Director General of Movements and Railways. He returned to railway service to become chairman of the LMS.

are working weeks of from 70 up to over 120 hours, young boys are being employed on footplates, and many men long past retirement age. This cannot be allowed to go on. The Society has asked the Board of Trade to return footplate men from Army Service to ease this terrible strain, and that no further young men be released, but be retained in the service for bringing down the hours to something within the range of physical endurance.[118]

Yet in 1918 the NER general manager, A K Butterworth, had to caution staff against employing men of military age, which amounted to a breach of the Defence of the Realm Regulations. An official of the company had temporarily engaged a man of military age and Butterworth warned that the Government viewed such incidents so seriously that it wanted the offender prosecuted in every case.[119]

The 20-year-old aspiration for an 8-hour day was finally agreed on 6 December, within weeks of the war's end, to come into operation on 1 February 1919.

By the end of December 1918, 184,475 railwaymen had joined the forces, over 30 per cent of the pre-war total of about 600,000. The percentage of employees who joined the colours was typically in the low thirties: on the LNWR, 34 per cent of the total staff; GWR, 32.6 per cent; LBSCR, 32.3 per cent. The proportion between departments varied much more markedly. Predictably it was high among hotel staff because many were closed or taken over for war use; 74 per cent of Midland Railway Hotels staff enlisted. Much more difficult operationally was the loss of half of the staff of the Burton & Ashby Light Railway, owned by the Midland, which reflected the tramway nature of the railway (see p 34).

It was not only the loss of operating staff which affected the railways. Though many middle-ranking managers and engineering staff were classed as reserved occupations, some of the railways' most able senior managers were purloined for Government positions: Sir Guy Granet (Midland Railway) became Director General of Movements and Railways and later visited the US at government request, in connection with food and transport problems there; Sir Sam Fay (GCR) became Controller of Military and Munitions Movements within the Department of Military Railways; the Midland's chief mechanical engineer (CME), Henry Fowler, and its carriage and wagon superintendent, David Bain, were recruited as assistants by David Lloyd George at the Ministry of Munitions; Guy Calthrop (LNWR) became Controller of Coal Mines when the Government took over control of the mines from 1 March 1917; and Sir Eric Geddes (formerly NER) had a series of senior appointments leading to First Lord of the Admiralty at the age of 41 (see Fig 2.6). When he became Controller of the Navy, Geddes became the only man other than members of the royal family to hold simultaneously the ranks of general and admiral. Few railways can have had its board of directors as depleted as the HR; five joined the forces.[120] It is estimated that about 2,000 men were loaned by the railways to the Government.[121]

The railways' only senior US manager, the Indiana-born Henry Worth Thornton, was also borrowed by the Government. Thornton had become general manager of the GER in 1914, and his abilities led to the eventual position of Inspector General of Allied Transportation and a knighthood, after becoming a British subject in 1919.

Collections were made to send parcels to railwaymen serving in the forces. In 1916 the GWR chief goods manager raised money to send a parcel of tobacco, cigarettes, sardines and chocolate to NCOs serving overseas.[122] These parcels were dealt with by the Military Forwarding Department based in Nantes and headed by the LYR's Antwerp agent with a staff of over 500.[123] At the 1916 AGM the GER's chairman, Lord Claud Hamilton, reported that the 37 staff who were prisoners of war (POWs) had been sent money or parcels of food each week through the American Express Company.[124]

The LNWR provided homes at low rental for its staff disabled by the war, using money partly raised by the sale of War Seals. The first to be built were 72 flats in a mansion block in Fulham. The nominal weekly rent of 6s 6d included medical care as well as rates and taxes. The flats had an open balcony and the block had heat baths and other medical treatment rooms, and a common entertainment room.[125] Among the fundraising efforts to pay for them was the fashioning of aluminium girders from shot-down Zeppelins into toasting forks, pipe racks, fern pot holders, shoehorns and so on, while others were mounted on cardboard. The Zeppelin debris was given to the LNWR by the War Office: 'special efforts have been made to maintain the identity of the origin of each article, and it is stamped showing it was manufactured from a fallen Zeppelin'.[126]

Service reductions

The ability of the railways to cope with wartime traffic despite losing so many staff, locomotives and wagons was largely achieved by significant service reductions, though these happened incrementally. For the first year of the war one could still join a restaurant car for Oban at Glasgow or ply Coniston Water aboard the Furness Railway's *Gondola*. Meals could be taken in 543 restaurant cars, and labour-intensive slip-coaches were still being discarded along the route of longer-distance trains. In 1915 the Cambrian even introduced two observation saloon carriages for journeys along its scenic coastal line to Pwllheli.

For the GWR to run 88,603 special trains on Government account during the war, it had reduced the total passenger train mileage by a third:

	Goods train mileage	*Passenger train mileage*
1913	20,169,166	32,419,547
1917	24,950,801	22,755,883

The GWR pointed out that the percentage increases in goods train mileage were markedly different between companies: between 1913 and 1917, the increases were just 2 per cent on the LNWR and 3 per cent on the Midland, but 23 per cent on the GWR. The GWR opined rather smugly that 'the superior power of our locomotives has enabled us to work most of this additional mileage without double heading, such as is necessary to a very considerable extent in the case of the Great Northern and Midland Companies'.[127] While true of the Midland, which always had a small-engine policy, it was not accurate when referring to the GNR; Gresley's class O2 2-8-0s had a higher tractive effort than Churchward's 2-8-0s.

Whatever the position between companies, the only way the demands from France for more men, locomotives, wagons and track could be met was by service reductions. In February 1915 the REC superintendents' subcommittee drew up a provisional list of specific trains to be withdrawn along with through carriages and dining cars, some operating on relatively short workings such as the GCR's 4.50 pm from Sheffield to Grantham. Travel was discouraged by suspending reduced fare arrangements for such groups as archery clubs, bible-class parties, church bell ringers, cycling clubs, freemasons, rowing clubs, shinty clubs and whist parties but retained for, among others, market tickets, emigrant tickets, fishworkers' tickets, theatrical companies, shipwrecked mariners, professional choirs, orchestral companies and 'hunting arrangements'. The following month the companies agreed from 1 April to withdraw dining cars on certain services providing companies on competing routes did the same, such as the GWR and LNWR between London and Birkenhead/Liverpool. Among the through carriages withdrawn were the 9.20 am from Horncastle to King's Cross (GNR) and the 10.00 am from Colne to Euston (LYR).[128]

Quality too suffered. A complaint discussed by the REC superintendents' subcommittee in early 1916 pertained to the suburban coaching stock in which troops often had to travel long distances. Trains without lavatories were supposed to stop for the men to relieve themselves every four hours, but it was found that this was insufficient, because 'many of [the men] have not recovered from the excesses of leave-taking for active service'. Consequently trains arrived in an 'insanitary condition'. It was agreed that corridor stock should be provided for all journeys over 150 miles, or halts made an hour after starting and then every two hours.[129]

According to a letter received in January 1916 by the RCH from Walsall and District Chamber of Commerce, long-term damage by railway congestion created by war traffic was likely to be inflicted on commercial activity, particularly on the export trade of the Midlands:

> Manufacturers are told by the Government of the importance of the export trade of the country being maintained as far as possible, so as to provide the means of paying for the country's large purchases abroad of munitions of War, but the present difficulties in getting goods collected and shipped render it most disheartening to manufacturers to produce goods at all.

> Another most serious aspect of the matter is however the prejudicial effect upon future trade. Merchants and buyers both in England and the Colonies, are protesting that the present long delays in the execution of orders, are having a most detrimental effect upon our export trade, and many markets are consequently being lost to American and other competitors.[130]

In 1916, the year that bank holidays were abolished and tourist tickets discontinued, further cuts in restaurant-car services were announced. In the previous year there were 543 restaurant cars in service; the LNWR had 105, the GNR 63, the GWR 56, NER 30, NBR 20 and the Caledonian 14. From 1 May all LNWR dining cars were withdrawn, luncheon baskets being provided instead, and the East Coast companies and GWR followed suit.[131] Their removal released men for war service, saved coal or increased train capacity, reduced maintenance and saved shunting movements. Following withdrawal of restaurant cars, the GER Hotels Department produced cardboard food-boxes with compartments, 'viands being packed in grease-proof paper bags'. A luncheon box for 1s 6d contained two ham or tongue sandwiches; one mutton pie; one fruit tartlet; cheese, roll and biscuits; and one apple.[132]

In response to the requirements set out by Eric Geddes following his September 1916 visit to France (*see* p 77), the REC proposed four measures: a drastic reduction in train services; a restriction on passenger travel; the pooling of railway company wagons; and the indiscriminate use of private owners' wagons (roughly half the wagon fleet of 1,450,000 wagons was privately owned). Despite opposition from the Private Wagon Owners' Association and from the GWR, because it was thought likely the measure would impede coal movements from South Wales, the Board of Trade authorised railway companies to use empty private-owner wagons from 16 March 1917. The GWR complained that common-user arrangements for railway company wagons militated against their effective maintenance.

The REC suggested that fares should rise by not less than 50 per cent, that no more special facilities should be provided for sports events and so on, Sunday services should be curtailed and lightly used lines might be closed. It called for a relaxation of rules on mixed trains, a reduction of leave to home forces, reduced passengers' luggage, an end of private saloons, slip-coaches, dining and sleeping cars, and no carriage of motor cars. The Board of Trade largely agreed, except for the draconian fare increases. The impact of leave traffic can be gauged from the 237 special trains the LSWR operated for the 164,780 men taking leave at Christmas 1914.[133]

At a meeting of the War Committee at 10 Downing Street in November 1916, the great increase in that year's passenger traffic over 1913 was discussed. A large proportion of this traffic was, according to the REC, 'joy riding' and soldiers and munition workers proceeding on weekend leave. The REC had a point: the attractions of London to soldiers based at camps on the LSWR in 1916 required the following special trains from Waterloo: four each to Bordon and Liphook, two each to Bulford, Dinton and Shawford, and one each to Tidworth, Eastleigh, Farnborough and Aldershot.[134] The Secretary of State for War, Lloyd George, 'urged the importance of cutting down the railway traffic in this country, not only in order to release railway workers for service with the colours (particularly engine drivers who were needed for railway traffic in France), but also to release a supply of locomotives urgently required for the British Expeditionary Force.'[135]

The Army Council decided to stop weekend leave of soldiers engaged on home service, but only on the understanding that it should be part of a plan to curtail facilities for the general public. Facilities in Britain had not been reduced to the same extent as France. Lloyd George also urged cutting down on much non-essential business traffic to release trucks for the BEF. Following a suggestion from the REC that 'the first thing to stop was carrying barrels of beer', Lloyd George thought that 'in the present state of public opinion it would occasion trouble if they were to cut off all beer', and Runciman pointed out that the railways were bound as common carriers by statute.[136]

It was agreed that the Board of Trade should take the necessary action to curtail passengers and goods traffic, which included ending weekend leave for munition workers. At Christmas priority should be given to sailors on active service and soldiers on leave from the front, then to munition workers and finally the general public. The change of government in December 1916, when Lloyd George replaced Herbert Asquith as prime minister, delayed the Board of Trade's implementation of these train service reductions,[137] but from 1 January 1917 train services were further reduced, luggage restrictions imposed, more through and slip-coaches and dining and sleeping cars withdrawn, seat reservations ended, and fares increased by 50 per cent except for certain categories of war workers and season tickets. Little-used stations and halts were closed. Deceleration of expresses would allow 10–20 per cent heavier trains. As a consequence of these service reductions, some railwaymen were reduced to 'inferior work', and the REC superintendents minuted that they should be paid 'either by maintaining their rate or paying them the lowest rate of the grade to which they belong'.[138]

Despite the service reductions, delays remained a concern. In June 1917 fruit growers expressed anxiety to the REC over the railways' ability to move expeditiously the 50,000 tons of fruit contracted by the Government for the Army and Navy.[139]

The smartness of staff also suffered from the priorities of war. In 1915 *The Railway Review* reported that 'men employed on the Burton and Ashby Light Railway would like to know when their next issue of uniform is coming, as the ragman has his eye on some of the men', and that uniforms for Maryport & Carlisle Railway staff from stationmaster down were nearly three months overdue. 'A large number are wearing their own clothes, and others who are still wearing their old uniforms hardly dare to be seen on a station platform or in the public streets for fear of being taken for a tramp and locked up by some vigilant constable.'[140] This was not simply a matter of appearance. A cleaner at a Scottish shed had such oil- and grease-saturated overalls that they ignited when they came into contact with a light: 'the poor fellow ran round and round the shed at such a rate that no one could catch him, and ultimately jumped into a pit full of water'.[141]

Service reductions included some complete closures, as much to liberate rails for France as to reduce train mileage. New rails were not being rolled in sufficient quantity, so the demand for them from France could only be met by lifting lines in Britain. A closed railway was an extremely rare sight then, but services over a few minor lines were withdrawn and the track lifted, usually for use abroad; among them were Eardisley Junction–Titley Junction, most of the Basingstoke & Alton Light Railway, Kimberley–Bennerley Junction, Selsdon–Woodside (Croydon & Oxted Joint), and the only railway which served a place with an exclamation mark – the Bideford, Westward Ho! & Appledore Railway in Devon. Also closed was the HR line between Keith and Buckie, but in this case the track was destined for use in new sidings at Dalmore, Invergordon and Muirtown in Inverness.[142] An alternative measure was to single a double-track route. Ledbury–Dymock was singled in 1917, as was Clarbeston Road–Neyland, and the track was lifted for dispatch to France.

More with less

The essence of the challenge for the railways was how to carry far higher levels of passenger and goods traffic with fewer resources, especially of staff. Those higher levels of traffic in turn created congestion at depots and goods yards, delaying the unloading of wagons. By the end of October 1914 the REC was receiving complaints from railway companies that large numbers of wagons were being held under load for various purposes, particularly at Woolwich.[143]

Demurrage – the practice of using wagons as storage on private sidings – became unacceptable. Even though a daily charge of 1s 6d per wagon was levied, many companies still found it cheaper than expanding their storage accommodation.

As a consequence some wagons were on the move for only a few days a month. This practice actually increased after the war began, because companies ordered further ahead or greater quantities to guard against longer delivery times or transit delays. Wagon shortages became apparent as early as November 1914. To retain a customer's business, railway companies had often adopted a relaxed attitude to the calculation and even collection of demurrage charges, but the REC was compelled to take a more robust approach to alleviate the situation, threatening one of the worst offenders, who owed £6,000, with court action.[144]

Paradoxically the worst offenders for wagon misuse turned out to be the War Office and the Ministry of Munitions, set up in June 1915. RCH returns for one week in January 1916 showed Government departments holding 5,000 wagons for an aggregate of 50,000 days. Munitions factories were renowned for using an entire wagon for a single consignment, rather than any attempt at aggregation; the worst instance was using a wagon for a case of cartridge signals weighing 41lb from Woolwich to Killingholme near Grimsby. In a non-government case, a barrel of gunpowder weighing 28lb rode in solitary splendour from Purfleet to Catterick.[145]

The increases in traffic were far from incremental or modest: between 1913 and 1918, for example, passenger numbers on the HR increased by 50.47 per cent and goods tonnage by 102.49 per cent. This was largely due to its strategic position on the supply line to the Grand Fleet at Scapa Flow, the creation of American mineworks at Inverness and Alness, and the need for timber from Highland forests.

At a time when railways were being asked to carry more, their physical resources were being reduced. New construction of locomotives and wagons was restricted at a time when both were being shipped to bolster railways critical to the war effort. In September 1915 the Ministry of Munitions was struggling with the 'shell scandal', and exhorted the REC to minimise the railways' expenditure on locomotives and the relaying of track to reduce the call on steel and engineering capacity.[146] Only half of the 200,000 tons of rail a year needed to keep abreast of rail renewals was available, so arrears and speed restrictions built up.[147]

The shortage of wagons encouraged the common use of wagons to reduce empty running and paperwork. From 3 April 1916 the GWR, LNWR, LYR, Midland and NER pooled all but very specialised wagons. But this initiative did not solve the problem, and in December 1916 railway companies were given the power, under the Defence of the Realm Regulations, to unload wagons that had remained under load for longer than a stipulated time (never more than four days) 'and the contents thereof to be warehoused or stored at the owner's risk' and any costs incurred charged to the trader. The railway company could even hold on to the goods until such charges were paid.[148]

From 2 January 1917 common categories of railway company wagons were pooled. Though this improved utilisation, it had an adverse effect on maintenance which could cause delays to traffic when a wagon developed a hot axle-box. Some indication of the arrears of maintenance is given by 44,835 wagons being under or awaiting repair in September 1919.[149]

Sir Douglas Haig's demand for more locomotives was discussed at the War Committee in December 1916. The President of the Board of Trade, Walter Runciman, was confident that he could supply 300, and with the service cuts agreed another 300 could be found. Demand for the release of locomotives grew in the last two years of the war. In January 1917 the GWR surrendered 72 Dean

Fig 2.16
The NER surrendered 50
0-8-0s of classes T and T1 for
use by the ROD. Most were
employed on limestone trains
from Marquise Quarries
between Boulogne and Calais,
and all were returned to the
NER in 1919. NER No 793
(ROD No 5793) is seen at
St Omer on 3 October 1918.

Goods 0-6-0s for France in deference to the request for locomotives of the same type. The GWR received 12 locomotives from other companies, leaving a net loss of 60. The LNWR contributed 70 for France and the Metropolitan, 2.

In August there was a request for 0-8-0s. The GWR had none, and its 2-8-0s were needed to haul Admiralty coal trains. The railways agreed to supply 22 0-6-0s for Salonica and 20 2-6-0s for France; the GWR would supply 17 of these, but wanted the Government to authorise materials to build replacements. The equipment surrendered by the railways for overseas theatres was substantial: the LNWR supplied 111 locomotives, 96 to France and 15 to Egypt, plus 6,370 wagons. The GCR sent 18 0-6-0 and 15 0-8-0 locomotives, 2,767 10-ton wagons and 500 covered wagons to France, and 35 brake vans to Egypt. By the end of the war the GWR had supplied 6,086 wagons for France and Egypt.

It wasn't only the loss of locomotives overseas; far more significant, if less widely reported, was the number of locomotives awaiting repair, usually for want of the materials and skilled men. By May 1917 about 3,000 locomotives across Britain awaited repairs, and the REC warned Sir Guy Granet, Director General of Movements and Railways, that there was 'an impossibility of avoiding a breakdown if steps are not taken by Government to secure that supplies are forthcoming, and that men are released from the Army for work in the railway shops'.[150] This elicited an instruction to the Ministry of Munitions to supply steel, copper and brass, but there was no promise that men would be released from the forces. It did little to alleviate the position: by the end of the war about 5,000 locomotives, or one-fifth of the locomotive stock, were awaiting repair.

Unavailability of suitable locomotives created the ludicrous sight of a Midland coal train being hauled by one of Johnson's elegant Spinners, its single 7ft 4in driving wheel designed for bantam-weight expresses. Equally enginemen often had to work on locomotives they had never even seen before, and both driving and firing of steam locomotives call for knowledge of the design's characteristics to obtain the best and most economical performance.

Some locomotives for domestic use were built, and the net increase in locomotives between June 1914 and 1919 on English and Welsh railways was 132, and in Scotland, 56.[151]

Over 600 locomotives and 15,000–18,000 wagons having been sent across to France, they had to be brought back again, and by 1919 wagons were being returned at the rate of 600–900 a week, though unsurprisingly all needed repair.

Ambulance trains

Anticipating heavy casualties from mechanised war, the War Office had begun preparing plans for an 'all-lines' ambulance train in 1912 by consulting the railways and the Royal Army Medical Corps which would staff them, so that the War Office had only to say how many it wanted when the need arose. The LNWR was given the job of designing a standard ambulance train for use in Britain. Since different braking systems were used on the Continent, as well as there being other technical differences, bespoke trains had to be built for service in France.

Within nine days of war being declared, a request had been lodged with the LNWR for a naval ambulance train, on 6 August. Men who were on holiday from Wolverton carriage works were recalled and worked day and night for 30 hours to enable No 1 Naval Ambulance Train to be dispatched at 4.30 am on 8 August to Chatham Dockyard. Similar feats were achieved by other companies; the SECR created two 11-vehicle trains for the Admiralty, each in 48 hours.

Though a standard specification had been drawn up, ambulance trains were made up from modified vehicles so differed between them and increased in length. For example, Swindon Works turned out the first two GWR trains by 9 October, each comprising six 40ft vans as ward coaches, two family carriages and one restaurant car. The GWR supplied two cooks for each train. Naval and military trains also differed: military cots were fixed to the sides of carriages,

Fig 2.17
The railways' carriage and wagon workshops turned out ambulance trains with extraordinary rapidity, working 24 hours a day. This LYR ambulance train has been posed with a 2-4-2T.

Fig 2.18
Ambulance train interiors
were largely standardised,
based on specifications
determined by the Royal
Army Medical Corps before
the war. Here soldiers
are being transported to
the French coast in an
unidentified train, c 1916.

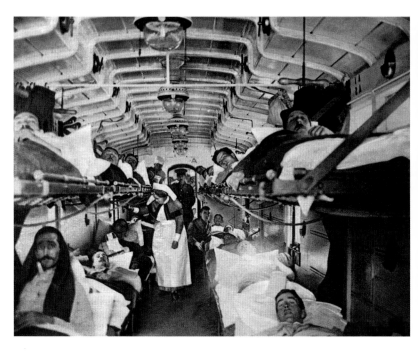

whereas naval trains had moveable cots that could be suspended from hooks
with pads to prevent lateral jarring.

A typical ambulance train for use in Britain would have a number of
linoleum-floored ward cars, a baggage car, a dining car, a kitchen car with
pantry, a complete pharmacy, a lead-floored treatment room, linen rooms, an
office, stores, hot and cold water supplies, and lavatories. Sometimes a separate
carriage or area would be set aside for those with infectious illnesses. They
would be dual braked to allow them to travel over all lines and electrically lit with
batteries capable of supplying light for 24 hours while stationary. Lights were
fitted with green shades. Ward cars were often made from parcel vans which
had suitably large doors. Typically they had capacity for 4 officers and 96 men
lying down and considerably more sitting up. In charge was a surgeon general
who received telegrams twice a week from all the larger military and Territorial
general hospitals, which stated the number of beds vacant in each. Some trains
had telephones to help communication between carriages.

Until the first ambulance trains were ready, complex ad hoc arrangements had
to be made for wounded soldiers arriving from evacuated hospitals in Ostend and
Antwerp. Landed in Kent, some were sent to Abergavenny, and the official detailed
to escort them had to make special arrangements even on London's Inner Circle
for a coach to be set aside for them. The GWR provided a bogie corridor coach
so that the men could lie down. The same official had to take 19 badly wounded
Belgians to Bedale in Yorkshire. The SECR provided a bogie saloon which was
met at Cannon Street by a GNR tank to take the coach round to King's Cross to
be attached to the 1.40 pm express, the coach being detached for the final leg to
Bedale on the Hawes branch. Red Cross volunteers accompanied the soldiers.[152]

The first large order was for 12 nine-vehicle ambulance trains of which the
LNWR built three; the GWR, Midland and GCR, two each; and the GER, LYR

and LSWR, one. All of them were converted from existing stock, as were most later ones. The first, built by the GCR, reached Southampton on 24 August only hours after the first wounded had been landed. They had been transferred to Netley Hospital (*see* p 48) by a train of pre-war WD stock. The other 11 trains arrived at Southampton by 30 August. Four more ambulance trains were required in January 1915.

The railwayman charged with setting out the technical requirements of operating ambulance trains on the Continent was Francis Dent. Besides being general manager of the SECR, Dent was a lieutenant colonel in the Engineer and Railway Staff Corps and a member of the REC. Responding to a War Office request, Dent was sent to France in September 1914 with a representative of the LNWR and GER to discuss technical issues with the Chemin du Fer du Nord and to assess what modifications would be necessary to allow British rolling stock to operate on French railways.

The scale of casualties took Dent to France again in December to discuss specifications for bespoke ambulance trains to be built in British railway workshops. He became the chairman of the Ambulance Trains for the Continent Sub-committee of the REC, which oversaw production of ambulance trains. The GER and LNWR carried out the work. A standard design was produced and eight trains were asked for in April 1915. Altogether the LNWR built seven ambulance trains for the Continent.

When in May 1915 more were required for France, the REC convened a subcommittee of representatives from the LSWR, GWR, LNWR and SECR to consider the provision and running of ambulance trains. New specifications were drawn up and the LNWR, GWR, GER and LSWR each undertook to provide one of the four new trains required by the War Office.[153] The length and capacity of continental ambulance trains was larger. A 16-coach train built in 1915 at the LYR's Newton Heath Carriage Works could accommodate 144 lying-down cases in the 4 ward cars, 256 sitting up and another 64 in a car for those with infectious illnesses. With staff, the train accommodated 530 people.[154]

It became customary to display newly built ambulance trains at major stations and charge the public a fee to walk through them, the money being given to medical charities or to funds to send comfort parcels to railway staff who were POWs. The GWR exhibited the two trains it built in November 1915 at 15 stations and charged 1s for a walk-through (3d for GWR employees).[155] The LNWR displayed part of its train at Euston and Cannon Street, and when the GER put its 16-coach train on display at Liverpool Street, 50,354 visitors raised £1,311 0s 7d to provide comforts for the railway engineering section of the Army in France.[156]

Most casualties from France were routed through Southampton, which became the base for 14 ambulance trains. The LSWR ran 10,332 ambulance trains carrying 1,848,623 wounded men, and of the 196 stations receiving patients, 40 were on the LSWR. The wounded from other theatres came through Avonmouth, Devonport and Liverpool, while Hull and Boston were used for British repatriated disabled POWs. The railwaymen assigned to operating ambulance trains remained railway employees, and from October 1914 received a bonus of 2/- a day.

The frequency of ambulance trains was naturally determined by the ferocity of fighting on the front. The Battle of the Somme in early July 1916 provided a particular period of stress. In the week from 9 July, 155 ambulance trains left Southampton Docks, compared with 29 trains on 7 July. The destination of the war's first casualties was the vast Royal Victoria Hospital at Netley near Southampton, built in the wake of the Crimean War, with its own railway station. But as the numbers of wounded rose, they were taken further and further afield, the longest haul being to Strathpeffer in the Highlands, where the Pavilion and the HR's Highland Hotel became hospitals.

Railwaymen witnessed the unloading even if the task of carrying stretcher cases was done by medical orderlies. As *The Times* recorded on 25 January 1915, 'the unloading of an ambulance train is always a sad sight ... They crawl along, moving very slowly. They are bowed and listless ... These men left England fine, alert, young soldiers.' Such sights may have motivated railway funding of hospital beds; the Tondu GWR Locomotive and Carriage War Distress Fund sponsored a bed in the local Coytrahen Red Cross Hospital.

A rather more breezy account was reproduced in the ASLEF magazine in 1918, describing life on an ambulance train after leaving a south-coast port with a mix of British and German casualties:

> The orderlies make the patients comfortable for their journey, and then collect the labels which are attached to each patient and hand them in at the office where a record is made. The medical officer comes round to each one with his cheery smile and jocular manner ... with a pleasant word for everyone.

> The patients have to be fed, and the orderlies rise to the occasion. Feeding patients is an art in itself when the train is travelling at the rate of 50 to 70 miles an hour. The carrying of soup in basins on trays, especially, necessitates a good deal of juggling. The orderlies delight to display their skill. ... Jam sandwiches go down with a relish, and there are many 'Oliver Twists' among the patients. [The orderlies] see men who experience hunger every day, and the ozone of the Channel is productive of not easily satisfied appetites.

> When all are fed and warm, inside as well as out, cigarettes are distributed, and some smoke while others sleep. ... Some of the patients are fond of passing away the tedious hours in recounting their experiences. Invariably, they make light of their wounds. ...we stop at one of our great railway centres. A large crowd of women and children and business men peer in at the windows, handing in gifts for the patients or wishing them good luck. A nursing orderly hands out some postcards and letters with the request that they be posted, most of them being roughly pencilled lines to relatives and friends. [At the destination] we find motor ambulances drawn up in readiness, with patriotic women of the W.A.A.C. [Women's Army Auxiliary Corps] standing beside them to drive away as soon as they are loaded. Men of the R.A.M.C. [Royal Army Medical Corps], the St. John Ambulance Corps and the Red Cross stretcher bearers are waiting to enter the wards with stretchers. The medical officer and the sergeant alight. 'Boards out!' roars the sergeant, and the orderlies adjust the boards at the doors so that the bearers may avoid the step. [We train staff] change the linen, make the beds, and, with brush and soap and water and elbow-grease, make our train spick and span for the next convoy, as we return to the disembarkation port once more.[157]

Wounded German POWs travelled with Allied servicemen, and one orderly, Alfred Pope Russell, wrote that he felt most sorry for them as they would have no one to visit them.

The last requests came after the US entered the war. In January 1918 the War Office requested 12 ambulance trains of standard type for the use of American forces in France, and a further 7 proved necessary. By the end of the war the railway companies had built 20 ambulance trains for England, plus 3 for the Navy, 2 for Scotland and 2 for Ireland, 31 for overseas use and 19 for the US Army in France.[158]

Military railways

Military railways had two principal functions: to train servicemen in the many skills required for railway operations in war, and to service training camps and stores of matériel, usually munitions, which required storage in secure locations. The oldest and largest network was the Royal Arsenal Railway, serving the Woolwich ordnance factory, research centre and testing range, which covered 1,285 acres by the First World War.

Many of the 1,100 buildings were served only by railway. These were laid to three gauges, though predominantly standard and 18in (457mm) gauges, which amounted to 147 miles of track at its greatest extent, some of it dual gauge. From 1859 standard-gauge lines began to replace plateways dating from 1824, and the first 18in lines were officially opened in 1873, drawing on the experience of the LNWR's system around Crewe Works. Both gauges carried passengers and freight, and the volume of traffic required over 90 standard-gauge 0-4-0 saddle tanks and over 80 18in gauge locomotives. A roundhouse reminiscent of the pioneer London & Birmingham Railway structure at Camden was built for the larger gauge in 1891–2.

Fig 2.19
Longmoor camp c 1912 with what is probably the A325 Petersfield–Farnham road in the foreground.

Fig 2.20
No locomotives were requisitioned for Longmoor until 1916, but some were hired in earlier. First to arrive, in October 1914, was the most improbable, LSWR Adams Radial 4-4-2 tank No 424, built by Beyer Peacock in 1882. It is thought to have remained at Longmoor until mid-1916, when it was transferred to the Fovant Military Railway in Wiltshire; it was purchased outright by the WD in June 1916. It was overhauled by the GWR's Swindon Works in November 1920, when it was given a GWR safety-valve bonnet and dome cover, as well as a coat of Brunswick Green, before being sent to Catterick Camp in Yorkshire.

It was the Boer War which spawned the first military railways to camps, such as the branch from Ludgershall to Tidworth in Wiltshire, which opened for military traffic to the newly created camp on 8 July 1901. It was built under an agreement between the War Office and the MSWJR, which staffed and operated the line.

However, the most famous military railway in Britain had its origins in a different role during the Boer War. The Longmoor Military Railway (LMR) in Hampshire arose from a camp created to receive returning troops from South Africa and was largely finished by 1903. The first railway, of 18in gauge, was built by the Royal Corps of Engineers to move complete huts around the camp, and the standard-gauge railway from Bordon to Woolmer and Longmoor followed in 1906–7. It was known as the Woolmer Instructional Military Railway until 1935. The agreement and connection with the LSWR at Bordon allowed main-line coaching stock to work over the LMR, and the first special trains bringing Territorial Army units to the camp ran in 1912. Companies came for annual training and to practise mobilisation, entraining and loading technical stores to identify shortcomings and anomalies.

When war was declared in August 1914, the five RE railway companies were mobilised. Training became Longmoor's principal activity, with emphasis on construction rather than operating, though it had a large instructional model railway built by model manufacturers Bassett-Lowke of Northampton.

The original strategy was for all railway support for the BEF to be provided by the French, but it soon became apparent that the operating resources of the French railways were hard-pressed to meet their own requirements. Consequently, the Railway Operating Division RE was formed, and the obvious base was Longmoor. The Railway Operating Troops Depot RE was formed in April 1915, and by March 1919 it had trained 494 officers and 26,089 soldiers. Many of the skilled engineers and technicians for this work came from British-owned railways in South America, with the complement of the Railway Construction Troops Depot rising from 300 in 1914 to 1,139 in 1918.

By early 1916 the War Office was so aware of the need for competent staff in the ROD, Railway Construction Corps and Railway Transport Establishments that it ordered the railway companies not to release any further railwaymen for general duties until 3,000 men had been supplied to these units.[159]

Fig 2.21
The station at Longmoor and
the 0-6-0ST *Woolmer*, built
by the Avonside Engine Co
for Longmoor, where it
remained until 1919, when it
went to Hilsea in Hampshire.
Though withdrawn from
Tidworth in 1953, *Woolmer's*
history prompted its
preservation and it is today
on loan from the National
Railway Museum to the
Milestones Living History
Museum at Basingstoke in
Hampshire. The coach in the
platform may be one of the
two light railway carriages
bought for Longmoor from
the Kent & East Sussex
Railway in 1909.

But Longmoor was more than a training centre; it was also used as a base to test equipment for construction and operation of trench systems and the application of internal-combustion engines in railway operations. It also supplied the officers and men to operate 12 light railways at other military camps, and the locomotives and rolling stock used on them were repaired at Longmoor.

Among other railways built purely for military purposes was the line from the East Coast main line at Peascliffe into Belton Park near Grantham. The 3rd Lord Brownlow offered the War Office the use of Belton Park, and after use by the BEF, it became the training school for the Machine Gun Corps, formed in October 1915. Besides barracks, the camp had instruction rooms, chapels, a post office, YMCA huts and a hospital. To operate the line, the GNR reported in December 1914 that it had purchased on behalf of the War Office a six-coupled shunting tank engine from Hudswell, Clarke of Leeds at a cost of £900 for the contractors' line. The GNR was prepared to work the line and look after maintenance on the understanding that expenses incurred would be submitted to the War Office.[160]

The GNR also served large camps at Harrowby and Clipstone, as well as what was then the naval aerodrome at Cranwell near Sleaford. The NER served Catterick, where the camp covered 25 sq miles and hosted as many as 45,000 men at a time. Catterick Bridge station on the Richmond branch exemplifies the way a rural byway could be transformed by war: in 1913 it handled 5,720 tons of traffic; during the war it averaged 160,000 tons a year. A new camp at Ripon was established in late 1914 with 4 miles of railway, which received 250,000 tons during the war.

On the LSWR a camp was built at Fovant in Wiltshire, primarily for the use of Australian troops, and connected in 1915 by a 2½-mile line to the Salisbury–Exeter line at Dinton. The Peckett 0-6-0T built for the War Office to work the line survives on the Northampton & Lamport Railway.

Responsibility for working the lines varied between the WD and the railway providing the connection. In March 1918, for example, the GWR agreed to a request from the WD to assume the working of the lines to the Wiltshire camps at Codford (4 miles) and Sutton Veny (5 miles from the junction at Heytesbury).[161]

Railway works and war equipment

The potential contribution the railways' workshops could make to the war effort was recognised by the President of the Board of Trade, Runciman. The size and capability of the railway companies' workshops ranged from the town-sized plant at Crewe, complete with Bessemer steelworks, to the cottage-industry scale of Cirencester and Machen. About two dozen substantial engineering workshops belonging to the railway companies were scattered across Britain, with a rather smaller number of independent contract locomotive builders employing 21,000 people. The latter met domestic demand when it exceeded a railway company's own capacity and built locomotives for dozens of countries around the world, though principally for the Empire.

It took little time for the first orders to be placed with the railways. In September 1914 the War Office asked the REC whether 12,250 ambulance stretchers of standard pattern could be produced, and a meeting of carriage and wagon superintendents divided the work between 11 companies. Deliveries began within 10 days. In the same month the railways were asked to build 5,000 'General Service' wagons which would be marked with an 'X'; they were supplied at the rate of 400 a week from December 1914, with company builds ranging from the LNWR's total of 650 to the GSWR's 40.[162] By October 1914 the GWR was already building road vehicles, adapting 60 two-horse vans and other vehicles. Gun carriages were urgently needed, and Sir Frederick Donaldson, Director of Army Ordnance at Woolwich Arsenal, and the LNWR's CME, C J Bowen-Cooke, dissected plans of gun carriages so that, at a meeting on 20 October, the CMEs of the Midland, GWR, NER, GNR, LYR and LNWR could decide how best to parcel out the work.

It soon became apparent that a body was needed to coordinate orders, so the Railway War Manufacturers' Sub-committee was established, comprising initially the CMEs of the principal railway companies and representatives of the War Office chaired by the GNR's C H Dent. Later the Ministry of Munitions and the Admiralty were represented. Requests for work were made through this subcommittee, though the actual order was issued by the REC. It was agreed that no profit would be levied on all work carried out for the Government.

The work ranged from picket pegs and posts to armoured and ambulance trains and included ambulance stretchers, road wagons for artillery, water-tank carts, harnesses, spare wagon wheels, luggage barrows, travelling kitchen limbers, gun carriages, naval gun mountings and trench howitzers.[163] The GWR also made saddle trees, aeroplane components, mattresses and pillows, howitzer gun carriages, 105 6-pounder Hotchkiss guns, copper bands for shells and ammunition wagons.

The railways offered to do more, but wanted compensation for costs of deferred maintenance work, which was difficult to calculate. As it was, most works were operating at full stretch. In 1915 Gorton Works in Manchester was kept running for 22 hours a day in double shifts for seven days a week with just three days' holiday a year and a Saturday afternoon and Sunday off once every three weeks.[164]

Inevitably Crewe Works assumed a major role. Part of it became HM No 9 Munitions Store, requiring the movement of 330,000 tons in 44,000 wagon-loads. The works manufactured components for guns, pressings for aeroplanes, 6in high-explosive shells made by women and girls working three eight-hour shifts, and the Bessemer mill turned out rail for other companies. In summer 1915 the Crewe MP, Ernest Craig, addressed the shops in turn, telling up to 2,400 workers at a time of the crucial importance of their high-class work.[165]

Fears of invasion grew following the departure of the BEF, creating a sense of increased vulnerability. In October 1914 Crewe Works received an order for two armoured trains for coastal defence based on South African experience; a trial run took place between Crewe and Chester on 26 December 1914. The first comprised two gun trucks made from Caledonian 30-ton boiler trolleys, two infantry trucks from GWR 40-ton coal wagons and a 200-gallon water tank between the frames to supply the 0-6-2 locomotive, sheathed in ½in (13mm) thick steel plate. Each gun truck had a Maxim and 12-pounder quick-firing gun with a range of 3 miles, and one truck on each train had a 1-ton coal bunker. The second armoured train was built to the same specification but the 0-6-2 condensing tank locomotive came from the GNR. One train was stabled on the Midland & Great Northern Joint Railway (M&GNJR) and the other on the NBR north of Edinburgh.[166]

With the munitions crisis of 1915 which led to Lloyd George becoming Minister of Munitions in May, most of the 32 railway companies which participated in war production became involved with production of shells or components. A major role adopted by eight railway companies was the re-forming of brass cartridge cases returned to Britain after firing. At first, split cases were scrapped, but Swindon Works devised a brazing technique which was adopted by others. By the end of the war, over 33 million cases of four different calibres had been re-formed, and 2 million brazed.[167] Private companies producing ammunition included Birmingham Railway Carriage & Wagon, Beyer Peacock, John Fowler, Gloucester Railway Carriage & Wagon, Hunslet Engineering, Hurst Nelson, Metropolitan Railway Carriage & Wagon, Ashbury Railway Carriage & Iron, Patent Shaft & Axletree, North British Locomotive and Vulcan Foundry. The Midland's locomotive works at Derby was an example of the way production methods were refined: it began by producing 3,000 fuses a week on its existing machines, but introduced new plant of automatic lathes and other equipment that allowed production to reach 30,000 fuses a week, carried out by 550 women among the workforce.[168]

The small works at Melton Constable produced roller bearings and aircraft parts as well as helping the Midland and GNR with locomotive repairs. The innovative Civil Engineer and Locomotive Superintendent William Marriott continued in his pioneering use of concrete, saving bricks, steel and wood which were all in short supply.

Besides the ambulance trains produced by various companies (*see* p 45), a Mobile Advanced Headquarters Train for Sir Douglas Haig was built at the LNWR's carriage works at Wolverton comprising 14 bogie vehicles, 11 of them former picnic saloons.

The pay disparities of war production work became a source of grievance at some workshops, since relatively unskilled munition workers were being paid higher wages than skilled workers in the railway plants. According to an August 1917 report on Swindon Works, 'the unrest which for some time existed ... has been aggravated by unskilled men working on the breaking of steel billets using specially installed machinery earning more through piece work rates than skilled men'.[169] The GWR began to take the view that now the Ministry of Munitions had its own establishments, 'the time has arrived for considerably restricting, if not of discontinuing, munition work at Swindon'. This ceased in December 1917 when the last 18-pounder cartridge case was made, bringing the total made since April 1915 to 1.63 million.

In November 1917 there was a suggestion that Swindon might become involved with aeroplane production, but it was recognised that the men would want the same remuneration as the new aircraft factories, and the Department of Aeronautical Supplies accepted that the railway companies would not undertake the work. Though war munitions at Swindon was being gradually discontinued,[170] the GWR did manufacture in 1918 some large covered vans for the carriage of dismantled aircraft; they were fitted with dual braking systems for work on the Continent. Though they may have been too late to be of use, their end doors later made them suitable for cars and scenery traffic.[171]

Inevitably the diversion of workshops to munitions had a deleterious effect on railway work, and in February 1918 the War Priorities Committee noted that:

... the attention of the General Services Committee [of the War Priorities Committee] has been very forcibly drawn to the serious shortage of Railway locomotives and wagons existing in this country and also in India, Egypt and the Colonies.

The Works which manufactured locomotives have during the War been engaged largely on the production of munitions, resulting in the complete dislocation of their plant, much of which is necessarily lying idle. They have also lost a large number of their skilled men, many of whom it will be difficult or impossible to replace.

After the War there will be an enormous demand for all kinds of Railway Stock, not only in the United Kingdom, but also in India, the Dominions and Colonies and particularly in Belgium. The Committee are of the opinion that preparations should be made without delay for this Country to meet that demand or much valuable business will inevitably be diverted to other Countries. The Committee put forward the following suggestions:

1. As the output of munitions is now being curtailed, orders should be issued to all Government Departments to release Railway Loco and Wagon Works as soon as possible from munitions contracts so that they may revert to and concentrate upon their normal manufacture.

2. That, in order to increase production, standard types of engines and rolling stock should be adopted and the manufacture of these concentrated in the existing Works.

3. Repairs only and not new construction should be undertaken at the Railway Companies Works, especially in view of the very largely increased number of locomotives at present out of repair.

4. The Government munitions works should, immediately after the termination of the war, be employed, so far as their machinery permits, in the manufacture of standardised engine and wagon parts, which in certain cases could be turned out in large quantities.[172]

The committee's recommendations were heeded. A letter from the Ministry of Munitions of War to the Secretary of the War Priorities Committee, dated 5 April 1918, noted that 'many of the contracts for the manufacture of gun ammunition components placed with locomotive and wagon works have recently been cancelled, to enable those works to revert to their normal manufacture'.[173] An exception was the NER-controlled 18-pounder shrapnel plant at Westmoreland Street, Darlington, partly because it was a purpose-built factory so did not interfere with railway work, but also because of 'the Railway War Manufacturers' Sub-Committee's desire to keep on these small contracts [for gun ammunition components] in order to employ the women who have been specially trained for the purpose. The machinery used is not serviceable for railway work.'[174]

An official record was presented to the Government in May 1920 detailing the work done by the railway companies. It ran to 121 pages and emphasised how the railways had responded to the demand for matériel at the expense of their own services and efficiency. The condition of the railways in 1919 proved a handicap that would resonate through the next two decades as the regulated railways struggled to compete with unfettered road transport. As Churchill commented in 1928: 'It is the duty of the state to hold the balance even between road and rail.' Fortunately for Britain in the next conflict, the consequences of ignoring the railways' call for a 'square deal' had not sufficiently impaired their ability to rise to another challenge.

Keeping up with prices

At the outset of the war, the NUR had proposed that the Railway Conciliation Scheme set up by Lloyd George in 1907 should continue. The first national railway strike in 1911 had succeeded in getting union representatives a place on the company conciliation boards, which dealt with matters of pay, hours and conditions. Discussions were being held to resolve grievances over the way they operated when war broke out, and the REC proposed a meeting with the NUR and ASLEF to discuss the amendments to the existing scheme.

The rise in the cost of living almost immediately put pressure on the railways, and in turn on the Government, to address the fact. At a meeting on 3 February 1915 between the REC, the NUR and ASLEF:

> ... it was represented that there was great unrest and discontent amongst the railwaymen arising out of the abnormal working conditions due to the War and the increased cost of living and that great pressure had been brought to bear upon the Societies by railwaymen throughout the Kingdom to at once give the notice provided by the Conciliation 'truce' agreement or alternatively to secure for them some additional remuneration to meet the increased cost of living.[175]

The union representatives asked for a War Bonus of 5s a week for all wage-earning employees. The President of the Board of Trade responded that the Government would be willing to share additional expense with the railway companies, but the GWR board was unsurprisingly strongly of the opinion that it should be treated as a working expense to be borne by the Government.[176]

The Government agreed to accept 75 per cent as a working expense, but later accepted 100 per cent as inflation continued.

The first War Bonus was agreed at a meeting between the REC, the NUR and ASLEF at London's Midland Grand Hotel on 13 February 1915: those on less than 30s a week or £80 per annum would receive 3s; those on more than 30s or an annual salary between £80 and £150 would receive 2s. Youths aged between 14 and 17 were excluded from the bonus, and in June a thousand youths at Swindon Works went on strike. It was agreed they should receive a 1s 6d bonus, applicable to all boys under 18 in railway service from August. Women too were denied the War Bonus, and 70 women carriage cleaners at Old Oak Common went on strike in April 1916 in protest.[177]

There was a strong presumption among railwaymen against strike action for much of the war, expressed in June 1915 by the NUR's first president, Albert Bellamy, when he told a meeting in Southampton that: 'There must be no strike during the war. If railwaymen were to strike at this moment they would be traitors, not only to their country, but to the thousands of their own members who were now serving their native land.'[178]

War Bonus arrangements were reviewed three monthly, with some increases under further agreements in June and October 1915, when the bonus was increased to 5s for those over 18 and to 2s 6d for those under 18. The agreement contained the undertaking that:

> The National Union of Railwaymen and the Associated Society of Locomotive Engineers and Firemen undertake that during the pendency of this agreement they will not present to the Railway Companies any fresh demands for increased wages, or general alterations in conditions of service, and that they will not give countenance or support either to a demand on the part of any of their members to reopen the settlement now made, or to any strike that might be entered upon in furtherance of such demand.[179]

Continued rises in the cost of living made short shrift of that commitment, and the NUR newspaper reported a demonstration in Hyde Park in August 1916 of 'between 6,000 and 40,000', organised by the London Council of the NUR, about rising food costs. One of the 30 speakers said that 'it would be a great misfortune if the railways were to be stopped', but there was resentment about war profiteering when the cost of living had risen by 70 per cent.[180]

Adding to the unrest on the railways were 'the wages paid in the munition works, docks, etc, when men employed side by side with the railwaymen, and in the case of the docks, on similar work, get two, three, or four times as much wages'.[181] The railway companies recognised that some or even all of the War Bonuses could not be withdrawn when war ended, yet every 5s added to the War Bonus meant a 2 per cent reduction in dividends on their ordinary share capital; 10s would obliterate the dividend.

So anxiety over the cost of the demand for an additional 10s a week bonus, made in summer 1916, was combined with sympathy for its justice and a recognition that the October 1915 agreement had been unwise in not allowing for revisions. On 19 June 1916 the secretary of the South Wales & Monmouthshire District Council of the NUR, G H Godwin, wrote to Herbert Asquith with a typical resolution about the cost of living and the comment that those 'in receipt of a standard wage, find it impossible to live, owing to the exorbitant prices asked for commodities and as a result our children are underfed and bootless, and this while other workers are in receipt of double our wage and others amassing fortunes, while we (patriotic) Railwaymen are on the verge of starvation'.[182]

The two main questions were: who should negotiate, and what would the position be after the war? The general managers were reluctant to negotiate and would only do so if the Government provided the railways with a guarantee for some period after the war. The NUR insisted on national, not company-level negotiations. On 19 July 1916 J E Williams, secretary of the NUR, wrote to Prime Minister Asquith: 'You will be aware that by the agreement between this Union and the Railway Companies we are prevented from putting forward fresh demands for increased wages until at least an opportunity has been given to discuss the matter with you.'[183]

It was accepted that the War Bonus should be reviewed three monthly and it was increased under further agreements in September 1916, April, August and November 1917, and April 1918. Up to the end of July 1917, the fixed sum per week was paid irrespective of hours worked, but under the August 1917 agreement the term 'War Bonus' was altered to 'War Wage' and overtime and Sunday duty were calculated on the fixed rate of pay plus the War Bonus.

The Government bore practically the whole cost of the War Wage paid to the wages staff and to salaried staff up to £500 per annum. The War Bonus was not paid to employees at some of the smaller railway companies, such as the Southwold and the Lynton & Barnstaple, and their employees objected, especially where, as at Barnstaple, railwaymen from larger companies were neighbours. Both railways argued that no extra strain had been placed on the men, as traffic had declined on both 'holiday' lines, but the Board of Trade Railway Department examined the issue in 1916 and accepted the case that during the period of control, the men should receive the bonus.[184]

Much more serious was the reaction of railwaymen at the way some companies were deducting a proportion of the War Bonus for poor timekeeping. For instance, a notice put up by the Caledonian Railway at St Rollox, Glasgow, in 1916 said that 'in the event of an employee not being available for duty during the entire working day, exclusive of overtime, a proportion of his weekly War Bonus, equal to 1/6th of the whole, would be deducted for each day, or part of a day, that the employee is not available'.[185] It took strong pressure from the Cabinet to resolve the matter. The Rt Hon Walter Runciman wrote from 10 Downing Street to W F Marwood, Secretary of the Board of Trade Railways Department, that:

> ... the General Managers may be hurt by the imperative tone of the Cabinet, but for your own private information you should know that my colleagues were very impatient with the Companies and said they could not tolerate friction and the General Managers ought to make a handsome settlement and avoid being subjected to something humiliating, if they don't do the handsome thing now.[186]

By 1 March 1917 the price of food had risen by 92 per cent over pre-war prices.[187]

For their part, the companies made good the pledges made to enlisting staff; for instance, GWR staff returning after being wounded and rendered unfit for their former role were given lower positions but 'paid the maximum rate of the position they are called upon to fill with the addition of an allowance equal to the difference between their old and new rates of wages'.[188] At the Midland's 1917 AGM the chairman, G Murray Smith, promised that:

> ... partially disabled men – and after two years of war there are many of these – who are unable to take up their old duties, will be and are, if possible, found work on the railway which it is in their power to perform. If a disabled man does not fit a machine, we try, by altering the machine, to make it fit the man, and we shall always try to find a disabled man who wishes to work some work to do.[189]

The excessive hours being worked encouraged the unions to make the eight-hour day an objective for a post-war settlement. The indispensable role of the railways made it imperative to try to avoid industrial unrest, and Sir Albert Stanley, President of the Board of Trade, pledged:

> ... the Government, the War Cabinet, and myself personally, to continue the present control of the Railways for a time after the cessation of hostilities, so that there would be an opportunity afforded within one month to bring forward a request for a shorter working day while the Railways were under control, and that any reasonable request for a shorter working day would have the immediate and sympathetic consideration of the Government.[190]

It was reported in October 1917 that the REC felt that Stanley had 'gone too far in the direction of encouraging the idea that an eight hour day would be granted after the war'.[191]

Skilled railwaymen were discontented with their wages compared with what was termed 'the District Rate' of other mechanics, often on piecework and earning higher wages. There was a month-long strike at Swindon in the autumn of 1917, when members of the Boilermakers' Society objected to a concession made to lower-paid men in the boiler shops. The union refused arbitration, but later settled after a Ministry of Labour intervention that entailed an entire revision of wages at Swindon Works.[192]

Further strikes occurred in January 1918 at Wolverhampton and Tyseley over a demand that a 12½ per cent War Bonus paid to men and women employed on munitions work in railway workshops be extended to all NUR members. A further increase of 4s was accepted, bringing the War Wage to 25s. In August 1918 introduction of a sliding scale based on the cost of living raised the War Wage to 30s, but this was deemed insufficient, and an unofficial strike began at Llantrisant in September 1918 and quickly spread, mostly on the GWR. Almost half of England and Wales was affected, though only 85 union branches – about a quarter of the total – were involved. On this occasion the demand for an increase was resisted by the Government, which offered to meet but not to reopen negotiations on the War Wage. The Executive Committee of ASLEF advised striking members to resume duty, and the strike was in defiance of the NUR and led to the resignation of its general secretary, J H Thomas, though he was persuaded to remain in office. At a meeting in Cardiff on 25 September members agreed to resume work, having been assured that no strikers would be victimised. London area strikers agreed on the evening of the 26th to return to work.

The first award under the sliding-scale scheme, of 3s, was made on 1 November 1918, 10 days before the war ended. The average railwayman's wage had more than doubled during the war, but so had the cost of living. Discontent was rife on the railways as the war ended, and would erupt in a damaging strike to the railway industry in 1919.

Using railway land

Every railway had land that was idle, around stations and alongside the track, and as the loss of merchant shipping created food shortages, railway employees were encouraged to cultivate it for food production. In July 1915 the Board of Agriculture and Fisheries wrote to the REC secretary expressing the hope that railway companies would facilitate and encourage their employees or competent persons to grow agricultural produce on waste land adjoining the railway.[193]

GWR tenancies rose from 1,507 covering 72 acres in January 1917 to 4,608 on 222 acres by May 1917. By the end of the war there were 6,387 on 307 acres.[194] Help with food production was volunteered by clerks in the General Offices at Paddington who became farm workers during their annual holidays in 1915.

The LNWR had 6,800 plots of land for staff use. Land for an additional 7,050 plots made available.[195] The LSWR established a Potato Growing Committee to encourage cultivation of hitherto unproductive land; potatoes were grown at such unpromising sites as the old locomotive works at Nine Elms. By the last year of the war, 7,000 LSWR staff had allotments alongside the line or on other ground free of charge, and the company supplied them with seed potatoes at cost price and money for prizes and lectures.

Food shortages encouraged Metropolitan Railway staff under its commercial manager to use land beside the railway between Harrow and Uxbridge, bringing

Fig 2.22
On 20 July 1918 the King and Queen visited allotments and piggeries in south-west London. This photograph was taken of a prize-winner on LSWR allotments.

15 acres into cultivation. A plough was bought, and women employed as bill posters supplemented men from various departments who volunteered for the paid work, planting half an acre with turnip seed and the rest with 14 tons of seed potatoes. The produce was to be sold to company staff.[196]

Britain's reliance on imports for 60 per cent of its food in 1914 was reflected in a reliance on Denmark for eggs. The need to maximise food production prompted the GER to create a Poultry Demonstration Train, which operated during October and November 1916 and was visited by 45,796 people at 37 stations throughout East Anglia. The four-vehicle train displayed models of poultry houses and other appliances; methods of hatching and rearing; egg production, table poultry and packages; and egg testing and grading. It ran with a restaurant car to serve coffee and as accommodation for the staff. It proved so popular that the number of station visits had to be increased.

The poultry train's success led the GER to buy the 480-acre Dodnash Priory Farm at Bentley in Suffolk as a poultry demonstration farm. The GER works at Stratford built the henhouses (each given a works number like a locomotive) and by 1920 the farm was producing 40,000 eggs a month, as well as chickens, turkeys, fruit and vegetables for the GER hotels, restaurants, dining cars and buffets. The farm was also a rest home for GER horses and had its own siding south of Bentley station. It was sold by the London & North Eastern Railway (LNER) in 1927.[197]

Damage from enemy action

The first damage to the railway was inflicted by Admiral Hipper's raid on Scarborough, Whitby and Hartlepool on 16 December 1914, which caused outrage for the attack on civilians and obloquy of the Royal Navy for its very occurrence. Railwaymen stuck to their posts, though a signalman at Whitby retreated after an 11in shell burst 6 yards from his box. Damage to the railway was most severe at Hartlepool.

Aerial warfare was still in its infancy during the First World War, with bombs initially dropped by hand and aimed by the naked eye. During the entire war, there were just 51 raids on Britain by Zeppelins, the worst year being 1916, but from May 1917 Gotha G.IV bombers and R-planes were also used. Though ports and industry were their principal target, most of the over 300 tons of bombs they dropped fell on civilian areas, killing 1,414 people. Railways were an obvious target, and the GER issued instructions that reports of hostile aircraft should be sent immediately to Liverpool Street station.

To reduce the visibility of targets, the Admiralty suggested to the REC in October 1914 that blinds in trains be kept down at night and asked whether measures to screen the glare from locomotive fires were possible.[198] The order to lower blinds at carriage windows had so little effect on passengers, who much preferred watching the action, that it was rescinded in March 1917. Instead train lights would be extinguished, a rule over which railwaymen had more control.[199]

A subcommittee was formed in September 1915 to decide on the best operational response to air raids. It concluded that traffic should be stopped within a target area, but the absurdity of this became apparent in March 1916 when bombs dropped on Dover and Ramsgate by a single plane resulted in all traffic in and out of London, and all trains on the GER, SECR and London

Tilbury & Southend Railway, being stopped. The procedure was changed to reducing speeds of passenger trains to 15mph, goods to 10mph, so that the firebox door would not have to be opened and attract enemy attention.

A Zeppelin raid on King's Lynn on 19 January 1915 damaged an empty M&GNJR train, and a raid on the line between Leigh and Southend on 10 May 1915 produced 'two sleepers scorched'. Even in one of the worst incidents on the LNWR, at Wednesbury on 31 January 1916, a section of track, a wall, a platelayers' cabin, the goods shed and weighing machine were 'all more or less damaged'.[200] More seriously, on 16 April an airship dropped three bombs on Lowestoft, killing three GER horses, and six bombs on Southwold, setting one of the narrow-gauge railway's wagons on fire.[201]

The first damage on the GWR was in January 1916, when Dudley goods shed was bombed, causing a small fire which was quickly extinguished. Zeppelin raids caused periodic 'lights out' and put a stop to work in March 1916 between Kidderminster and Worcester, and in London and Swindon. Reports suggest that more damage, usually to glass, was caused by shrapnel from anti-aircraft guns than by German bombs. Zeppelin raids caused delays to trains, which might be stopped until the threat passed; Ocean Specials from Falmouth to Paddington were held for over four hours at Savernake and Lavington during April 1916.[202] On 23–4 September 1916 a Zeppelin dropped four bombs on the North London Railway (NLR) at Bow, badly damaging trackwork and destroying seven carriages.[203]

Raids on London increased during 1917. The worst raid of the war took place on the late morning of 13 June 1917, when 20 Gotha G.IV bombers

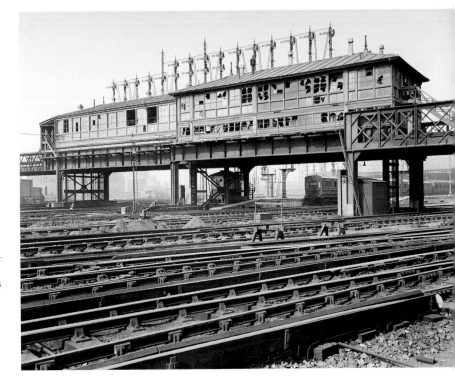

Fig 2.23
Bomb damage to the railways during the First World War was relatively slight. Some glass has been smashed and windows blown out in London Waterloo A signal box.

Fig 2.24
Those who had to cope with the devastation of Second World War bombing would have been wryly amused that this slight damage to track at York Road in Lambeth should have warranted an official photograph.

dropped 7 tons of bombs on London. Three of the bombs landed on Liverpool Street station, killing 16 out of a total of 162 people. Though in retrospect the danger seems minimal compared with the Blitz, the more affluent bought or rented houses in safer commuter towns and villages, increasing the number of season ticket holders travelling into the capital by almost 25 per cent between January and October 1917 for distances of 13–25 miles, and over 100 per cent for those over 25 miles.[204] The 50 per cent increase in fares from 1 January did not apply to season tickets. Up to 7,000 of those who stayed to face the music could find shelter in the basement of the goods warehouse at Marylebone, which the GCR made available; it was one of the largest railway buildings to be destroyed in the Second World War.

By the end of the war, 24 railwaymen had been killed in bombing raids: 12 on the GER and 10 on the Midland, 8 of them from 5 bombs dropped on St Pancras in a single 1918 raid.[205]

Railway docks and ships

As vertically integrated companies, many of the pre-grouping railway companies owned extensive docks, and collectively they accounted for more than half the country's dock facilities. The LSWR owned the most important port for the First World War at Southampton, which it had bought in 1892. The ports were requisitioned from November 1914, most becoming conduits for supplies and matériel, but the GER's Parkeston Quay in Essex became the most important naval base between Dover and the Firth of Forth. The GCR's Grimsby Docks became an RN Reserve Trawler or Mine-Sweeping Section, and its docks at Immingham became a submarine and torpedo-craft base.

The railways owned some of the largest warehouses in the country, and these became part of the supply chains to sustain the country. The railways sometimes waived storage charges at their warehouses in ports. Free storage was given to 4,602 boxes of cheese given by the government of Quebec in October 1914, and free subsequent storage of 'gifts from Colonies to Mother Country' included canned salmon from British Colombia, sugar from Barbados, Jamaica and British Guiana, flour from Ontario and Manitoba, maize from Southern Rhodesia and potatoes from New Brunswick.[206]

Many of the pre-grouping railway companies had significant shipping interests to complement their dock facilities. At the outbreak of war there were 218 railway-owned vessels, and by mid-October 1914 the Admiralty had requisitioned 64, which rose to 126 during the course of the war.[207] The REC expressed concern that they be restored in as supplied condition or the companies reimbursed for the cost of replacement. Compensation was also expected. Most of the railway vessels had been used on ferry services to the Continent or Ireland, but a smaller number provided tourist services, most particularly along the Clyde. The speed and shallow draught of many railway vessels made them ideally suited as troop and hospital ships, and the manoeuvrability, shallow draft and reasonably high speed of paddle steamers made them ideal minesweepers.

The position by 21 October 1914 was as shown in Table 2.1.[208] Requisitioned ships continued to be manned by their own crews with a leavening of Navy personnel.

Three GCR ships were interned at Hamburg at the outbreak of the war, allegedly before expiry of the British ultimatum. The SS *City of Bradford* was intercepted by German patrols off the Elbe in August 1914, taken to Hamburg and incorporated into the Imperial German Navy, and she served as a floating workshop renamed *Donau*. She was returned to the GCR in 1919 and refitted. The SS *City of Leeds* arrived in Hamburg unaware of the outbreak of war and was taken as a prize. Captain Lundie, and the crews of the other ships, were held prisoner at Ruhleben in Germany until the end of the war and only returned to England in 1918, but three stewardesses were released early in 1915 after

Table 2.1 The position of railway-owned ships on 21 October 1914

Company	Ships owned	Requisitioned by the Admiralty
GCR	13	7 (War Office had 1)
GER	11	8
GWR	11	2 (War Office had 3)
LBSCR	4	2
LNWR	15	4
LSWR	17	3
LYR	33	20
Midland	6	2
SECR	15	11

representations from the GCR through the American Consul in Hamburg. The *City of Leeds* was recovered by British forces in January 1919 and returned to Grimsby. The third ship, SS *Bury*, became accommodation for naval pilots and was returned to the GCR after the war.

Three of the SECR's steamers helped evacuate Belgian refugees from Ostend on 14 October 1914, the day the Germans entered the town. Five of its vessels were lost, including the SS *Hythe* in the Dardanelles after its conversion to a minesweeper. Three steamships, the *Engadine*, *Empress* and *Riviera*, were fitted up as seaplane carriers and served in the Battle of Jutland. The SECR SS *The Queen* was involved in the heroic rescue of almost 2,000 Belgian refugees from the torpedoed French liner *Amiral Gantéaume* on 28 October 1914 following a boiler explosion. The King asked to meet its captain, Robert Carey, who was also presented with an inscribed silver plate by the French and Belgian governments.

Mines were laid both offensively and defensively, and enemy-laid mines were cleared by paddle steamers sailing in parallel with a serrated-wire sweep between them to cut the tethers of the mines, which would rise to the surface and be detonated by rifle fire. It was tedious and obviously dangerous work. The Scottish west-coast paddle-steamer fleets were the main source of minesweepers, the NBR providing 10 and the Caledonian and GSWR 8 apiece, with 4 coming from the LSWR and 2 from the Furness. Five of the railway minesweepers were sunk by mines, two were torpedoed and two sank after colliding with other vessels. Ten railway steamships were adapted to become minelayers, creating minefields off the British coast and in the eastern Mediterranean.

The LBSCR fleet of passenger and cargo ships was requisitioned by both the British and French governments. Of 10 GWR Channel steamers, 7 were commandeered by the Admiralty; 1 was lost through a collision at Scapa Flow and 3 served in the Mediterranean and the Dardanelles. The three turbine Channel steamers, TrSS *St David*, *St Patrick* and *St Andrew*, all survived the war as hospital ships, later termed 'ambulance transports'. The TSS *Lynx* achieved distinction by ramming a submarine, as did the TSS *Ibex*, which sank an enemy submarine by gunfire, for which the crew received a £500 reward.

Of the LNWR's 15 ships, 9 were requisitioned and 3 were lost, the TSS *Slieve Bloom* through a collision off Anglesey with an American destroyer, the USS *Stockton*, at night in March 1918. Drafted as a hospital ship, the SS *Anglia* was returning from Calais to Dover with 385 injured soldiers in November 1915 when she struck a mine. Despite the help of a torpedo gunboat and a collier, 134 people were lost, and the ship was designated a war grave in 2017.

In December 1914 the captain of the GER SS *Colchester* ignored a signal from a German submarine to stop while sailing from the Hook of Holland to Harwich. Requesting maximum power from the stokers and engineers, he outmanoeuvred the submarine, and he was presented with a gold watch by the GER chairman, Lord Claud Hamilton. It was engraved: 'Presented to Capt. Lawrence by the Chairman and Directors of the Great Eastern Railway Company as a mark of their appreciation of his courage and skilful seamanship on 11 December 1914.'[209]

One of the most remarkable stories concerned the former LNWR SS *Hibernia*, which had become the armed patrol boat HMS *Tara*. On 5 November 1915 the ship was torpedoed in the eastern Mediterranean. All but 10 of the 89 LNWR crew (supplemented by RN officers and ratings), nearly all from Anglesey, managed to land on the North African coast, beyond the Egyptian frontier. This was thanks to the U-boat which had taken the *Tara*'s lifeboats in tow, while other crew clung to the deck of the submarine. The survivors were given water and biscuits and handed over to the Senussi. Back home nothing was heard of the survivors other than that they had succeeded in making it ashore. On 26 November they were sighted at El Aziat, west of the Gulf of Sollum, and on 27 January 1916 came news that the 95 survivors were in the hands of the Senussi and were being well treated, if short of food. They were compelled to eat snails and desert herbs and had only five days' rations left when they were rescued by a brilliant 195km motorcar raid under the command of the Duke of Westminster. Of the 89 LNWR men, 5 died of disease. On their return to the UK, the men were given a public welcome at Holyhead. On 17 May 1916 the LNWR entertained the *Tara*'s survivors to lunch at the Euston Station Hotel, at which Sir Gilbert Claughton, the LNWR chairman, paid tribute to the men. They then attended a performance at the London Coliseum. The Duke of Westminster sent a telegram: 'Mind you give my kindest greetings to all the men, and mind you give them snails for a remembrance.'[210]

Few incidents of the First World War aroused greater wrath than the sequel to the capture of the GER SS *Brussels* in June 1916 by German torpedo boats operating from Zeebrugge. Along with Belgian refugee women and children, 44 officers and men were captured, and Captain Charles Fryatt was charged with attempting to ram a submarine on a voyage the previous year. On 27 July 1916 he was executed by firing squad in Bruges, which the Prime Minister denounced in the Commons as an 'atrocious crime against the laws of nations',

and the King's condolences and his 'deepest indignation' at the outrage were sent to his widow by Lord Stamfordham. It was reported by New York papers as a 'crowning German atrocity' and 'a deliberate murder'. The five stewardesses on board were regarded as fighting women, and after two nights in Bruges town hall were taken by cattle truck and fourth-class carriage to Cologne for Holzminden internment camp. Intervention by the Secretary of State for Foreign Affairs secured their release and they reached Holland on 1 October on their way to England.

In July 1919 Fryatt's body was exhumed and taken by special train to Antwerp with GER officers aboard. A destroyer delivered the coffin to Dover, where the SECR placed it in parcels van no 132, which had already carried to London the body of Edith Cavell and would later carry the body of the Unknown Warrior. At Charing Cross it was met by the GER's chairman, Lord Hamilton, and most of the senior management of the railway. The coffin was taken on a gun carriage to St Paul's Cathedral for a service accompanied by the GER Musical Society and was attended by hundreds of merchant seamen. It was then taken along streets lined with crowds to Liverpool Street, where the Fryatt memorial tablet was draped in flags. Chopin's *Funeral March* was played as the train left for Dovercourt Bay station and interment of the body in Upper Dovercourt churchyard. Fryatt's name was given to a street in Zeebrugge, a hospital and pub in Parkeston, and a mountain in Alberta. The Railway Heritage Trust is funding the restoration of Fryatt's grave to be completed by the centenary of the repatriation of his body.

Serving the fleet

Scapa Flow in the Orkneys had been used by the Admiralty since the Napoleonic Wars, and two Martello towers had been built to defend it. The decision to develop it as a northern naval base was taken in 1904, based on its threefold ability to control the entrances to the North Sea, place the Grand Fleet beyond reach of a surprise attack and avoid the risk of a fleet based in the Firth of Forth being bottled in by a minefield. However strategically sound the choice may have been, it took little or no account of the difficulties of supplying the fleet with coal, ammunition and personnel. It relied on the largely single-line HR, whose resources were usually taxed only by major sheep sales, tourism and the peregrinations of aristocrats, many in search of field sports.

Coupled with the naval base at Invergordon, the Highlands became an area of such strategic significance that from 25 July 1916, the area to the north and west of the Caledonian Canal and the Borough of Inverness were declared a Special Military Area. Only members of the armed forces in possession of a travel warrant and civilians with an official pass or a permit book could be booked to stations north of Inverness.[211] Despite such precautions, seven people were arrested as spies at the HR's Station Hotel in Inverness, some thanks to the vigilance and shrewdness of staff.

However, it was not coal for the Grand Fleet at Scapa Flow that placed such strain on the HR, because the port of Grangemouth was chosen in mid-1915 as the principal destination for rail-borne coal, to be forwarded by coastal steamer – the HR could never have coped with the millions of tonnes of dry steam coal that the Royal Navy required. The coal's calorific value was secondary to it being if not smokeless, close to it – in pre-radar days, funnel smoke glimpsed through binoculars was usually the first sight of the enemy. This characteristic was found only in coal mined in the Rhondda Valley and its environs. Consequently the long-haul burden fell on the GWR, LNWR and Caledonian, though remarkably the coordination of the transport was entrusted to Wm Mathwin & Son, coal exporters and shipping agents based in Newcastle upon Tyne.

In the weeks before war was declared, much of the fleet at southern naval bases was moved to Scapa Flow and other Scottish inlets. Plans for this eventuality had been made since 1911. Stockpiles of suitable coal had been created at Newcastle and other unnamed places where North Sea warships could be rebunkered. The first recorded 'Jellicoe Train', as the coal trains became known after the fleet's commander-in-chief, Admiral Lord Jellicoe, left Pontypool Road station on 27 August 1914 for Grangemouth.

The assembly points were Quaker's Yard near Merthyr Tydfil and Pontypool Road, at both of which sidings were built specifically for Admiralty traffic. The route for Scotland-bound trains was then via the Shrewsbury & Hereford Joint line to Chester, Warrington and north down the West Coast main line to Carlisle, where most proceeded over the Caledonian, although some took the GSWR line via Dumfries. From October 1915 some were also routed via Normanton to reach the East Coast main line, and from summer 1916 a proportion went via Hellifield on to the Settle & Carlisle. When the Shrewsbury & Hereford line was at capacity, trains were routed via the Brecon & Merthyr line through Torpantau to Talyllyn Junction and the Cambrian Mid-Wales line to Moat Lane Junction, regaining the GWR at Gobowen. The Cambrian kept its signal boxes open 24 hours a day to handle the traffic, and its locomotives worked as far as Crewe.

Fig 2.26
Photographs of Jellicoe coal trains are as rare as hen's teeth. This photograph by F E Mackay of Webb B class compound 0-8-0 No 500 hauling about 38 wagons was taken on Shap, in the Westmorland fells, being banked by a locomotive that will have come on behind the brake van at Oxenholme or Tebay.

By early 1918 an average of 79 special trains a week was being run, carrying 32,000 tons of coal, but this proved insufficient and it was increased to 109 trains a week to deliver 41,100 tons.[212]

Other ports which received Admiralty coal included Birkenhead, Burntisland, Chatham, Devonport, Glasgow, Gosport, Holyhead, Hull, Immingham, Leith, Lowestoft, Newcastle, Southampton and the Thames estuary. The scale of Immingham made it an obvious choice as a reserve port: between 2,000 and 4,000 coal wagons of Welsh coal were kept there, as well as a stack that reached 35,600 tonnes, ready for immediate dispatch through the dock coaling facilities.[213] One of the routes to south-coast ports entailed trains travelling over the Severn Bridge between Lydney and Sharpness. Hull coal was routed via Banbury and the GCR over the critically important link to Woodford Halse, which carried 491,986 wagons during 1916 alone.

To begin with, much still went by sea: in the calendar year 1914, 3.7 million tons was loaded on to colliers, warships or supply vessels at Cardiff, compared with 105,351 tons dispatched by rail to naval establishments. Growth prompted the Government to exclude merchant shipping from Grangemouth after requisitioning of ports in November 1914. The number of Admiralty coal trains run by the GWR from South Wales was:

1914	309
1915	1,729
1916	2,454
1917	3,421
1918	5,763

The 1918 average was 110 trains a week, and by the end of the war 13,676 Jellicoe Specials had been operated, a monthly average of 268, carrying over 5 million tons of coal.

Before the war, the Admiralty had taken a hire option on 4,000 wagons from a character of questionable probity named Henry Gethin Lewis, who anticipated the demand for wagons and built up a fleet that numbered 14,000 by the middle of the war. It is estimated that keeping the Grand Fleet in steam coal required 14,000–16,000 wagons at any one time. As recorded elsewhere, availability of wagons was a major problem throughout the war, and reliance on private owners' wagons was fraught with difficulty since there was no control over their maintenance; the need to detach a crippled wagon from a train could throw timetables and operations into disarray, and as early as 8 September 1914 problems with the wagons were being reported. Hot axle-boxes were the main problem.[214]

Ammunition for the Grand Fleet was routed through Inverness, which entailed construction of a new 1,000-yard branch to the harbour in less than a fortnight. Trains of ammunition arrived from factories in southern Scotland and England for transfer to vessels for delivery to warships.

The passenger equivalent of the Jellicoe Trains was the 'Daily Naval Special' train between London and Thurso. At first, attempts were made to accommodate naval ratings on service trains, but this descended into such disorder that a special naval train was instituted from 15 February 1917, running every weekday in each direction and scheduled to take 21½ hours for the 716¾ miles, which made it the longest-distance regularly booked train ever run in Britain.

Stops were made for connections at Crewe, Preston, Carlisle, Stirling or Rosyth, Perth, Inverness, Dingwall, Alness (for the US Naval Base at Dalmore), Invergordon and finally at Helmsdale and Forsinard for locomotives to take water. Those travelling to Achnasheen and Kyle of Lochalsh for the west coast took a local train from Inverness. Initially the Naval Special ran non-stop by the Caledonian route between Carlisle and Perth, but so that men from Rosyth Dockyard would not have to travel back, from 21 May 1917 until 30 April 1919 it was routed via the North British Waverley line, dropping off carriages for Rosyth at Inverkeithing. Trains left Euston at 6 pm and arrived at Thurso at 3.30 pm the following day. The southbound train left Thurso at 11.45 am and reached Euston at 10.05 the following morning. In winter, to allow for daylight embarkation at Thurso, the northbound train left Euston at 3 pm.

The corridor-stock train generally consisted of 14 LNWR vehicles, supervised by a master-at-arms, though it sometimes had to be run in 2 or 3 portions. The average number of passengers was 300, yet sometimes it would leave either end with just 40–50 passengers, picking up more en route. Sleeping accommodation was provided for officers. Some compartments were fitted with iron bars and locks for ratings who had outstayed their leave or infringed naval discipline. Up to 35 prisoners a night might be carried. The total number of men carried between 15 February 1917 and 30 April 1919 was about 475,000, according to the records of the Naval Transport Office in Inverness.[215]

Having a dedicated train also simplified arrangements for feeding the men. Tea was served before leaving Euston, 'bag suppers' were provided at Crewe and officers were served a sit-down breakfast at the Station Hotel in Inverness (owned by the HR). Bag dinners were distributed at Inverness for men heading for the west coast. Southbound officers had tea at Inverness Station Hotel and were handed dinner baskets at Kingussie, before a stop at Perth for 10 minutes for tea and sandwiches on the platform. Southbound trains might also have torpedoed or shipwrecked survivors. Light refreshments were served by voluntary workers at other points en route; a brass plaque at Dingwall station records the 134,864 sailors and soldiers who were supplied with tea by the Ross and Cromarty branch of the Red Cross between 20 September 1915 and 12 April 1919.

The Naval Special encountered what was then a typical Highland storm in 1918 when on 12 January a severe blizzard trapped a snowplough at Scotscalder followed by the Special. Locomotives trying to reach the stranded train also became stuck fast, and the men had to walk across country to Thurso. It was a week before the line was fully reopened.

Naval leave specials were run for the bases at Rosyth and Invergordon, the longest run being the 721 miles between Plymouth and Invergordon, with stops at Taunton, Shrewsbury and Perth for refreshments. When the whole personnel of the Grand Fleet was given 12 days' leave in December 1918, staggered in parties of 14,000 at a time, the NBR had to run as many as 32 special trains from Rosyth or Port Edgar, in addition to simultaneous trains for Army leave.[216]

The HR also came under strain from non-coal traffic for Thurso associated with the Grand Fleet, supplies to the base at Invergordon and the military camps at Cromarty, Invergordon and Nigg, and timber traffic. For the first three years of the war the goods yard at Invergordon dealt with a daily average of 72 wagons, most a consequence of the decision to use its location on the Cromarty Firth as a repair base for the Grand Fleet. A floating dock capable of holding the largest warship in the fleet arrived in September 1914, and many new sidings were installed to serve the two piers and Admiralty buildings covering 145 acres. This northern equivalent of Devonport employed over 4,000 workmen, with some of the married men housed in a model village of 126 cottages.[217]

At the beginning of the war whole trainloads of timber, much of it felled in northern Scotland, were required for construction of floats on boom-defence works at Scapa Flow and elsewhere. The demand for pit props rose as more coal was required for industry and transport. During 1918 alone the HR handled 293,561 tons of pit-wood, much of it felled by the Canadian Forestry Corps; with other types of timber, the total was 403,560 tons.[218] The Newfoundland Forestry Battalion had a camp between Dunkeld and Dalguise, and camps for German POWs with forestry experience were created at Carrbridge and Lentran.[219]

Even though the HR was not asked to carry coal for the Grand Fleet, it gained new flows of coal traffic for fishing drifters. Before the war this had been carried by coastal steamers, but with the submarine threat this was considered too risky, with the consequence that at times almost every far north line station was blocked with coal wagons from collieries further south. The pressure on the HR main line was so great that many trains were routed via Aberdeen, despite the much greater mileage; on one Sunday alone the GNSR took over 21 troop specials off the HR at Keith for camps in the south, and during the five years from 1 August 1914, 48,440 loaded and 9,033 empty wagons were routed via Aberdeen because the HR main line was so congested.[220]

The strain was further increased after the US entered the war in April 1917, with the decision to create a vast minefield known as the Northern Barrage. This envisaged laying 100,000 mines over about 380km between the Orkneys and the Hordaland coast of Norway. Minelaying began in March 1918, and 70,000 had been laid by November when it stopped. Over four-fifths of the mines were supplied in component form by the US using the rail-connected Dalmore Distillery near Alness, and specially constructed sheds at Muirtown Basin, Inverness, as assembly points. Before the Dalmore site could be used, 4,500 casks of whisky had to be moved by train to a distillery at Edderton, 21 miles north of Alness. Most of the mine components were unloaded from US vessels at Kyle of Lochalsh and railed to Dalmore, usually in a train of 11 12-ton SECR wagons hauled by LSWR locomotives. The work required about 1,700 American naval ratings to be based at Kyle, and about 400 trains of mines were dispatched. Some mines came up the Caledonian Canal from Corpach. Among the more unlikely items carried over the Kyle line were hydraulic chairs for US Army barbers' shops and equipment for US hospitals in Britain, as well as more predictable boxes of chewing gum.

At the AGM in 1916, the HR's chairman, William Whitelaw, told shareholders that:

The Highland line is organised to be overworked for four months in the year, and to be, comparatively speaking, at rest for the other eight. It has now been overworked for nineteen months without rest, and I am glad it has fallen to my lot to bear testimony to the work of all ranks in our employment throughout this period of unequalled strain and difficulty on the Highland system.[221]

Before F G Smith was asked to relinquish his position as HR locomotive superintendent, for designing a locomotive supposedly too heavy for the line's structures, he arranged with the REC the loan of a motley collection of locomotives. About 50 locomotives, one-third of the HR's own fleet, were out of service awaiting repairs, so the influx of over 40 locomotives from 6 companies was welcome, but inevitably problems arose over spares.

Perhaps the strangest Army specials from the Highlands were the 7 trains that conveyed from Invergordon to Winchester 161 Russian officers and 2,993 men sent by Kerensky's short-lived government to fight on the Western Front. They had arrived on 4 October 1917 in three ships which also carried 300 presumably pro-tsarist refugees who were sent by special train to London. On 9 July 1918 Invergordon received another curious collection of largely Serb troops, but also French, Polish and Czech soldiers who had ended up in Russia; the 470 men were taken by a single train to Southampton en route to France.[222]

The ship also carried 331 civilian refugees of 10 nationalities who were sent by a Home Office-arranged train to London, along with 522 bags of mail from Russia. Russia was the probable destination of the contents of two special trains from London which arrived at Invergordon in December 1916 and January 1917: the first was of four vans of bullion guarded by a military escort in four coaches; the second had three bullion vans and five corridor coaches of guards.

In handling all this traffic, the HR was so acutely short of staff that shifts of 12 hours often extended to 14–16 hours, and at times 3 crossing loops between Perth and Inverness had be switched out for want of signalmen.[223] In evidence to the Select Committee on Transport in October 1918, Sir Herbert Walker expressed the view that 'certain companies, such as the Highland, have had very heavy burdens placed upon them in the shape of traffic ... I think the Highland has been hit more than any other company.'[224]

Sustenance for servicemen

Trains carrying troops and sailors made scheduled stops for the men to visit buffets, but where these did not exist or opening hours meant that servicemen went without, volunteers often stepped in.

Within a fortnight of the war beginning, Banbury had a refreshment room for servicemen open from 7 am to 10 pm, apparently in response to the sight of a trainload of troops drinking the contents of the station's fire buckets. Relays of Red Cross nurses and volunteers served tea, coffee, lemonade, milk, cake, sandwiches and fruit, and supplied postcards for notes to family and friends. In the first year the room received about 350,000 troops.

Similar facilities were established at London termini. A stall for light refreshments was set up in April 1915 on the Lawn at Paddington and soon catered for 45,000 servicemen a month. It was open 24 hours a day and staffed by women volunteers, supported by monthly collections from the public at the station and donations of cake, eggs and hampers of fruit. After the war Viscount Churchill and other directors held a reception and tea in the GWR general meeting room at Paddington for Mrs J J Runge OBE and her 130 assistants to mark the winding-up of what had become an institution at Paddington. A diamond brooch was given to Mrs Runge. The surplus funds were given to the fund for relieving members of the company's staff who had been incapacitated during the war.

Free refreshments were provided at Lady Limerick's buffet at London Bridge for some 63,000 men a month, and at Waterloo, Lady Brassey had a buffet in a subway. Similar facilities could be found at Edinburgh Waverley, Glasgow Queen Street, Darlington Bank Top, Leeds, Newcastle, Perth and York,[225] and even at smaller stations such as Monk Fryston and Church Fenton on the NER.

When the *Yorkshire Evening Press* reported the absence of comparable facilities at the county town, on 15 November 1915 the 'Ladies of York' opened a Soldiers' and Sailors' Canteen on Platform 3 (now 1). It was made up of two carriages donated by the NER, and served tea, coffee and food to servicemen in uniform. Run by volunteers, it was open 24 hours a day, 7 days a week, until it closed on 23 May 1919. During this time it served 4½ million soldiers and sailors – an average of 18,000 per week. In its first year of opening it spent

Fig 2.27
Volunteers staffing the free buffet for soldiers and sailors at Paddington station, one of numerous similar facilities women established throughout Britain.

£7,630 on tea, coffee and food – about £330,000 today. As the *North Eastern Railway Magazine* remarked, 'the women of the canteen didn't only provide sustenance for troops; in many cases, they were a much needed friendly face. A cup of warm tea and a kind remark would have gone a long way for many of these boys, who had likely been away from home for a long time.'[226]

Fundraising for these facilities ranged from organ concerts to a fête laid on in June 1916 at Invermay House in Perthshire in support of the 'Perthshire Patriotic Barrow' at Perth station. A speech was given by Lady Beatty, wife of Admiral Sir David Beatty, and the occasion raised £450; the average cost of providing each serviceman with free sustenance at Perth was 1d.

Some of the refreshment places kept visitors' books, and two have survived from Peterborough East station tea-room run by the city's Women's United Total Abstinence Council. They contain poems, jokes and pencil sketches, including a brilliant one of Charlie Chaplin by Private W V Wood of the 62nd Cyclist Company. The stories behind some of the 600 signatories have been traced and placed on the internet thanks to a Heritage Lottery Fund grant.[227]

Prisoners of war

Movements of German POWs began on 10 August 1914 with the arrival of the first at Dorchester's empty artillery barracks in Poundbury. Others were accommodated the same month at Queensferry, Lancaster, Horsham, York, Bradford Moor, Olympia (London), Edinburgh and Fort George. Some old

Territorial Army camps were used, such as the remote Stobs camp in the Borders, which brought unexpected traffic to stations accustomed to only a few dozen passengers a day. Other accommodation was established in country houses such as the requisitioned Donington Hall in Derbyshire or Dyffryn Aled in Denbighshire.

German POWs are recorded carrying out some railway work. In 1916–17 about 1,500 POWs prepared the trackbed for an extension to Blackdown of the Brookwood–Bisley Camp Tramway which was worked by the LSWR.[228] Men from the camp at Black Hall near Kerry in Montgomeryshire rebuilt the moribund 2ft (610mm) gauge Kerry Tramway to move timber to Kerry station. They were also involved in timber-felling and railway operations.[229] A *Times* correspondent described the arrival of a couple of hundred of the rank and file with about a dozen officers at Camberley station for the march to a compound at Frith Hill. Before receiving POWs, this Surrey camp had been used to intern German and Austrian nationals, 600 of whom were brought down from London by special train on 23 October 1914. They had been moved to the Isle of Man and the camp closed before it was reopened in 1915 to receive POWs, but details of how POWs were handled by the railways are scant.

By the end of the war, it is estimated that there were 115,950 POWs in Britain, and most of these will have been taken by train to their camps and to embarkation points after the war ended. Repatriation of German POWs began on 30 August 1919, and most had been returned home by November, a much quicker process than with the later conflict.

Railway hotels

Large buildings, such as country houses, were requisitioned or voluntarily loaned to the nation during the war, and most railway hotels were among them. Hotels in the south were well located to become hospitals, such as the GER hotel at Harwich, as well as the Railwaymen's Convalescent Home at Herne Bay. The GCR's 500-roomed Hotel Great Central at Marylebone became a convalescent home for wounded officers from 3 October 1916.

The HR hotel at Dornoch was closed to guests in July 1916 and taken over by the Canadian Forestry Department, and its Strathpeffer hotel was taken over by the US Army. The GSWR's Turnberry Hotel was taken over from January 1917 as a school of aerial gunnery.

America enters the war

The US entered the First World War on 6 April 1917 after President Wilson asked Congress for 'a war to end all wars', but because of General Pershing's insistence that American soldiers be well trained before combat, it was not until the following year that US troops began arriving on the Western Front in significant numbers.

Though ships delivered US troops into the harbours of Bordeaux, St Nazaire and Brest, many were routed via Britain and especially Liverpool, which had to cope with huge numbers of Empire and, from March 1918, US troops. Moreover, between April and September 1918 almost 800,000 Australian troops

Fig 2.28
Soldiers of the US 316th Field Artillery Regiment (81st Division) boarding a train in the up platform at Knotty Ash & Stanley station on the Cheshire Lines Committee Liverpool–Widnes line, en route to Southampton on 14 August 1918. When the USA entered the war, a large depot was established in fields to the east of the line at Knotty Ash, because there was plenty of suitable grazing land for the horses after their Atlantic crossing.

arrived through Liverpool, and the LNWR provided 1,684 out of 2,333 special trains for American troops.[230] The largest convoy arrived on 31 May 1918 with 33,000 troops requiring 64 special trains. US troops arrived with such large kit bags that on average a baggage train had to be run for every three troop trains.

Plymouth and other western ports also received US troops; the LSWR alone handled 1,695 troop specials for their forces, conveying 868,577 men. On 10 July 1918 the arrival of an American troop convoy saw 53 trains pass through the Winchester area within 24 hours.

Demobilisation

The task of demobilising a conscript Army numbering nearly 3.8 million men kept the railways busy after the end of hostilities. Plans had been developed by Lord Derby from August 1917, mindful of the impact of returning soldiers after the experience of Russia. His proposal was that men with industrial skills should be discharged quickly, and some railwaymen are likely to have been in that category. However, since these were also likely to have been called up as a last resort towards the end of the war, those who had been in uniform longest were likely to have to wait longer. The process caused such discontent that riots or small-scale mutinies occurred in Calais, Folkestone and Seaford, and there were demonstrations in Whitehall. After Churchill's appointment as war secretary in January 1919, a more equitable system was introduced based on length of service, age and number of wounds, which helped to defuse the anger.

The principle adopted by the War Office and REC in 1917 was that demobilisation should take place not from regimental depots but from 20 dispersal areas, each with one or more camps and served by a dispersal station. Ideally men were sent to the port nearest the dispersal centre, which was the one closest to his home. This was supposed to minimise train travel and guarantee full trains, and the railways agreed to handle 20,000 men a day from the ports, plus another 20,000 troops already in Britain. The four principal ports used were Southampton, Folkestone, Tilbury and Immingham.

To Prees Heath near Whitchurch on the single-track line south to Shrewsbury, for example, the LNWR ran 1,587 special trains conveying 343,458 officers and men between 3 January and the first week of July 1919.[231] It was agreed with the War Office that railwaymen would be demobilised through the REC, and by the end of 1918, 2,001 men had returned to the GWR.

Part of the demobilisation problem was that the planners had not thought to consult the French about the process, and they were none too cooperative, offering to move troops only to a port of their convenience and not Britain's choice. In fairness, the French Nord and Est railways had to contend with the destruction by the retreating German armies of 5,600km of track, 1,510 bridges and other works, and 12 tunnels.[232] Any sensible sorting would have to be done on British soil, so the carefully worked-out timetables had to be rewritten.

Delays in sending Empire contingents home also caused trouble. In March 1919 several Canadian soldiers were killed during a riot at a camp in Rhyl, and there was another riot of Canadian soldiers in Epsom several months later in which a policeman was killed.

A year after the war's end, the British Army had fallen to under 900,000 men, and by January 1920 there was only one dispersal centre left open. In common with every facet of life in Britain, the railways' task immediately after the war was affected by the outbreak of Spanish influenza in March 1918. The global pandemic is estimated to have killed between 50 and 100 million people, of whom about 250,000 were in the UK.

Railway stations played a part in demobilisation by being receiving points for greatcoats retained for the journey home from camp. Providing a soldier handed the coat in within 28 days, £1 would be paid as part of his post-war gratuity. Rather absurdly, given the attendant cost and minimal prospect of reuse, trainloads of greatcoats had to be sent from dispersal centres to ordnance depots.

The 125,000 horses in France also needed repatriating, and the plan was to return 12,500 a week through Southampton, Tilbury, Surrey Commercial Dock and Hull, take them by train to quarantine centres and thence to sales around the country, again by train. Train schedules were set up to serve the quarantine centres allocated to each port, those from Hull being Edinburgh, Glasgow, Ayr, St Boswells, Cupar, Newcastle, Croft Spa, Catterick, Ripon, Doncaster, Sheffield, Clipstone and Grantham. As with the demobilisation of troops, these plans had to be abandoned when the Ministry of Shipping could not provide the necessary tonnage. So many conventional ships had been assigned to bringing back troops that the decision was taken to return horses by train ferries from Calais. The REC dispatched a train of cattle trucks to Calais within 24 hours, but this system was supplemented by horses coming through more ports than the four originally planned. Moreover, sales were often held at the quarantine sites rather than sale yards; in the latter case, the purchaser would often have been within walking distance of their stables, but not the former. Consequently a straightforward plan became immensely complex for the railways.[233]

In some places dinners were held to welcome home colleagues. The staff of the GWR Goods Department at Hockley held a dinner for 124 at the GWR Hotel in Birmingham; 36 members of the clerical staff had served, of whom 6 had been killed. Another event was held at the Grand Hotel, Birmingham, to thank station staff at Snow Hill and Soho for the help given to the Voluntary Aid Detachment during the war. Stops for refreshments at Snow Hill station had been made by 2,390 ambulance trains containing 380,000 wounded men.[234]

The Ministry of Transport was formed by an Act of 15 August 1919 and the formal transfer of transport functions from the Board of Trade took place on 23 September. The REC ceased to exist on 1 January 1920 and its place was taken by a short-lived Railway Advisory Committee consisting of the general managers of the 12 principal companies and four trade union representatives. Two years later, the grouping of the railways took place, bringing the curtain down on the names of most of the standard-gauge companies that had endured the First World War.

Fig 2.29
Troops disembarking at Folkestone Harbour. By 1919 over 9.7 million British and Allied troops had passed through the harbour, as well as 850,000 Red Cross and other war-time workers. Folkestone was also the harbour which handled most mail with the Western Front.

3 | First World War theatres

In August 1914 there can have been no clear idea what railway support or equipment would be required to sustain campaigns in the dominant overseas theatre on the Continent, or in other theatres of war. No one could have anticipated the static nature of the trenches that stretched from the North Sea to the French/Swiss border. The density of the railway network over the northern third of the Western Front on which the BEF was deployed, for roughly 160km between Dunkirk and Chaulnes (midway between Amiens and St Quentin), coupled with the immobile nature of trench warfare, gave rail transport an unequalled role in the campaign.

It was expected that French railways, then all still in private ownership but placed under military control on the outbreak of war, would meet the railway transport requirements of the Allies in the country. It did not take long for this reliance to be questioned, and as the need for support became more urgent, it was clear that there were two fundamental requirements: the ability to repair and build railway lines, which fell naturally to the RE, and an organisation to operate them, for which no appropriate body existed in 1914.

At the outbreak of war, the RE numbered about 24,000 including Territorials, and as part of contingency planning for war, RE officers had been attached to British railways for training and experience. To begin with, the War Office was satisfied that the RE would meet requirements; when the NER's deputy general manager, Eric Geddes, offered the Director of Movements a fully trained unit of skilled civilian railwaymen of all grades from the company, he was told that military railway personnel were competent to deal with the situation in France and railway units were not needed. Geddes saw his offer as a first step towards creating 'the great civilian transportation machine' which eventually provided Haig with, in words the general wrote in May 1917, 'that "mobility" which will enable us to out-manoeuvre the enemy and enable me to bring a superior force of guns and men at the *decisive moment* to the *decisive point*, before the enemy can take counter-measures.'[1]

As a lieutenant colonel in the Railway Staff Corps, Territorial Force, Geddes had worked on mobilisation timetables and communications between the railway companies while he represented the NER on the REC, rather than the general manager, Kaye Butterworth. Geddes had had a colourful past, including expulsion from various public schools, and had met Lord Kitchener in India in 1904. In December 1914 Kitchener as secretary of state for war summoned Geddes to London to discuss the railway situation in France. Kitchener wanted to send Geddes to France, but opposition from the General Staff at the War Office deferred the involvement of civilians with practical industrial knowledge. As a military attaché at the British Embassy in Paris, Colonel Le Roy-Lewis, wrote: 'The appointment of anybody who does not belong to the Military Trade Union is as welcome to soldiers, as the appointment of a bishop drawn from the ranks of stockbrokers would be to the clergy.'[2] The shell crisis of 1915 would put an end to such parochial reservations.

In October 1914 Kitchener sent Brigadier General Sir Percy Girouard to France to report on the BEF transport system. He advocated a centralised control system under General Headquarters (GHQ) with the French retaining operation of their railways, though with more executive input from the British. The early decentralised command structure of the BEF was influenced by Sir John French's experience of the Boer War and treated each mode of transport independently. Railway movements were initially organised by the Inspector General of Communications. Lacking radio communications, it was difficult for him to respond quickly to a request for supplies, so the Quartermaster General was put in charge of the tactical control of railway movements, which would be arranged with the French by the Inspector General of Communications, who retained control of the ports.[3]

One of Girouard's observations led to an early contribution to military logistics by an English railway. He witnessed at Boulogne the inefficiency of trans-shipment methods between ship and train in Bassin Loubet, the area of the port handling British supplies, which the SECR general manager, Francis Dent, no doubt observed during his visit to France in December 1914. The War Office commissioned a study from Dent, who concluded that the port could be re-formed to handle 5,000 tons a day, and the Army accepted his offer to bring this about, despite some scepticism. Consequently the SECR took over operation of Bassin Loubet in April 1915.[4] Ten SECR 0-6-0 tank engines were sent over with their own crews, but the lion's share of the work was done by 25 hired Belgian locomotives drawn from a pool of over 2,000 Belgian locomotives spirited across the border in advance of the German invasion.

It soon became apparent that independent control and operation of the link between ports and supply depots would benefit the BEF, which led to the founding of the Railway Operating Division (ROD) in January 1915. It grew to 67 companies, with 18,400 men and about 1,500 locomotives serving the BEF on the Western Front. Besides recruitment, from about May 1916 men with railway experience were transferred from other units, so the ROD came to include representatives from almost every railway in Britain and many overseas railways, especially those in India, Ceylon, Africa and Argentina, usually with a background in locomotives or in workshops. Separate operating units were provided by Australia, Canada and South Africa.[5]

The strain on French railways in meeting the logistical requirements of the BEF was evident as early as March 1915, when the French transportation authorities requested rolling stock and other help.[6] From August 1915 a ROD company of LNWR men took over operation of the Nord Railway's line from Hazebrouck to Poperinghe in Belgium; the line continued on to Ypres.

The man who would make such a difference to transport in France was finally brought into government employment during the summer of 1915 when Lloyd George recruited Geddes into the Ministry of Munitions. Lloyd George later described Geddes as 'one of the most remarkable products of the Great War'. Geddes was one of a number of 'men of push and go', with little time for red tape and a knack for improvisation to get things done, who were brought in to raise production. Geddes was placed in charge of rifles and machine guns and later analysing trouble spots, though Lloyd George's failure to appreciate the difficulties of increasing production when component production and assembly were geographically dispersed soured their relationship for a while.

But Geddes's achievement in raising machine-gun manufacture and setting up the National Factories scheme was irrefutable. When Kitchener died with the sinking of HMS *Hampshire* in July 1916, Lloyd George took over as secretary of state for war and took some men from Munitions with him, including Geddes.

The shortcomings of the BEF's transport network became most apparent in 1916, when the Somme offensive begun on 1 July faltered for want of munitions being delivered where they were required. Urgently needed stores in quayside warehouses became buried by subsequent deliveries, and Amiens became a major bottleneck with 30km of trains stuck in sidings and loops. This in turn caused a wagon and locomotive shortage, prompting requests for supplies of both from Britain. The mud which plagued the men in the trenches also afflicted the roads, which became quagmires after rain and could immobilise horse and lorry. Haig's diary during 1916 contained many comments on transport difficulties, exacerbated by the increased amounts of ammunition being shipped to France.

Despite a reluctance to risk the replacement of high-ranking soldiers with civilians, Haig accepted the need for a transport expert to visit France to advise on better coordination. Geddes went to France in August 1916 and again in September, accompanied by former NER colleagues. They produced a report setting out the necessities of the situation in France: coordinated management of railway, water and road transport and the ports was needed, along with 300–350 locomotives (nearly all of the same type), about 20,000 trucks, 1,600km of track and personnel. The investigation showed that considerable development of railway facilities would be necessary to supply the required 300,000 tons of supplies per week for the British Army in 1917. Geddes also recommended expansion of the network of light railways whose value he had witnessed in India. They would allow him to meet the requirement of 2,200 tons of matériel per mile of front per day. Fulfilling these requirements would call for service reductions and more economical use of resources on Britain's railways (see p 39).

In September 1916 Geddes was appointed Director General of Military Railways and within days Director General of Transportation with the honorary rank of Major General, a move strongly resisted by some members of the Army Council. But the support of Lloyd George and Haig, with whom Geddes established a good relationship, allowed him to make the necessary reforms. Geddes's deputy was the Midland's Guy Granet, who would succeed to the top post the following year. He had a keen analytical brain and rarely accepted the status quo; he had transformed the efficiency of traffic management on the Midland, and 'was said to be one of the most persuasive expert witnesses who ever gave evidence before a parliamentary committee'.[7] Geddes made a visit to Flanders in December 1916, this time accompanied by John Aspinall, Sam Fay and Robert Turnbull – an impressive combination of railway experience and acumen – to plan the supply routes for the spring offensive the following year.

By the end of 1916 very little railway work had been done by the British Army; 965km of track had been sent to France for additional running lines and sidings. Up to the end of September 1916 the British Army had laid running lines between Hazebrouck and Ypres (30km) and Candas and Acheux (23km), the Contay line (13km) and some extensions in the Somme area to railheads in the Montauban and Guillemont area. Britain was in the process of supplying 13,000 of the 22,000 wagons needed for an advance through Belgium. Only 34 steam and 7 internal-combustion locomotives were in France for British Army purposes in September 1916, though arrangements were in hand for another 170.[8]

As the war ground on, the French were less and less able to meet the needs of the BEF, giving priority to their own forces and civilians, especially during the harsh winter of 1916–17, when the canals froze and railway wagons rather than barges had to deliver coal to Paris. By the end of 1916, French railways had had to suspend their commitment to provide rail transport for the Allies, and the ROD took over most military traffic and even some civilian services on the Nord. ROD locomotives would eventually work as far as Cherbourg in the west, Cologne in the east and Paris or even further in the south.

The area behind the French and British lines was divided into two zones: the French would work all lines south-west of a line from Hazebrouck through Lille, Valenciennes and Mauberge, while all railways north-east of that line up to the Rhine would be operated by an International Commission, using largely Belgian locomotives, later supplemented by other Allies. ROD crews would have felt reasonably at home with the Belgian locomotives, since 1,384 of the country's locomotives were based on designs by the Caledonian Railway's locomotive superintendent, J F McIntosh. The extent of French railway operated by the ROD rose from 160km at the end of 1916 to 534km by the end of 1917 and 1,312km by the end of 1918, following a significant reduction during the German offensive that spring. There was no demarcation line for operations; all coal trains were worked by French crews, for example.

British and French experts disagreed over the number of wagons that Britain needed to supply: the French said Britain would need to supply 54,000 wagons for the advance; British experts said 41,000. France requested assistance at the Nord locomotive workshops, for which the LNWR built two 45-ton cranes at Crewe, and the part-built workshops for the Chemins de fer de l'Etat at St Etienne-du-Rouvray, midway between Rouen and Oiessel, were taken over in February 1917. They were finished by British units and opened to complete the first two imported locomotives in July with a staff of about 1,000 plus 300 German POWs. During 1917, 135 new locomotives were erected and 5 were repaired, with 97 new engines built before May the following year, when St Etienne-du-Rouvray dealt with just repairs.[9]

The primary railway task of the RE was the repair of damaged lines and construction of new ones, for which 45 RE Railway Construction Companies were created for work on standard-gauge lines. Though about 25,000 railwaymen joined the RE, it is impossible to give precise figures for the men employed in railway work, since it was common practice to use Pioneer battalions, men being 'rested' from the trenches, colonial troops and the large Chinese labour force when opportunity and need coincided. But it is estimated that about 29,000 men were involved in railway construction work.

It was over the winter of 1916–17 that railway construction by British forces in France began in earnest. Before September 1916, no light railway track had been constructed, but by the following May 80km of track a week was being laid to forward supplies from the railheads (see below). Haig told Geddes he needed three elements – men, munitions and movement. He believed he had the first two but not the third, and had accepted the means by which to remedy the position. By February 1917, under the new Transportation Directorate, permanent way, locomotives and rolling stock were pouring into France, and by the end of the year British locomotives were hauling 60 per cent of trains for the BEF in France. Canadian and US locomotives were being assembled from July 1917.[10]

British railway troops built standard-gauge railways at the rate of:

	miles	km
1914	1½	2½
1915	103	166
1916	417	671
1917	800	1,287
1918	1,300	2,092

Fig 3.1
Rail-mounted guns were used by all combatants in the First World War. Seen ready for action at Arras, this is one of two 14in Mark III guns made in 1918 by Armstrong Whitworth at Elswick Works, using naval barrels ordered by a foreign country but not delivered. Weighing 248 tons, the gun's recoil mechanism and multi-axle bogies allowed it to be fired without track reinforcement. It had a range of almost 22 miles.

Geddes reorganised transport under a single directorate, bringing in trusted subordinates with skills in different modes and enabling the Director General of Transport to decide which type of transport was most suitable for each consignment. The ROD was expanded, and success in improving the supply lines enabled the BEF to mount four major offensives in 1917, rather than the single one of the previous year. Geddes's reforms were helped by the relatively static nature of the Western Front, which created consistent routes for supplies, thus replicating peacetime operations. The exception was the final kilometers before the front line, which were largely supplied by light railways. By February 1917 Haig was able to express satisfaction with the reserves of ammunition, and favourable US reports on the British organisation of transport led to the Americans adopting the British system. In March 1917 Geddes was made Inspector General of Communications in all theatres of war.

The vital importance of railway supply routes was illustrated at Passchendaele from 31 July 1917 by a major object of the offensive being the disruption of the enemy's supply lines; the intention was to close the German 4th Army's supply route through the junction of Roulers. Taking British figures, a single division

required 200 tons of stores and supplies a day, and between May and October 1918 a weekly average of 1,800 trains were run for British Army traffic carrying about 400,000 tons, plus another 130,000 tons by light railways.

The German advance in spring 1918 threatened the important railway centres of Amiens, St Pol and Hazebrouck. This forced the hasty provision of three separate routes for north–south traffic by doubling and quadrupling existing lines and by some new construction amounting to 320km between April and July. Work was hampered by enemy aircraft which concentrated on important junctions and points, such as the bombing of the viaduct at Etaples. The counteroffensive in August 1918 changed the focus to rehabilitation of lines in recaptured territory, which the Germans had done all they could to destroy, as well as laying delayed-action mines. Among the most damaging of enemy actions was the explosion of 2,000 wagons at Luttre. Military traffic had to be diluted with supplies for the civilian population in recaptured areas. During the last quarter of 1918, 1,770km of line were reconstructed in a huge effort by British and Canadian railway construction troops, working day and night.[11]

By the end of the war, Britain had sent over to France 1,205 locomotives and 52,597 wagons.[12] The GWR alone had sent 95 locomotives, 6,567 goods wagons and 238 coaches overseas. The GCR's Robinson class 8K 2-8-0 was the 'standard' design chosen by the ROD, and 521 were built to the order of the Ministry of Munitions from 1917. Of these, 305 were shipped across to the Continent and all were returned to Britain, though some were sold to China and Australia as well as British railway companies.[13] Some were built by the GCR's works at Gorton, but most were built by outside contractors.

In terms of personnel, the standard-gauge lines were being worked by 18,400 men serving in 67 operating companies of the RE, supported by 6 workshop companies staffing 3 large repair facilities. The ROD continued to operate some Nord lines until February 1919, and ROD locomotives ceased working beyond Mons on 1 April. However, the last ROD locomotives were not repatriated until January 1921.

Military ports

The amount of traffic destined for France prompted construction of a new port at Richborough on the River Stour in Kent to create a cross-Channel barge service to Calais (55km) and Dunkirk (87km). The idea appears to have come from Follett Holt, who had constructed the train ferry system across the Parana River to link Argentina and Paraguay. Under Granet's aegis, construction at Richborough began in June 1916, creating a port that covered 2,200 acres threaded by 60 miles of railway lines in five yards. The port was linked to the SECR by a branch south of Minster Junction, inland from Ramsgate. By December a service of towed barges laden with guns and ammunition began; wherever possible the French canal system was used to reach depots nearer the front line, using a fleet of 242 barges, some with a 1,000-ton capacity. At its peak in 1917, inland water transport along the Western Front moved 56,000 tons a week.

The train ferries entered service on 10 February 1918, feeding an average load of 900 tons into the French railway system at Calais and Dunkirk. Adjustable link spans with two tracks were built to link ship and shore. Three four-track train ferries, SS *Train Ferry No 1, 2* and *3*, were designed in 1917 by

Fig 3.2
The cross-Channel train ferry service between the bespoke port of Richborough in Kent and Calais began on 10 February 1918, but it continued to be supplemented by the Southampton–Dieppe route. Taken at Southampton on 11 April 1918, the photograph shows the ferry is carrying Army lorries and ambulances as well as carriages of the LYR-built ambulance train.

W G Armstrong Whitworth at Elswick in Newcastle upon Tyne, which also built the first two; the third was built on the Clyde by Fairfield Shipbuilding at Govan. Loading could take place whenever the link span gradient was easier than 1 in 20, and average loading time became a remarkably slick 18 minutes. The ferries had a capacity of 54 standard 10-ton wagons and were used primarily for heavier loads, such as Rectank wagons of 35-ton carrying capacity; these transported tanks from the Metropolitan Carriage, Wagon & Finance Company's Oldbury Works in Worcestershire to the Tank Corps HQ in France. To begin with it took an average of 14 days for a Rectank to make the return journey, but this was gradually reduced to an average of 5½ days.[14]

When the war was over the GER offered to buy the ferries and they were sold after the grouping to the Great Eastern Train Ferry Co, which began a service between Harwich and Zeebrugge in 1924. All three found a role in the Second World War (*see* p 111).

Light railways

The French and Germans were much better prepared than the British for the conditions that would develop on the Western Front. The French military chose the 600mm (2ft) gauge railway as the means of linking standard-gauge railheads with front-line strongholds, as would the 1930s Maginot Line with its internal and external 600mm (2ft) lines to bring in shells and supplies.

Fig 3.3
The LNWR's Crewe Works turned out 132 'Crewe tractors' based on the Ford Model T, but they had limited haulage capability and this load looks optimistic. No 39 was photographed on 19 August 1917 hauling shells for the 9th Regiment, 'A' battery, Royal Garrison Artillery, at the end of the Battle of Langemarck during the 3rd Battle of Ypres.

RCL Publications

The French relied heavily on systems developed by two French pioneers of military/industrial railways, Captain Prosper Péchot and Paul Decauville, whose eponymous company at Corbeil specialised in equipment for portable railway systems using prefabricated track. Péchot had designed a Fairlie articulated locomotive, lending his name to the Système Péchot of trench railways which is thought to have extended for about 7,500km.

The Germans had gained experience of the benefits of such railways in German South West Africa during the Herero Wars of 1904–8 when the 567km 600mm (2ft) line between Swakopmund and Tsumeb proved its value. Prior to 1914, a large supply of 600mm (2ft) equipment was built up in preparation for an outbreak of hostilities, with about 250 Brigadelok 0-8-0Ts in readiness.

In contrast, the British Army had put its faith in the lorry to transport supplies. The RE had taken an interest in Sir Arthur Heywood's 'Minimum Gauge Railways' proposals, but the War Office had rejected the idea and by 1913 Army Regulations stated that the lorry was the approved method of supplying forward units. When the roads of France became impassable with mud, the folly of the choice became evident.

Following the recommendation of Eric Geddes, responsibility for light railways was vested in a new Directorate of Light Railways towards the end of 1916, leaving standard-gauge railways to the ROD. Brigadier General Philip Twining, RE, was made Director of Light Railways and Roads based at Montreuil-sur-Mer, near Etaples, and took charge of the network of 600mm (2ft) lines, previously under the War Department Light Railways, which numbered over 40 companies. Each army had an assistant director of light railways and under him a superintendent of light railways, assisted by an Army traffic superintendent, a locomotive superintendent and a tractor superintendent. Then came the various commanding officers of operating companies and district traffic and locomotive superintendents.

For British railwaymen, these narrow-gauge systems were unfamiliar, the country having far fewer narrow-gauge railways than either France or Germany. But many recorded their affection for the quaint 'Heath Robinson' systems with their uneven track and diminutive locomotives and wagons. Trains were controlled by telephone, and though there were no brake vans, the train crew included a guard. The busiest period was dusk to dawn, when smoke and steam were less likely to mark a target for artillery. Derailments were an almost nightly event, which fostered an expertise in re-railing. Trains took supplies up towards the front line and returned with men for rest billets and litters carrying the wounded. Despite the small loading gauge, these light railways could handle huge quantities; about 1,000 tons a day was handled on a 30km stretch between Maroeuil near Arras and railheads near Vimy Ridge. As an indication of the demands placed on the railways, from the beginning of the August 1918 offensive to the armistice, 700,000 tons of shells were fired.

Geddes's recommendation for the expansion of light railways took effect from 1916: at the end of that year there were just 155km of 600mm (2ft) railway; by the end of 1917 there were 1,310km of line carrying, by September, 210,808 tons a week.[15] Steam locomotives were used in the rear and petrol-engined tractors closer to the front line to minimise the visibility of steam. The men usually lived in wooden huts, sandbagged partway up to offer protection against shrapnel, and they were usually away from company headquarters with little to entertain them. Shells were taken up at night, and supplies of corrugated iron, timber, wire netting, cement, iron stakes, barbed wire, concrete slabs and poison gas cylinders were also carried. Men were carried, 35 to a wagon, in trains of 4–6 wagons.

Standardised locomotives were developed by each country. Having lost much of its productive capacity to the Germans, the French Government contracted Baldwin to build a Decauville-type locomotive. This became the Baldwin 10-12-D 4-6-0T, and in 1917 the American Locomotive Company

Fig 3.4
The most common locomotive on the light railways was the Baldwin 4-6-0 side tank, which had been built initially for the French military light railways in Morocco. The first 45 were ordered in August 1916, and another 450 followed by April 1917. ALCO of Schenectady, New York, built a further 100. No 636 is seen here leaving a standard-gauge yard on 7 March 1918. The hose on the back of the bunker allowed water to be lifted from tanks or shell holes.

Fig 3.5
The Péchot-Bourdon development of the Fairlie-type locomotive was chosen in the hope that if one unit was disabled, the other could continue to operate. The first 50 were constructed in 1906, and a further 280 during the First World War by the Baldwin Locomotive Works in Philadelphia. An example is preserved in Dresden Transport Museum.

(ALCO) built 100 2-6-2Ts which ran better in either direction than the 4-6-0Ts. Decauville designed the Progrès 5T 0-4-0T and an 0-6-0T of which large numbers were built. Péchot's Fairlie articulated 0-4-4-0T was designed with a colleague to produce the Péchot-Bourdon locomotive; 62 were built between 1888 and 1914, and the Baldwin Locomotive Works in Pennsylvania built another 280. The shortcomings of the Krauss-designed Zwillinge 0-6-0T, which could be used back to back with a single crew, had become evident during its use in German South West Africa from 1898, and led to the adoption of the 0-8-0T Brigadelok design with Klein-Lindner articulation of the front and rear axles. Over 2,000 were made during the war. Locomotives were fitted with flexible pipes so that they could fill up with water whenever an opportunity arose, often from water in shell craters. Internal-combustion-engined tractors were made for the British lines by Baguley, Motor Rail, Dick Kerr and Westinghouse.

Life for uniformed railwaymen in France

Footplate work in France was a trying experience: preparation of locomotives was difficult, especially at night, when flare lamps were prohibited and any opening of a firebox door could invite enemy attention; there were often no pits for access underneath the motion and wheels; coal was frequently poor and the water unsuitable for boilers; and the 33 different classes of locomotive made it impossible to have a stock of standardised spares. Differences in language, signalling systems and operating methods compounded the challenges. Hours were often excessive: a 12-hour shift was the norm, but continuous turns of 60 hours were not unknown, and after the final push extended distances, a living van was attached to the locomotive to carry two crews. Working well behind the lines was no guarantee of safety; the junction of St Pol north of Amiens was shelled in 1918, even though it was 40km behind the front line. As aerial power developed, trains and supply depots became favoured targets.

A ROD driver recalled that 'French enginemen, who often acted as our pilotmen won the admiration of our men for the courteous and efficient manner in which they carried out the duty. A share-out of their coffee was usually their first act, and our tin of "bully", to which they were very partial, would then change hands.' Another wrote that:

... engines of nearly all English and Scotch Companies are at work there, also Canadian and American ... Let me say at once that our conditions of work are very different from those at home, and often a crew will come to work at night, and this is when most work is done, and have to prepare a type of engine they have never seen before, and this, too, with only the aid of a handlamp, no naked flame being allowed.

The system of signalling whilst working over the French railways places much more responsibility on the Driver, and over our own lines in the vicinity of the 'line' no fixed signals are used, so that the efficient working reflects credit on the footplatemen. A new danger, too, or at least one much intensified of late, is the dropping of bombs or aerial torpedoes by enemy aircraft. This often makes the position most unpleasant, considering the nature of the goods carried, and often being their special target.[16]

Many of the locomotives transferred from British railways proved unsuitable for operation in France; the larger continental loading gauge and narrow footplates of British locomotives made shunting operations difficult, and this was compounded by the universal use of screw rather than three-link couplings on wagons. The GWR 2-6-0s and NER 0-8-0s were apparently favourite classes.

The only British steam locomotive captured by the Germans was Midland Railway 0-6-0 No 2717, when a German counter-attack during the Battle of Cambrai overran a salient bisected by the Péronne–Marcoing railway in November 1917. The driver, J Woodhouse from Oxenholme, had to abandon the engine near the Gouzeaucourt level crossing, and the locomotive became a German machine-gun post. Woodhouse saw his old charge at Charleroi after the armistice before it was returned to the Midland.

The ROD's locomotive workshops and stores were created at Audruicq, a small town between Calais and St Omer, where huge stores of locomotive spares were held. Training in operations and footplate work was given in the extensive yards. An adjacent munitions dump must have added to fear of aerial attack, which was justified by a successful hit on 21 July 1916, when the explosion blew fragments of 400 railway wagons over a wide area. The Director of Light Railways and chairman of the REC, Lieutenant Colonel V M Barrington Ward, was appointed Distinguished Service Order (DSO) for driving a locomotive into the exploding ammunition dump to rescue men who had taken refuge in dug-outs.

On ROD lines trains were controlled by 'signalmen' in a hut or dug-out at each end of a block section, using telephone, red or green flag and lamps. Written orders to proceed were tied to a hazel branch made into a loop and caught by the guard in the brake van, which under French practice was placed next to the locomotive. He would then give the driver the order to proceed. Additional brake vans were added according to the train weight and nature of the route, because French railways relied on the van brakes rather than stopping a train to pin down brakes on wagons, as in Britain. Again in contrast to British practice, French brake vans were not fitted with stoves, so many guards scrounged a brazier to provide some warmth, at the cost of suffocating fumes.

The German offensive in spring 1918 severely disrupted the system and much of it was lost, but with the counteroffensive, the German Heeresfeldbahn systems were gradually taken over and the Allied 600mm (2ft) lines left far behind.

Fig 3.6 (right)
The yard at Westonhoek in Belgium gives an idea of the scale of the 600mm (2ft) gauge light railways. On 7 March 1918 rakes of wagons loaded with ammunition await forwarding to the front, having been transhipped from standard-gauge wagons, on the left.

Fig 3.7 (below)
The British-built contribution to the steam fleet of the light railways was the 4-6-0 side tank developed by Hunslet of Leeds from a design of 1905 for a Rhodesian gold mine light railway. Hunslet's munitions work meant it lacked the capacity to build more than 155 during the course of the war, hence the Baldwin and ALCO orders. The Hunslet was apparently the most popular design with engine crews. No 359, is seen at an unidentified base.

RCL Publications

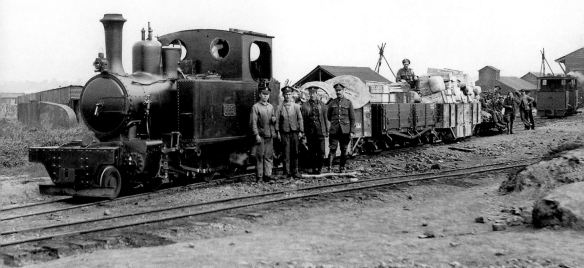

RCL Publications

Fig 3.8 (right)
Both the British and French governments recruited Chinese workers, the former for the Chinese Labour Corps. The Chinese labourer on the right would be the gang foreman with enough English to translate orders to the others unloading 15in shells from standard to narrow gauge, on 7 March 1918. About 140,000 Chinese worked in France and most were repatriated by 1920.

Fig 3.9 (below)
Narrow-gauge lines were also used to transport the wounded in canvas-sided converted vans, recorded here on 7 March 1918 with Hunslet No 318. The left-hand side was for an attendant and walking wounded.

RCL Publications

RCL Publications

The German systems even had signals and brick-built signal boxes, but in retreat they had made such a comprehensive job of destruction that they were of limited use. The armistice ended the need for reconstruction.

After the armistice, ROD trains were run to Cologne, where a GWR Dean Goods 0-6-0 and a Caledonian 0-6-0 were based for some months at the depot at Nippes just outside the city. They finally left, coupled together, in March 1919, hauling the staff train and returning to Audruicq via Liège and Mons, where care had to be taken when coaling from an old German supply which had been mixed with small black bombs by retreating German troops. At Audruicq the locomotives were 'stripped' for return to Britain.

Railwaymen on the front

Periodically railwaymen were sent overseas in a civilian capacity after volunteering for a particular task in response to a call from the War Office for a bespoke set of skills. In April 1916 the War Office requisitioned men for service in the ROD, Railway Construction Corps and Railway Transport Establishments.

Early in 1917 the War Office issued a request for 3,000 civilian platelayers for construction of temporary railways in France. A letter was sent to railway companies asking for volunteers to form companies of 250 men. The rates of pay included bonuses and all travel, board and food. The men would remain civilians but under the direction of a railway officer, and the work would usually be of short duration. Eight companies were formed, Nos 1 and 2 being exclusively LNWR men.

In March 1917 a company of 250 platelayers from the GWR assembled at Paddington and went to France for three months. The engineer-in-chief reported that they:

> ... carried out a very fine piece of emergency work at Steenwerck [in French Flanders], working 11½ hours per day for ten consecutive days and completing the work before scheduled time. At this place they had the honour of being nearer to the firing line (about 4½ miles [7km]) than any other English railway Company, and they showed a fine spirit, working cheerfully, even after shells had fallen in their camp ... No. 3 was a most efficient Company, and I cannot speak too highly of both the officers and men comprising it.[17]

They were visited by the GWR chairman, Viscount Portal, in May. A report of a similar visit that year by a *Daily Mail* journalist was reproduced in the ASLEF journal:

> Within a few hours after a fresh British advance the railway workers make their appearance. They find bridges blown away, tracks obliterated and booby traps everywhere. Heavily armoured locomotives haul up material. The track is cleared, the craters made by German explosives filled, fresh bridges thrown across the gaps, and in an incredibly short time here is a new route ready to hand over to the Railway Operating Department [*sic*].

The construction of extensive systems of railways behind the lines is comparatively a new thing. At first the Army relied mainly on motor-lorries. One train can haul as much as 200 motor-lorries. It employs four men in place of 400, saves heaps of money and, incidentally, avoids the continual tearing up of roads which a big motor-lorry service means.[18]

A sense of the widespread deployment of railwaymen, few of whom would previously have left Britain, is given by the decorations awarded to some of the 22,941 Midland staff; in addition to British decorations, others were awarded by France, Belgium, Italy, Portugal, Romania, Serbia, Greece and Russia.[19]

NER pals battalion

The pals battalions were created to encourage enlistment by the promise that recruits would serve alongside friends, neighbours and colleagues. The only example on the railways was the 17th Service Battalion, Northumberland Fusiliers (NER) Pioneers. Within a few days of war being declared, over 2,000 NER men had joined the colours. On 8 September 1914 the NER management issued a circular inviting those who wanted to serve in an NER unit to return an attached slip. The circular stated that the company was prepared to make adequate provision for wives, families and dependants; to keep men's positions open for them; to pay their contributions to superannuation and pension funds; and to provide accommodation for the families of men who were occupying company houses.

The circular stated that 1,100 men were needed; almost 3,000 responded. Official sanction to form the 17th Battalion came on 11 September, and recruitment began on the 14th. Accommodation was found at the King George Dock in Hull, which had been opened on 26 June 1914 by the King and was the joint property of the NER and HBR. The latter agreed to two warehouses being fitted up as barracks for the battalion. The recreation room soon had a billiards table and harmonium, but some found it difficult to adjust to barracks life: 'It is a rather trying experience going to bed in company with about five hundred men – some more or less "merry" – especially after being used to home life, and in addition having to sleep in blankets on a bag filled with straw.'[20]

The whole battalion was assembled by 1 October and in November was moved to Patrington on the Withernsea line, where the men were billeted. A sergeant took them along the streets and civilians would shout, 'Here, I'll take two in here.' They ended up at Kilnsea guarding the coast for three months at a time while invasion was expected, causing nervous sentries to fire off a few rounds at comrades at night, fortunately without ill-effect. The German bombardment of West Hartlepool on 16 December increased anxiety.

When trench warfare had become the established mode of combat along the Western Front, it was decided to convert the 17th into a Pioneer Battalion, the role of which was defined by the War Office as 'to fight as infantry, and in addition to provide organised and intelligent labour for engineering operations', so on 11 January 1915 the title of the battalion became the 17th Northumberland Fusiliers (NER) Pioneers. This raised the rate of pay by 2d a day to reflect its skills.

Back in Hull in February 1915, training continued, including a course of platelaying at Hessle, reached by special train each day. In June the battalion moved to Brough Park at Catterick Bridge for drills and route marches, before moving on to Bardon Moor, near Leyburn in Wensleydale, to build rifle ranges, living under canvas amid the heather. In August the battalion moved to wooden huts on Salisbury Plain, again building rifle ranges and practising manoeuvres. In mid-November the battalion went to France.

After a snowy night in 16-man tents situated in 'a swamp' outside Le Havre, the battalion was transported in cattle trucks, 35 to a truck, to the 'mud-hole' of Pont Remy for a 16km march to Ailly-le-Haut-Clocher, before moving on to Belloy-sur-Somme. There, in an estaminet, troops were treated to *café au cognac* with such lavish hospitality that the Adjutant had to be summoned. As he entered the scene of ructions, a relieved Madame 'greeted him with "Merci, merci, Monsieur le Capitaine". The Adjutant's reply – "Mercy, madam, mercy! There's no blooming mercy in the British Army" – became historic.'[21]

Diary entries record the usual horrors of trench life: 'liquid mud up to the knees', the plague of rats and mice. The battalion had brought out 'war dogs' and one proved such a good ratter that he killed 36 in an hour. Between trench duties, the battalion built roads, dug-outs and 'trench tramways'.

During the Battle of the Somme in 1916, the battalion's story merges with the division, but the 17th was in divisional reserve, to be employed in opening up communications (trenches and extension of the Authuille Wood tramway) between Allied lines and positions won. One soldier wrote on the evening of the battle: 'All of us addressed by our own officers and told of tomorrow's events. Pessimistically inclined making wills. There is a strange feeling about the whole night. I cannot explain it. It is not to be explained – only felt...'[22] Though the battalion received relatively light casualties, some were in the trenches for eight

Fig 3.10
A track panel is lifted over the heads of fasteners, showing the system of building light railway, with unskilled tasks often carried out by infantry who were out of the front line.

days without even taking their boots off, living on bully and water, and getting little sleep.

Months of garrison, trench and tunnelling duties as well as building trench-mortar emplacements followed during the Somme offensive, before the battalion joined two railway companies of RE to convert the Beausart–Aveluy line from metre to standard gauge and later extend it to Mouquet Farm. The battalion was based at Acheux, and working the nocturnal materials train from Acheux to Mesnil was remembered as a dangerous job, because the train, in earshot of the Germans, could provoke shell showers.

On 4 November 1916 the 17th Northumberland Pioneers became a Railway Pioneer Battalion, and a succession of railway building and modification tasks followed: a 600mm (2ft) line from Aveluy to Pozières; building a standard-gauge line from Aveluy to Acheux; and after a move to Berguette, the construction of railway workshops for both standard and narrow gauges on a new line 2½km from Berguette station. Prefabricated parts were sent by canal barge from England and brought right to the site, all pieces being carefully numbered to assist erection. Heavy concrete foundations had to be laid for the lathes and drilling and milling machines, in which the battalion was helped by 'a gang of Hun prisoners [who] worked well all the time'.[23]

The battalion was then posted to Poperinghe, where the famous Talbot House provided an oasis of rest and comfort and a 'ripping little church'. The men enjoyed a review put on by the 55th Division: 'The British soldier is a wonder; here, about ten miles [16km] behind the line, and the worst point of the whole front, we see a show that beats many I have seen at home.'

On 3 April 1917 work started on the standard-gauge Great Midland Railway from Peselhoek, 3km north of Poperinghe, eastwards to the Yser Canal, which entailed filling the near dry canal. It was completed by 12 June and the battalion was then put on light railways and 'Decauville work' in various areas between Poperinghe, Ypres and Elverdinghe, with some construction work having to be carried out at night.

Among the preparations for the big push at Passchendaele scheduled for 31 July, detachments were sent to a training camp for light railway construction near Watou. 'Here all sorts of tips for the rapid laying of light lines were shown, and different units demonstrated their special schemes … The instruction was not too strenuous, and some apparently thought they had little to learn.' Following the occupation of St Julien, a light railway was extended across the Yser Canal to the village.

The battalion moved near the Belgian border to work on defences at Nieport; the men bathed nude in the North Sea before moving back to the Salient and St Julian. The battalion 'became railway troops' on 15 November 1917 and worked on light railways with other companies until the German offensive of April 1918, which was anticipated and aroused much apprehension during March. Towards the end of the month the bridge over the River Steenbeck, swollen to twice its normal width, collapsed as a train was crossing it, and the driver and fireman were drowned.

After the offensive began, the 17th was moved to Hazebrouck on 14 April, and it was a few days before the German advance was halted, partly due to a failure of their supply lines. As the Allied advance accelerated, the 17th was engaged mainly on making sure roads were open for supplies, replacing bridges destroyed by the retreating Germans.

Other railway companies

Though the NER formed the only pals battalion, the LNWR supplied a complete company of the RE, known as 115th Railway Company RE, drawn entirely from the Engineering Department. It went to France in 1915 and subsequently to Palestine and Egypt. The LNWR also formed the first complete Railway Operating Corps of 3 officers and 267 men (227 from the Traffic Department and 40 from the Locomotive Department), who left Euston for camp at Longmoor on 14 July 1915.[24] The North Staffordshire Railway (NSR) started a drilling and shooting corps.

In June 1915 the GWR was asked to find the men to create the 116th Railway Construction Company RE. Within a few days 220 platelayers, 12 carpenters and 6 blacksmiths were enrolled and sent for training at Longmoor (*see* p 50). The three GWR officers (out of six) were R C Kirkpatrick, the chief assistant to the divisional engineer at Wolverhampton; E Lake from the divisional engineer's office at Plymouth; and Allan S Quartermaine from the chief engineer's office at Paddington.[25] The regime was: drill before breakfast at 8; parade at 9 for inspection, special orders read out, followed by drill or musketry instruction; sometimes a route march, with about a dozen playing mouth-organs; lunch at 1; 2–5, more drills, marches or lectures; tea at 5, then free. Concert usually arranged each week. Roll call at 9.30. Lights out at 9.45. Beds were straw palliasses with three blankets.

The men's first assignment was to lay sidings for ammunition at Portsmouth, after which they went to Blaydon near Newcastle to lay sidings for a new munition works. They were billeted in the Drill Hall and Church Room at Blaydon, and the kindness of local people made a great impression on them. The company was at sea on Christmas Day 1915, and the men were allowed one bottle of beer each 'as a luxury' and plum puddings and cigarettes provided by the GWR Gifts Fund. It landed at Port Said in Egypt and travelled in open trucks to El Ferdan, a passing place on the Suez Canal, to lay a 2ft 6in (762mm) railway for 8km east from the canal. One of the officers, by special application, was 'able to obtain porridge, milk and sugar for breakfast as additions to the bacon and bread' because of the manual nature of their work. During sandstorms the cooks found their gasmasks useful as they struggled to make their pots boil.

A detachment was sent to Port Said to construct a similar railway along the shoreline while the rest of the men went to El Kantara to lay a standard-gauge railway from the Suez Canal to Katia, an oasis in the desert 50km to the north-east. They were reinforced by the Port Said detachment and worked alternate shifts with the 115th Railway Company of LNWR men. They were to work together for the next three years as 50km became 950km, running on to Haifa with branches to Beersheba and Jerusalem. Though there was not a bridge for the first 200km, there were plenty of cuttings and embankments. Sand was used as ballast until Palestine was reached and a supply of stone. The longest stretch laid in a day was 3.2km, but 1½ was the norm, using unskilled Egyptians for much of the labouring. Operation was by the ROD, using locomotives from the Egyptian State Railways, the US, LNWR and LSWR. The heat could reach 48°C in the shade, and flies, insects, sand and dust were trials. Dysentery, malaria and septic sores were a scourge, resulting in almost every man going to hospital at some point.[26]

A second GWR company was formed for overseas service in summer 1916 at the request of the War Office; known as the 275th Company Royal Engineers

Railway Troops, it consisted of 200 platelayers, 2 fitters, 2 engine drivers, 2 firemen, 1 clerk, 1 draughtsman and 2 cooks.[27]

Though not formally a GWR company, the Wilts Royal Engineers Territorial (Swindon) Company, renamed the 565th Wilts Army Troop Company RE(T) in September 1915, must have been composed largely of GWR staff to judge from the space devoted to its war in the *GWR Magazine*. When war was declared, the unit was in camp at Purbrook, Portsmouth, having just completed a week's training. It was sent back to Swindon and then almost immediately to Weymouth to work on defences around Portland. After rebuilding the outer defences, the company had a month's strenuous training before being sent to France to work on a defensive scheme at St Omer. The men were then sent to work so close to the front line at St Eloi near Ypres that they were not allowed to smoke or talk above a whisper. They were then assigned the maintenance of floating bridges across the canal north of Ypres, which the Germans tried to shell and eventually succeeded in one case, but enough material was on hand to repair the damage in 1½ hours. It was so lively that almost every day the unit returned to camp one or two men short, and by the time it was reduced to 50 per cent capacity, it was struggling to perform its duties. Their billet in farm buildings was shelled, so the men had to create dug-outs, but a barrage of 8in guns also found them. They were glad to be ordered to move to Dranoutre in Belgium in June 1915 for a relative rest.

There they created a system of defence lines around Kemmel Hill and north for about 10km with the help of 400 civilians. Half the company was sent to Bailleul to work in an engineering shop and sawmill, fabricating observation towers, huts, gun platforms and trolleys; eventually about 800 men were employed. This released some of the company to work on defence lines at Nieppe, building concrete dug-outs and machine-gun posts.

In October the whole company was installed in a camp at Bailleul to construct a new sawmill at Steenwerck, as well as undertake minor assignments on light railways, water supply systems and the erection of a new hospital at Trois Arbres.

In July 1916 the company moved to the Somme, working on water supply pipes and associated pumping stations. The mud was so bad that if a horse strayed off the road it could drown while standing up. The following spring the company moved to Faucaucourt and then Villers-Carbonnel to create a new Army HQ on a site beyond the old German front line, where a large number of dead were still lying. A camp for 2,000 men was built before the company moved on to La Chapallette to construct heavy steel bridges over the Somme at Péronne, for which it was given 12 days. On the seventh it was ordered to Dunkirk, by which time three of the four bridges were finished and the fourth was ready for launching.

At Dunkirk the company converted the Terminus Hotel at Leffrinkouke into an Army HQ, but enemy shelling put an end to the seaside idyll. After work on water supplies in the docks, a large detachment was sent to build a musketry school in Abbeville. In November 1917 the unit was transferred to the Cambrai front to fill mine craters near the Hindenburg Line. Construction of a new line of defence between Vaulx Vraucourt and St Leger was the next task before more water supply work, including cleaning wells for returning civilians.

The concealed machine-gun battery positions the men created 'did terrible execution' when the enemy launched a major assault on 21 March 1918. This entailed night work to construct trenches and make a coherent system out of a maze of original British and German front-line trenches; one of the new linking trenches was named 'Swindon'.

When the Hundred Days Offensive and the final chapter of the war began in August 1918, the company returned to water supply duties, with some men working 36 hours without a break to provide water for horses when neighbouring systems broke down. As the advance progressed, the company was sent to Ruyaulcourt to build a heavy ramp to the Canal du Nord by Havrincourt Wood. Here the greatest single loss of life occurred when a barrage killed 8 men and injured 20. A week's rest at Boyelles was sanctioned before the company joined the New Zealand Tunnelling Company RE in constructing the largest heavy steel bridge on the Western Front, at Hermies. The span was 180ft and the launching weight 140 tons. Within six days the first traffic was crossing the bridge, and it was fully completed in nine.

More water supply, camp and bridge work followed, and a bridge over the railway at Douai was being repaired on Armistice Day. Soon after Christmas the demobilisation scheme was put into force, and individual men began leaving for home. Those remaining joined the Army of Occupation in Germany and were stationed at Troisdorf before being sent home around March 1919.[28]

By the end of the war British personnel had laid over 2,300 miles of standard-gauge track and 1,300 miles of narrow-gauge track.[29]

Palestine

The development of military railways in Palestine by the RE began in early 1916 when there were no railways east of the Suez Canal. Until then, positions east of the canal had been defensive, and the plan was to improve communications to help the Egyptian Expeditionary Force (EEF) of British and Empire units achieve a decisive victory over the Turks. In December 1915 Sir George Macauley was appointed Military Director of Railways for Egypt, having been Under-Secretary of Egyptian State Railways and a former officer in the RE, who helped to construct the Sudan Military Railway in 1898. Eight short 2ft 6in (760mm) gauge railways were built along the east bank of the canal with help from two RE construction companies, in order to link military depots with the Egyptian State Railways.

The standard-gauge Sinai Military Railway was begun at El Kantara on the east bank after two Turkish attacks on the canal had been defeated in February and March 1915. Two RE companies with 500 Europeans were employed on construction works assisted by 18,000 Egyptians and Sikh Pioneers, mainly on earthworks. The single-line railway ran along the coast to Romani, which was attacked in August; the three-day battle turned out to be the final battle in defence of the canal before a steady eastward advance by the EEF. El Arish (150km) was reached by Christmas 1916, and Rafa, on the border of Egypt and Palestine and 200km from El Kantara, was taken on 9 January, with the railway catching up in March. Deir el Belah (222km) was reached in April 1917 and Haifa (412km) in December 1918. Engineers faced building the railway across swampy soil, wadis which could become raging torrents overnight, and undulating country requiring steep gradients and tight curves.

Construction works entailed more than the railway; water from the Nile had to be piped across the desert, and blockhouses with barbed-wire entanglements were built to protect the line. However, it took three battles over seven months to dislodge the Turks and Germans from Gaza, allowing railway construction to proceed north as close as possible to Jerusalem to enable General Allenby to take the city in December 1917. A line was continued as far as Acre, partly by rebuilding earlier sections of track.

Traffic was sufficiently heavy to justify doubling of the line between El Kantara and Rafa in the second half of 1917. The 412km Sinai Military Railway was one of the largest railway construction projects of the First World War, so it is no wonder that it called on the resources of so many RE units: the 96th Light Railway Operating Company, 98th Light Railway Train Crew Company, and the 115th, 116th, 265th and 266th Railway Construction Companies, as well as companies of Sikh Pioneers.[30]

Operation was not straightforward either. Few men were doing what they were trained to do: many drivers were cleaners; stores clerks and wagon labellers were employed as signalmen; and there was one instance of a clerk being given the job of driving. Local staff were often inebriated. After peace, it became the ROD's job to teach native labour to take over their jobs, but it was an uphill task: 'signals were habitually ignored, vacuum brake pipes were left uncoupled, and oil cans were either never taken out of the tool box, or else the engine from funnel downwards was bathed in lubricant'.[31] Injectors invariably failed as one passed one's 'home' station, allowing time with the family while an assistant engine was summoned. On one final journey back to Kantara, the Arab crew had managed to allow the water level to fall below the crown of the firebox and caused a fusible plug to melt, which stranded them in the middle of nowhere.

Other theatres

Though Palestine was the largest non-European construction project, railway units became involved in the operation and maintenance of railways further afield.

Operations against the Turks in Mesopotamia started in November 1914 when a force from India captured the Fao fort at the mouth of the Shatt-el-Arab and subsequently occupied Basra. In June 1915 Amara was taken and in July, Nasiriyah. The tide turned with the retreat to Kut-al-Amara from November and the fall of Kut in March 1916, with the surrender of 2,970 British and 6,000 Indian troops through exhaustion of supplies. The plan to use rivers and especially the Tigris as the main means of supply, supplemented by railways, was undermined by the extremes of climate and frequent flooding due to silting. A plan to build a railway in 1915 had been rejected by the Indian Government but was authorised after the fall of Kut. Metre-gauge lines were built under the direction of General G Lubbock, who was appointed Director of Railways in Mesopotamia in September 1916.

A line was driven 225km north from the port of Basra to Nasiriyah, followed by Kurna–Amara (112km, an exception at 2ft 6in gauge but later converted to metre gauge); Kut–Hinaidi (6km south of Baghdad) opened on 24 July 1917 and soon after it reached the city (175km with 13 crossing places and sheds for 24 locomotives at Kut and 6 at Hinaidi); Basra–Kurna was begun in February 1917 and opened on 1 January 1918. On the western bank of the Tigris was the standard-gauge Baghdad Railway, promoted by Germany, which was extended south to Baghdad South and north to Tikrit and Sharqat. Much of the equipment – rails, locomotives and stock – came from India, though LSWR 0-6-0 locomotives found their way to the standard-gauge lines at Baghdad.

In East Africa British forces in 1915 captured the 1,145km, metre-gauge German Central Military Railway from Dar es Salaam to Ujiji on Lake Tanganyika, and the 355km Usambara Railway. The 148km Voi Lake Railway was built to connect Uganda with the Usambara Railway.

Frequent attempts were made by the Germans to disrupt traffic on the Uganda Railway, and a goods train was blown up on 16 May 1916. Preventive measures included removal of ballast so that a mine could not be placed without its being exposed, whitewashing of ballast to show whether it had been disturbed, more patrols and larger maintenance gangs, and guards placed at all bridges and culverts throughout the entire length of the railway. An armoured vehicle of ½in steel plate was run with each mail train, with guard trucks run in front of the locomotive – these were originally filled with sand and placed to detonate a bomb on the track, but the Germans altered their bombs so that a certain number of axles had to pass over before the striker struck the detonator, making two vehicles necessary.[32]

Though India never became a theatre of war, the railways contributed to the war effort, not only in the supply of equipment but also raw materials. For example, from Khanai on the North Western Railway a line was built by the Baluchistan Chrome Mines Company specifically to extract chrome ore from its mines at Hindubagh, which opened in September 1917. What became known as the Zhob Valley Railway was later extended to Fort Sandeman and became part of the North Western Railway in 1921.

4 | Second World War home front

The Second World War was a more morally clear-cut conflict than the First; as a *Manchester Guardian* editorial the day after Germany invaded Poland summarised it, 'The Nazi system, its brutal prosecuting spirit, its colossal immorality in international relations, are something which even the most cynical feel that in sheer self-preservation we must resist.' This may have helped to suppress the discontents and periodic rancour that coloured life on the railways during the first global conflict.

Four years after the First World War had ended, 120 railway companies had been grouped into the 'Big Four': an enlarged GWR, London Midland & Scottish Railway (LMS), LNER and Southern Railway (SR). Inevitably this made coordination much simpler than during the earlier world war. Very few lines had been closed, which was just as well, given the need to conserve petrol and rubber, especially after 1942 when motoring other than for business purposes was severely curtailed. As LNER General Manager Sir Charles Newton said after the war: 'In 1939 there were over 3,000,000 motor vehicles upon the roads of this small and highly congested island, and the load transferred to the railways was correspondingly heavy.'[1] This was the inevitable consequence of rationing of fuel because of the costs in foreign exchange as well as lost lives and ships.

Britain's railways were again taken under state control with an order on 1 September 1939 under the Emergency Powers (Defence) Act 1939, placing authority with the Minister of Transport through a Railway Executive Committee. Even before the REC was formed on 24 September, the railways had handled the first wave of reinforcements for overseas garrisons: on 1–3 September, 22 specials arrived at King George V Dock in Glasgow with about 10,000 men, following the recall of regular and Territorial troops from summer training camps from 23 August.[2]

The mobilisation plan for the Army and Air Force was carried out over 24 days according to a scheme worked out with the War Office. The Admiralty had already brought the fleet up to full strength. The BEF had been set up after the Anschluss in March 1938, and planning for the movement of the small but highly trained army had been done by a small unit of selected officers in the War Office, with just seven confidential clerks and typists, who had worked out every detail of the arrangements. The Secretary of State for War thought 'their ingenuity, their precision, and their patience would have baffled *Bradshaw*'.[3]

The movement of the BEF to France in September 1939 took place over 27 days (9 September–5 October) and conveyed 102,000 men with armoured fighting vehicles and guns. The BEF was routed predominantly through Southampton, with smaller numbers through Harwich, Dover, Portsmouth, Avonmouth and the South Wales ports.

The operation entailed 261 special trains to Southampton over the 27 days. The heaviest day was 15 September, when 18 trains arrived carrying 6,921 men from Portsmouth, Cosham, Farnborough (2), Chichester, Amesbury and Andover Junction, Edinburgh, Brentwood, Digby, Brentwood and Bedford, Halifax, Westenhanger, Saffron Walden, Formby, Richmond (Yorkshire, 2), Blackpool and Netley.[4]

The first REC comprised Sir James Milne (GWR deputy chairman), Gilbert Szlumper (SR general manager), the recently retired Sir Ralph Wedgwood of the LNER as the REC's chairman, Charles H Newton (LNER), Sir William Wood (LMS president) and Frank Pick of the London Passenger Transport Board (succeeded by Lord Ashfield). In August 1941 Sir Alan Anderson became Controller of Railways and chairman of the REC, with Sir James Milne as deputy chairman.

The REC was initially based at Fielden House in Westminster, but Frank Pick offered the bombproof disused Underground station at Down Street in Mayfair. The Piccadilly Line station had closed in 1932, and once its suitability had been approved it was converted by Sir Robert McAlpine & Sons into offices, dormitories, kitchens and mess rooms, accessed by two lifts and also a short platform at which those on REC business could alight from the train cab. Down Street was shared with the Prime Minister and the War Cabinet until the Cabinet War Rooms were brought into use on 15 October 1940.

The REC was advised of the general requirements of naval, military and Air Force traffic and other essential government traffic, and the priority to be accorded to each, by railway control officers within the RCH. Special sections were created to liaise with the three fighting services to understand and implement their requirements. It proved difficult to find time to recruit people with aptitude or some railway experience because of the burdens on senior staff at HQ, divisional and district levels. Twice daily reports were sent to the REC on congestion, damage and working difficulties.[5]

A paper headed 'Most Secret' and written by an LMS member of staff, with a foreword by T W Royle, chief operating manager and later a vice president of the LMS, was highly critical of the situation in which the railways found themselves. Prior to the war, as war production was being increased:

> ... the railways laboured under the serious handicap of lack of information as to the requirements of the Government Departments for transport and the needs of the production programmes. The large production Departments, i.e., the Ministry of Supply, the Ministry of Aircraft Production, and Admiralty Establishments, were working independently, their requirements were frequently in direct conflict and wasteful from a railway point of view, and no information was forthcoming as to the output to be expected from the factories, the mines, and the Government depots of various kinds. The last thing which seemed to be thought of was prior advice to the railways of what should be expected so that the necessary provision could be made, and the attitude seemed to be – if indeed thought were given to the matter – that the railways had unlimited resources.[6]

Its writer acknowledges a dawning realisation of the transport implications of conflict, 'but at no stage were forecasts [produced] of the probable requirements of the Fighting Services and Government Departments, of the volume of imports or the output of industry generally, sufficiently reliable materially to assist the railways'. The paper complains of the difficulty:

> ... experienced in obtaining essential materials, and in securing action on matters affecting the public or traders which needed a Government pronouncement or regulation for their enforcement. Delays of a year or

more were not uncommon when a month or so should have sufficed to bring about a reform required by the railways to enable them to do their war-time job.

Consistency of policy in Ministerial circles was not engendered by the frequency with which the holders of the office of Minister of Transport were changed. In the first stages of the war this office maintained its pre-war reputation for brief occupancy, and no sooner had a Minister gained some familiarity with railway problems than he was moved to other fields. In April, 1939 Dr Leslie Burgin, the Minister during much of the period of preparation for war, vacated the post and was succeeded by Capt. Euan Wallace, who occupied it for thirteen months; during the next twelve months, two other Ministers, viz., Sir John Reith (five months) and Lieutenant-Colonel J.T.C. Moore-Brabazon (seven months), had come and gone.

In contrast to the First World War, passenger services were reduced and decelerated almost immediately on the LMS, LNER and SR, from 11 September, and on the GWR from 25 September. No express was timed to exceed an average speed of 45mph. Pullman and restaurant cars were withdrawn from 11 September and then some services gradually reintroduced from 16 October.

Air-raid precautions (ARP) had been under way all year since the January 1939 announcement that enough steel had been ordered for construction of 400,000 four- or five-person Anderson shelters. The railways assumed the key role in their distribution, which was complicated by the components being manufactured by five firms across the country and requiring assembly into sets of parts before distribution. Railway staff had already seen protection works applied to railway installations to the tune of £3–4 million, 50 Underground stations had works to prevent flooding should water mains burst, and protective clothing was issued to some staff.

Detailed arrangements had been drawn up and timetables printed to evacuate 4 million people from industrial areas to 1,200 detraining stations. Emergency headquarters outside London were prepared for the four railway companies. The SR moved into the Regency country house of Deepdene, near Dorking, which had been turned into a hotel in the 1920s; underground caves mentioned in John Evelyn's diaries were adapted into a bunker for the telephone exchange and Traffic Control. Diagrams of important junctions were placed on walls, and there were radio receivers in every room and dedicated 'Control' lines to every signal box. The GWR moved into six country houses west of Reading, with Beenham Grange at Aldermaston as the headquarters. The LMS took over The Grove, a Georgian house near Watford, after the Easter 1939 invasion of Albania by Italy, though the move of its HQ did not take place until the weekend of 2–3 September. The LNER moved into a mansion named The Hoo, near Hitchin.

Staff practised ARP and blackout procedures, including hoods over locomotive cabs to mask the glare from the firebox, and trains were created to provide instruction in, and facilities for, decontamination from poison gas. The first, in a bright yellow livery, had been displayed at Euston in November 1937. Additional breakdown trains were assembled, and the scrapping of locomotives and wagons had been deferred to ensure adequate resources – about 20,000 locomotives and 1¼ million wagons. Locomotive men, signalmen and others out on the line were issued with helmets and some with gas masks.

Fig 4.1
The driver of GWR Castle class 4-6-0 No 5085 *Evesham Abbey* is wearing the gas mask and helmet issued to locomotive crews at the beginning of the war when gas attacks were feared.

Ambulance trains were quickly created: in all, 886 carriages were converted for use in 39 ambulance trains, divided into Overseas Ambulance Trains (OATs) for taking patients from casualty clearing stations to base hospitals or shipment home, and Home Ambulance Trains (HATs) to link ports with military hospitals and then hospitals near patients' homes. The initial order for 8 HATs and 4 OATs was placed on 2 September 1939 to LMS drawings. The HATs comprised 9 gangway-connected coaches, later increased to 11, and the OATs, 16 vehicles. All 136 vehicles were taken from LMS 57ft-long stock for conversion. The LMS work was done at Derby and Wolverton; Swindon on the GWR; Doncaster and York on the LNER; and Eastleigh and Lancing on the SR. Each railway concentrated on one type of vehicle, and two HATs and four OATs were built within three weeks.

Evacuation from cities

The bombing of Guernica in 1937 during the Spanish Civil War had provided a foretaste of what might be to come, and preparations for the evacuation of mothers and infants, schoolchildren and their teachers, the sick and the aged from major industrial centres began in September 1938 following the Munich crisis.

The first evacuations were in Scotland on 31 August 1939, the day before war was declared. The authorities had booked 338 trains to carry an anticipated 237,000 evacuees from Glasgow, but in the event, only 118,333 turned up. Among the more desirable destinations in rural areas was Culzean Castle in Ayrshire, which received sick children from the Southern General Hospital.[7]

On 1 September, the first of 617,480 mostly children made their way to 72 central area London Underground stations to reach trains waiting for them at such suburban main line railway stations as Ealing Broadway, New Barnet, Richmond, Watford, Harrow-on-the-Hill and Wimbledon, rather than terminus stations. London's four days of evacuation trains were matched by similar evacuations from other urban centres (Table 4.1).

Table 4.1 The number of trains and children evacuated from cities in September 1939

	No of trains	No of passengers
London	1,577	617,480
Birmingham	170	46,934
Bradford	96	15,800
Hull	95	24,114
Leeds	98	21,697
Manchester	302	115,779
Medway Towns	54	9,754
Merseyside	382	161,879
Portsmouth, Gosport and Southampton	172	36,917
Runcorn and Widnes	19	10,477
Sheffield	26	3,954
Teesside	27	11,175
Tyneside	271	73,916
Wearside	34	10,659
Dundee	47	16,872
Edinburgh	129	31,125
Clydebank and Glasgow	322	123,639
Rosyth	2	2,187
Total	**3,823**	**1,334,358**

EVACUATION
OF
WOMEN AND CHILDREN
FROM LONDON, Etc.

FRIDAY, 1st SEPTEMBER.

Up and Down business trains as usual. with few exceptions.

Main Line and Suburban services will be curtailed while evacuation is in progress during the day.

SATURDAY & SUNDAY. SEPTEMBER 2nd & 3rd.

The train service will be exactly the same as on Friday.

Remember that there will be very few Down Mid-day business trains on Saturday.

SOUTHERN RAILWAY

Fig 4.2

SR passengers were clearly expected to know the Up and Down directions. The reference to business trains on Saturday recalls a time when many offices were open for at least Saturday morning.

The plan called for trains of 12 coaches to accommodate 800 passengers, and in the case of Ealing Broadway, for example, the 60 trains a day would leave at 9 minute intervals between 8.30 am and 5.30 pm. In the event, 58 trains on the first day tailed off to 28 on the last because the total was less than half those registered for evacuation. Trains were queued up funnel to tail lamp on relief and goods lines between Ealing and Acton. Stationmasters at reception stations kept volunteers and staff informed so that the feeding and billeting arrangements could be timed for arrival.

Weekend trains quickly became busier as parents visited their children. The 'Phoney War' allowed the children's return, and on 1 January 1940 the railways even resumed selling cheap fares such as walking-tour tickets and anglers' day tickets.

Once the fall of France looked inevitable, it was obvious that the children taken to East Anglian towns could be on the front line in an invasion. On 19 May 1940 the LNER carried 4,400 children in seven trains from Ipswich, Clacton, Walton, Felixstowe and Woodbridge to South Wales, and the following month all evacuees and domiciled children within 10 miles (16km) of the East Anglian coast – 19,254 in 27 trains – were moved to the Midlands and South Wales. Plans drawn up to move adults, entailing 311 trains, did not have to be implemented.

Other evacuations took place, of ministries, the Bank of England and art treasures from London's museums. On 3 September 1939, 1,200 staff of the Bank of England were moved to the large Victorian country house of Hurstbourne Park at Overton in Hampshire. Chalets were built close to the station to house 450 people, requiring a large amount of building materials, and Overton station became a busy station at weekends.

Gallery paintings were loaded at Camden Goods station for the journey to Bangor and their storage at the University of North Wales and various country houses, including Penrhyn Castle. Wagons were fitted with specially modified buffers to reduce vibration, and the paintings were placed in specially made containers. The train ran under a special headlamp code and was closely monitored, though few knew of its contents. As German bombers reached Liverpool, the paintings' safety was called into question and they were transferred to free-standing buildings constructed within caverns blasted out of the rock at Manod slate quarry near Blaenau Ffestiniog, accessed by a narrow-gauge railway.[8]

Food supplies

Another precaution planned before the war entailed substantial freight movements: food supplies. Stores were divided into three categories – National Reserves, Emergency Dumps and Evacuee Emergency Rations – and their location was often on railway property or close to it. As soon as war was declared, the Ministry of Food sent staples to the hundreds of designated stores: corned beef to Caterham and Ewell; flour and biscuits to Redhill; and various items to Tunbridge Wells, for example. With the fall of France, stores in the South East and coastal areas had to be moved again, usually westward. By January 1941, SR staff at Exeter had handled and stacked 10,000 tonnes of food.[9]

Fig 4.3 (above)
An orderly queue at London's Liverpool Street station on 1 September 1939, the first day of evacuation of children to safer places in the countryside and smaller towns.

Fig 4.4 (right)
Such poignant scenes of evacuation were a gift to photographers; this one was taken on 18 May 1940 in the second wave of evacuations. Each child had a label attached to their clothing, stating their name, home address, school and destination, and some had their date of birth.

Fig 4.5
'Dig for victory' poster.

The pressure on food supplies and the 'Dig for Victory' campaign brought more railway land into production as allotments. By 1943 there were 13,000 plots on 600 acres of SR land, and produce competitions unleashed a wholly disproportionate determination to win, then as now.

Adapting railways to 'blackout'

Of all the frustrations and handicaps experienced by railwaymen during the war, none exceeded the impact of the blackout. Safe railway operations at night call for plenty of light at key points, but that was made impossible by the blackout, which was the most persistent drag on efficiency throughout the war.

A Lighting Committee consisting of representatives of the Ministry of Transport, the Home Office, the Air Ministry and the railway companies had carried out tests from 1937 to ascertain the minimum light levels required for tasks. A total blackout was obviously impossible, so three categories of location were created: a very few were exempted and would have lights extinguished only when there was an air-raid warning; fully restricted, which became known sarcastically as 'Gloomy Glim'; and the rest, complete blackout. Glass in station roofs was painted or replaced with less hazardous opaque material where possible, and the white line to make the platform edge more visible became more common, though it was not a wartime introduction. Large amounts of glass were removed from other vulnerable buildings. At Eastleigh 50,000 sq ft of glass in the works was removed from the roofs and replaced with felt, but the artificial light proved so unsatisfactory that moveable shutters were installed in some places.

One of the duties of passenger guards has been to make sure that all carriage doors are fully shut before giving the driver the 'right-away'; the time taken to fulfil that duty on a station with no lights caused significant delay. At the start of the war no light was allowed in the guard's van, so he had to read labels and sort parcels and luggage by the light of a hand lamp.

Every evening signalmen had to block up signal-box windows with frames of wire mesh and wood with a peephole at each end of the box, making it hard to check passing trains for hot axle-boxes and the imperative tail lamp, let alone maintain contact with a shunter's lamp signals.

It was bad for footplatemen, who lost their landmarks at night, and they had to contend with anti-glare sheets consisting of a top sheet and two side sheets. They were instructed to keep them in place during the hours of blackout, and during air raids the coal door in the tender, cab-roof ventilator, gangway doors and, whenever possible, the firebox doors should be closed. This caused such uncomfortable conditions as well as drowsiness that enginemen requested a change in the regulation when there were so few bombing incidents at the start of the war. From November 1939 it was agreed the side sheets could be opened, and this became a permissive instruction when the frequency of raids increased.[10] Electric-train drivers had to coast over points and crossings to minimise the risk of arcing flashes.

There is little doubt that the blackout contributed to some serious accidents: one of the war's first occurred on 13 October 1940 when a double-headed Euston to Stranraer boat train overshot signals at danger approaching Bletchley and crashed into a locomotive shunting a carriage. Four people died. The report dwelt at length on the impact of the blackout, and the driver of the pilot locomotive was acquitted of manslaughter charges.

But it was worst for shunters. Marshalling and goods yards were dangerous places at the best of times, with numerous hazards even for the wary or careful: signal wires, point rodding and point hand-levers to trip over, the constant movement of wagons. The mental map of a yard built up over years became even more important – and made it more difficult and dangerous to recruit new staff. Add in slippery conditions after rain or snow, and then darkness, and consider the tasks to be performed. It was impossible to read wagon labels or chalked instructions, so whistle codes between shunters were developed to convey the siding number when it was too dark to see the chalk numerals. Uncoupling wagons with a pole or using a brake stick to retard a rake of loose-shunted wagons and prevent them crashing into others was a skilled task in good light, but how do you judge the effort needed to brake a wagon when you can't see the distance? It was made worse by searchlights; when they were switched off after a raid, it took some minutes for the eyes to readjust. Unsurprisingly there was an increase in accidents: in the year to the end of

Fig 4.6
Removing glass from the train shed roof at York, which both took away a danger to those below and prevented light attracting the attention of bombers. The roofscape behind is the LNER-owned Royal York Hotel, with the Minster in the distance.

August 1940, the LMS alone attributed 1,894 accidents to the blackout and 2,190 over the following 12 months.[11]

During October 1940, lights in the London marshalling yards such as Feltham, Willesden and Brent had to be extinguished every night, in aggregate for 299 hours or three-quarters of the total hours of darkness.[12] At Camden goods shed, the normal procedure had been to complete loading of wagons just before midnight and then start unloading inward wagons for morning deliveries. Delays because of air raids threw this procedure into disarray with a domino effect; trains could not be received, which caused delays further back. Wagon productivity suffered.

It was soon realised that it was safer to keep trains moving during air raids. To begin with, the procedure for a passenger train was to stop at the first station to let passengers off if they wished and then proceed at 15mph, while freights would stop at the next signal box and proceed at a maximum of 10mph. From November 1940 the daylight maximum was abolished and the nocturnal limit raised to 30mph.[13]

Passengers were instructed to draw down carriage blinds by both day and night during raids, which provided some protection against flying glass, but passengers couldn't find seats when blinds were drawn, which delayed departures. ARP notices at the start of the war gave the draconian command that 'all internal lights in trains will be permanently extinguished throughout the period of the War'.[14] Blue bulbs were fitted in carriages which made reading impossible, though these were replaced by hooded white lights to restore legibility. Windows in buildings had to be screened, electric bulbs on platforms were replaced by a dim blue light and gas lamps were shaded. Small wonder that a poster had to be produced warning passengers to check there was a platform in front of them before stepping off a stationary train.

LMS signal boxes had their windows covered in cellophane and hessian, a precaution which proved its worth for the stationmaster at Manchester Victoria on 23 December 1940:

I was on duty at Victoria West Junction signalbox. At about 11.50pm I was on the telephone when suddenly the signalman shouted. I saw a blue flash, followed by a terrific explosion. Then the window facing the station blew in on me and wrapped itself around my head. Thanks to the cellophane covering, it saved my face and head from serious injury.[15]

The most vulnerable signal boxes where staff would have to remain at their post even during air raids were provided with a steel shelter placed on the working floor of the box. They could take cover here when not carrying out duties. The shelters were made of ¼in steel with a hinged door and roof, and a seat, but no floor was provided. Slots allowed the signalman or -woman to see the block instruments. Brick, steel plates and sandbags were used to provide additional protection at vulnerable points, and some crucial boxes, such as Crewe North and South junctions, were reconstructed with more substantial walls and a 4in-thick concrete roof.[16]

Consideration was given to the plight of railway horses during air raids. At the request of the Government, the RSPCA called together principal horse owners, and humane killers were given to railway horse superintendents. Stables were made as gas-proof as possible at short notice.

Fig 4.7
A cautionary London Underground poster, ironically designed by the Berlin-trained Hans Schleger (1898–1976), who followed the Bauhaus design principle of simple concepts and a reduction to essentials. Schleger left Germany during the rise of Hitler, settled in England in 1932 and became a British citizen in 1938.

IN THE BLACKOUT

Before you alight make sure the train is in the station. Look for platform

The severity of blackout regulations and their enforcement was relaxed by 1942, though coastal and southern stations still had to take rigid precautions.

Dunkirk and movements from Channel ports

The successful evacuation of so many troops from Dunkirk has become the epitome of a victory snatched from the jaws of defeat, with the rescue of seven out of every eight soldiers on the beaches. Sources disagree over the total number, but they range from 319,116 to 338,226, rescued by 220 Allied naval vessels and about 650 other ships and boats.

As the probability of an evacuation increased, a first meeting was held at Dover on 20 May 1940 between naval staffs, liaison officers from War Office Movement Control and the Ministry of Shipping to discuss the organisation of a large-scale evacuation. A meeting the following day took place at the War Office to consider arrangements after arrival. Train planning had to be done without knowing the total number or the ratio between ports. An improvised pool of 186 trains was sent to disembarkation points along the south coast, many to Ashford, where military and railway authorities would decide the ultimate destination of each train. The SR provided 55, the GWR 40, the LMS 44 and the LNER 47, and they needed to be stabled near the coast with 186 locomotives and crews with the appropriate route knowledge available. The critical junction of Redhill became the strategic centre where drivers were told where they were going: half went to SR destinations, especially Aldershot and Salisbury Plain, 37 per cent went to the GWR, and the rest to the LMS and LNER. Preparations were made to close Redhill station to the public, which became necessary, and an emergency control room was set up at Dover. Yards were emptied of unnecessary wagons to make room for the trains, and the down line between Hothfield and Ashford stabled trains almost funnel to tail lamp, ready to proceed to the ports. A bus service replaced down trains, and the Redhill–Reading line was to be cleared of all passenger and freight trains.[17]

The order for evacuation of the BEF was given by Anthony Eden, British War Secretary, at 04.10 on 26 May, starting what was codenamed Operation Dynamo.[18] Between 7 am that day and 4 pm on 4 June, 620 trains carrying 319,056 officers and men left the south-east ports. Ships landed troops at Sheerness, Weymouth and Harwich, as well as the most commonly used ports of Margate (38,000 men, 75 trains, plus 21 ambulance trains), Ramsgate (43,000 men, 82 trains), Folkestone (35,000 men, 64 trains) and Dover (200,000 men, 327 trains). The peak days were 31 May (107 trains) and 1 June (110 trains), and Folkestone presented the greatest operating problem with the 1 in 30 gradient up from Harbour station, requiring three locomotives. These trains had to be slotted into the stream of trains from Dover heading for Redhill. Most trains avoided London, using the cross-country route through Redhill, Guildford and Reading, and many left ports without knowing their destination.

At Dover Marine, ambulance trains were kept constantly at Platform 3, and arriving evacuated civilians had to go through Customs and Immigration to make sure they were not spies or fifth columnists. So many dogs had attached themselves to soldiers in France and Belgium that a special lorry service had to be set up to take them away from the quays.

Fig 4.8
Signal boxes in areas likely to be subjected to air raids were equipped with what were nicknamed 'tin coffins'. One of these steel boxes in which to take shelter can be seen to the left of Audrey Hallam, working an unidentified signal box, probably on the GCR, with a single-line Webb & Thompson staff instrument on the right.

Fig 4.9
Belgian soldiers rescued
from Dunkirk stand beside
a rake of LNER coaches at
Margate station, awaiting
a train for London on
4 June 1940.

Special trains of coal had to be run to replenish the engine-shed stocks at Dover and Redhill, where 300 tons of ash accumulated over the eight days. Locomotive rostering became unusually ad hoc. Redhill locomotives ended up as far afield as Exeter, and men were on the footplate for as long as 18 hours without respite. One driver and fireman were on their locomotive for 28 hours, and considerations of route knowledge sometimes had to be waived. Low water supplies at Ashford necessitated a stop at Tonbridge, where the stationmaster's wife organised supplies of food and drink for the soldiers, funded by contributions from passengers in other trains calling at the station.[19]

At Headcorn the Royal Army Service Corps organised a 24-hour refreshment service headquartered in a barn near the station. For nine days 40–50 women of the neighbourhood produced beverages and tens of thousands of sandwiches for 40 soldiers to hand to those on the trains as they called at the station. One evening 5,000 pies were delivered to Headcorn for the soldiers, but it became best known for the supply of tea in tin cans and the command to 'Sling them out' at which hundreds of cans clattered on to the platform, to be collected and washed before the next train.

Requisitioned railway ships played their part. The three train ferries that had plied the Channel from Richborough during the First World War (*see* p 82) were all in action. The SR's PS *Whippingham* took the record for the number of troops evacuated, 2,700 men on 4 June. The LNER's 1899-built Clyde paddle steamer *Waverley* was sunk by enemy planes, and five SR vessels were lost while helping with the evacuation from France. The experience of one crew member can stand for all. A former carriage cleaner at Brighton, Mrs Lee, had become a steward on the SR's *Paris*, which had been converted into a hospital ship. As the *Paris* was repeatedly bombed and machine-gunned, the ship had to be abandoned and Mrs Lee was thrown into the water, where she managed to avoid more machine-gun fire. Though picked up by a lifeboat, she was again flung into the water, where she spent an hour and a half before being rescued by a tug, which took her to Dover.[20]

More evacuations took place after Dunkirk. On 11 June two LMS steamers, *Princess Maud* and the *Duke of York*, rescued 1,700 men from St Valery-en-Caux, 80,000 were taken from Brest to Plymouth and 2,500 packed into the GWR's *St Helier* from St Malo to Southampton. LNER *Train Ferry No 2* was sunk by gunfire during the attempt to rescue the Highland Division from St Valery-en-Caux, and half her crew were saved. The Channel Islands were evacuated during June 1940 by LNER *Train Ferry No 3* and five SR cargo steamers, and also by the planes of Jersey Airways, which was jointly owned by the GWR and SR. Among the last evacuees from Jersey were 38 of the 49 railway company staff on the islands aboard the last ship to leave, the *Isle of Sark*, on 28 June, with 647 passengers on board.[21]

Though not part of the Dunkirk evacuation, unquestionably one of the most important trains of the entire war ran after the evacuation of forces and

Fig 4.10
Local bakeries had supplied large quantities of baked goods for these evacuated soldiers receiving refreshments at London's Addison Road station on 31 May 1940.

the King and Crown Prince from Norway. A special train left Falmouth in the evening of 21 June 1940 carrying 35 of the world's top scientists and the world's entire supply of heavy water, which had been brought from Norway via Paris and Bordeaux to prevent it falling into the hands of the Nazis. The 20th Earl of Suffolk had led the mission to rescue eminent scientists from France, and had been joined by the Russian Lew Kowarski and the Austrian-Jewish Hans van Halban, who had escaped from Paris with 52 gallons of heavy water in jerry cans. A tramp steamer, the SS *Broompark*, carried this extraordinary cargo – along with $10 million worth of gem diamonds from an Antwerp bank – to Falmouth. On the overnight train to Paddington the heavy water was under military guard and was hidden with the Crown Jewels at Windsor Castle, until being shipped out to Canada later in the year. Had the water not been spirited away, it could have been Germany and not the Allies that developed the first nuclear bomb.[22]

Bournemouth and Plymouth would later receive 17,000 men who rejected General de Gaulle's appeal on 18 June for French soldiers evacuated from Norway and Dunkirk to resist their country's occupation and join the Free French Forces. The majority preferred repatriation to Vichy France.[23]

Fear of invasion

Following Dunkirk, efforts focused on protecting the railway and contrary measures to disable it should the enemy invade. Units to defend Britain were initially formed on an ad hoc basis, but they achieved more formal status with the radio announcement on 14 May 1940 by the Secretary of State for War, Anthony Eden, that a force known as the Local Defence Volunteers was being formed, and invited suitable recruits to join. Railwaymen made up 10 per cent of what became known as the Home Guard – 156,046 of the 1.5 million it eventually numbered, with 25 battalions composed entirely of railway staff. A further 130,000 railway staff were trained in civil defence work. Men joined in their spare time and guarded vulnerable points on the railway, helped by their knowledge of safety and operations to avoid a repetition of the fatalities on guard duty that had occurred during the previous conflict. They also took over the manning of some anti-aircraft guns, with 1,617 men on the SR alone being trained in their use. A locomotive, LMS Patriot class 4-6-0 No 5543, was named *Home Guard* by Lieutenant General Sir Henry Pownall, Inspector General of the Home Guard, at Euston station on 30 July 1940.

Garrisons were strengthened, those in Northern Ireland requiring 23 trains to Stranraer in June 1940 and the use of railway steamers. By late 1940 the War Office had stationed a few armoured fighting vehicle trains at strategic points in the south and East Anglia for use in the event of invasion. The trains comprised 2–3 passenger-carrying vehicles, including guard's compartment, a covered stores van and ramp wagons with 5–9 Warflats, which could carry two medium tanks and a maximum weight of 50 tons.[24]

The geographical spread of the railway made staff invaluable eyes and ears: 'The Army were much impressed with the potential value of Signalmen as look-outs for hostile troops by reason of their location in elevated signal boxes in all parts of the country, and the availability of an independent telephone system by means of which reports could be transmitted quickly to Station Masters and District Control Officers.'[25]

After the last Allied troops had been evacuated from Norway, the whole of the east and south-east coasts needed defending, though some stretches of coast were made more vulnerable by nature. The deep water and gap between sandbanks off Weybourne, west of Sheringham, had made this section of the Norfolk coast a promising landing ground for centuries, as reflected in the rhyme 'He that would Old England win / Must at Weybourne Hope begin.' A ramp for unloading tanks was built at Weybourne station, which served a nearby camp housing an anti-aircraft artillery range; with Stiffkey just along the coast, it formed the principal training range for Ack Ack Command.

To provide mobile coastal defence, 12 standard-gauge armoured trains were created by Derby Works, using armour plate from Ashford Works,[26] and deployed along the east and south-east coasts. Sir Nigel Gresley chose the former GER Class F4 2-4-2T as the locomotive to be sandwiched between armoured coal wagons. The wagons were reinforced with 4in of concrete and an outer skin of ³⁄₁₆in mild steel plate. Armaments were a quick-firing 6-pounder Hotchkiss gun and an assortment of Vickers machine gun, Lewis gun or Bren gun. Derby Works produced 7 of the 12 in just 10 days, while Stratford Works armoured the locomotives.[27] Initially operated by the RE and Royal Armoured Corps (RAC), from late 1940 they were manned by railway company crews and soldiers from the Polish Armed Forces in the West until taken over from 1942 by Home Guard units made up of railway employees. A 10-day course of instruction was devised

Fig 4.11
Members of the Palmers Green and Winchmore Hill LNER Local Defence Volunteers at what is thought to be Palmers Green station with a Gresley class N2 0-6-2T. Note the blacked-out lamps.

by the Coast Artillery School at Shoeburyness for the initial units of 1 officer, 7 NCOs, 39 RAC soldiers and 8 REs, the last including two sets of driver and fireman and guard/shunter.[28]

Though the trains were lettered and the units operating them were numbered, War Office departments used different sets of numbers for the units. To make matters worse, letters and digits were not in a matching sequence. This recipe for confusion was not rectified before 44 men arrived in Inverness from Yorkshire to discover they should have been sent to Norwich.[29]

From the first batch of six trains, five went to Eastern Command and one to Scottish Command, and vice versa for the second batch. Eastern Command deployed its trains to stabling points at Ipswich, Saxmundham, Melton Constable, Norwich, Canterbury and Ashford. The last location was considered the most critical in that its duty encompassed the most likely invasion area, travelling a route that took in Dungeness, Appledore, Rye, Hastings, Lewes and return, stopping for water six times.

Unaccustomed to such long journeys, the F4 on the first of the Scottish Command trains arrived at Inverness from Stratford with overheated bearings, so they had to be attended to before deployment along the line to Elgin. The first foray north towards Invergordon did not go well, with two derailments during the day at Inverness and Clachnaharry, through driver inattention, and a broken wireless mast on a bridge. Another F4 expired at Ais Gill on the Settle & Carlisle before the other trains were assembled at Carstairs and sent off to stabling points at Aberdeen, Edinburgh, Stirling, Forfar and Glasgow, though some were soon reassigned as each command argued the case for more trains.

It had been decided that no more than the original 12 would be built, so 3 of the Scottish trains were handed over to Northern Command and 3 of the Eastern ones to Southern. The Northern trains were based at various times at

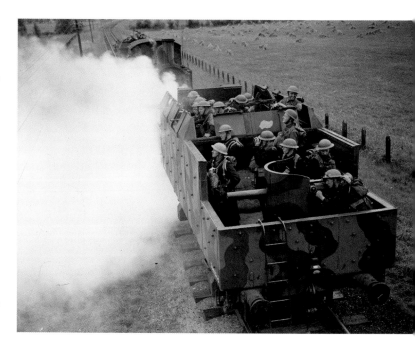

Fig 4.12
Armoured Train C near Saxmundham in Suffolk on 14 August 1940, with the cylinder drain cocks of LNER class F4 2-4-2T No 7214 releasing a cloud of steam. The train is equipped with two 3in (76mm) guns and Bren guns manned by a crew of 26. The train was based at Saxmundham to patrol the line between Wickham Market, Beccles and Lowestoft, the branches to Framlingham and Aldeburgh, and inland to Harleston on the Waveney Valley line.

Market Weighton, Morpeth, Alnmouth and Louth. The trains were periodically placed on public exhibition, partly to encourage support for National Savings. While schoolchildren were being shown a train at Blyth on Tyneside, the 6-pounder was accidentally discharged and the shell went through the roof of a nearby dwelling, fortunately without injury to the occupants. The Southern Command trains went to Devon and Cornwall, based variously at Barnstaple, Plymouth, Wadebridge and Newton Abbot.[30]

The proximity of the 15in (380mm) gauge Romney, Hythe & Dymchurch Railway to a likely landing area for an invading force placed it in the front line as the Somerset Light Infantry built defensive works around it. The railway enthusiasts in the battalion formed a railway section and effectively took over the railway from June 1940. Two former Ravenglass & Eskdale Railway ballast wagons were sent off to Ashford Works, with the 4-8-2 *Hercules* to have armour plate fitted and two Boys anti-tank rifles and four Lewis guns mounted. Until the fear of invasion passed in autumn 1941, the armoured train had steam up at all times, and its crew claimed to have shot down a Dornier Do 17.[31]

Lessons were learned from the invasion of France, when French railways tried to evacuate locomotives, carriages and wagons from threatened areas, which led to hopeless congestion and confusion and a large amount of stock falling into enemy hands.[32] The order was given to evacuate only locomotives, and to reduce those movements after an invasion the precaution was taken of moving idle locomotives away from the coast each night, so engines based at Hull were moved to Selby and those at Scarborough to Malton, for example.

To deny the enemy use of the railways, structures and equipment at locomotive depots were marked with red paint to denote the weakest spot for a sledgehammer to disable it. Bridges were prepared for demolition with the stipulation that the damage should be repairable within a week. By August 1940 the LNER alone had prepared 108 bridges, including the Tay and Forth viaducts, but the policy was changed to the provision of anti-tank barriers, blocks and ditches. The railways built pillboxes, trenches and barbed-wire barriers along stretches of coastal railway.

The exceptional vulnerability and importance of the Forth and Tay bridges prompted the instruction that passengers had to place all but the smallest items of hand luggage in the guard's van while crossing them; the guard's suspicions would presumably have been aroused by anything that could be an explosive device. A camp was set up at Dalmeny to protect the bridge against saboteurs, but there was only one incident when a flaming mass was seen shooting out of a carriage window. It transpired that the passenger was carrying a roll of celluloid film which had spontaneously combusted, and he had thrown it out of the window.

Inevitably London Transport (LT) staff made an exceptional contribution to home defence: of the wartime staff of 75,000, 42,000 were engaged in civil defence duties and 25,000 engaged in fire-watching, while 30,000 served in the board's Home Guard Unit of seven battalions; 1,500 were loaned to government departments and industry, and 400 craftsmen went into aircraft production. Of the 22,500 staff serving with HM forces, 768 were killed, and 426 were killed during air attacks on London, 171 while on duty.[33]

Besides guard duty, the Home Guard carried out demolition and salvage work, manned anti-aircraft batteries, anti-tank guns and armoured trains, and provided guards for ammunition trains.

Even when the threat of invasion had passed, there was still the fear of sabotage, though not one incident seems to have occurred. However, the SR bomb damage register for 14 July 1944 records what was probably a foolish hoax, with a touch of *Dad's Army* about it:

> The signalman at Meldon Junction today had his attention drawn by a woman to a note picked up under the viaduct. It was written in good French and said 'If you want to blow up the bridge meet me at ...' Signalman has forgotten the time mentioned. Stationmaster at Okehampton and local police aware and DSO had contacted latter who do not attach much importance to the matter, which, however, they are following up. S. Rly Home Guard advised and are providing men to guard the viaduct.[34]

Fig 4.13
A sentry at what is thought to be the south end of Copenhagen Tunnel on the approach to King's Cross.

The aerial threat

For railwaymen the greatest distinction between the world wars was the scale of the danger from the sky. Minimal damage was done to railway infrastructure or trains during the first conflict; the second was a very different story. Besides the blackout, the threat posed three challenges for the railway: providing shelters for staff; the demands that would be placed on it by the need to evacuate civilians and casualties from urban areas; and the need to reinstate services in the wake of damage to infrastructure and trains.

Shelters were built at key points on the railway system, with an eventual capacity of 500,000 people. The LMS earmarked old locomotive boiler barrels as auxiliary bomb shelters. Instruction began early, and more than 170,000 railwaymen were fully trained in ARP duties and over 300,000 as fire guards. The SR began detailed planning for ARP in early 1938. Eastleigh had the largest workshops, covering 220 acres, and appeals were made for volunteers. 'A good number offered their services.' Squads were formed in firefighting, fire watching, first aid, demolition, rescue and decontamination, and railwaymen volunteering for ARP training were sent on a two-day course at the Brunswick Institute in London and later at the Railway Institute in Eastleigh. Decontamination training was given at Southampton on two-day courses, and the Time Office was converted into a cleansing centre. Additional facilities had to be created for female staff 'when they were employed', and showers were installed in lavatories.[35] The feared gas attacks never materialised, and the 47 coaches converted into mobile cleansing vans were never used.[36]

Concrete slabbing trenches were made around Eastleigh's locomotive and carriage and wagon workshops, and the two power houses were given blast protection. The first alert came on 7 June 1940, and by the end of the war Eastleigh had had 1,699 alerts. The worst day was in October 1940 when the locomotive running shed was bombed and two members of staff in the offices were killed.

Naturally the LMS regarded its divisional and district control offices as crucial to operations, and the most vulnerable. Accordingly some were made into fortresses with roofs 10ft thick. Communication channels were duplicated or even triplicated, so that speedy and precise dissemination of warnings would limit their impact to the smallest possible area. This anxiety was borne out on 23 December 1940, when the divisional control office in Manchester was destroyed and the standby emergency control office was simultaneously flooded. All telephone communication was put out of action and a control room had to be rigged up in nearby cellars and railway arches, but it was days before the paralysis of traffic across several counties eased.

At Edinburgh Waverley control rooms were built in the Scotland Street Tunnel built in 1847 by the Edinburgh, Leith & Granton Railway and closed in 1925. It contained a traffic office with centralised traffic control and telephone links to all signal boxes, goods yards, and major stations and offices.[37]

Anxiety over the vulnerability of communication wires to bombing prompted a request as early as 1936 from the railway companies for wireless telegraphy. It was vetoed, and the alternative of multiple telephone and telegraph wires was not authorised until January 1939. When bombing started, it was realised that 21,000 miles of new lines were still required.[38] To speed repair to damaged wires, a list of railwaymen owning motorcars or bikes was kept. Staff were told they

Fig 4.14
The still-smouldering LNER warehouse at Goodmans Yard on the approach to London Fenchurch Street gives an idea of the havoc and loss of facilities with which the railways had to cope on a daily basis throughout the Blitz. The warehouse had been built by the GER in 1861.

might have to use their initiative if lines of communication were broken, which produced a curious mix of highly centralised control and local improvisation.[39]

The destruction of signal boxes was less disruptive and more localised in its impact, but the largest signal box at Birmingham New Street, with a 152-lever frame, was practically destroyed in an evening raid, probably in April 1941. A linesman's room was set up as a temporary block post with signalling instruments, and points were manually operated and trains signalled by hand under instruction from the temporary block post until two emergency boxes were installed and operational 11 days after the incident.[40] Bow Junction box in London was twice burned out, and existed as a corrugated-iron shell for some time.

To effect repairs to bomb-damaged bridges and trackwork, stockpiles of supplies such as cutting and welding equipment, rails and sleepers, and standard bridge parts were created at strategic sidings, with some of the material already loaded on wagons. The LMS had 10 centres with enough materials to relay 22 miles of plain track, 130 crossings and 130 points.[41] Viaduct piers were assessed for the foundations of trestle footings should the structure be damaged, and those trestles were kept in readiness. Mobile canteens and living accommodation were set up for engineering staff.

A paper on the most effective ways of restoring services was written by the SR chief engineer for the REC chairman and dated 30 June 1941. It set out the preparations made before the war and itemised the suitable materials and plant on hand. To maintain services on the SR's 2,133 route miles, 4,105 miles of running line, about 3,500 steel bridges and 5,600 arches, depots had been set up at five locations around London within a 10- to 15-mile radius, with suitable cranes, rails, sleepers, points and crossings, and reserves of filling material. A nucleus staff of four to six people would be on duty, with others on call.

To reduce the risk of loss, stores were moved to less vulnerable areas: the SR dispersed timber, diesel oil, engine fittings, upholstery materials, carpets and wood patterns to stores at Itchen Abbas, Micheldever, Wilton, Tongham, Farnham, Wherwell, Privett and Fordingbridge.

Instructions to LMS trainmen, signalmen and persons in charge of level crossings were that they should remain at their posts during an air raid, and so should others 'until danger is imminent in the immediate vicinity of the place at which they are working'.

Guernica's population when German and Italian planes destroyed the town was just 7,000. Estimating the casualties that might arise from comparable raids on cities the size of London or Birmingham was impossible, but in October 1939 the REC was planning to provide 34 Casualty Evacuation Trains (CETs) with an average capacity of 300 stretcher cases each, primarily for the evacuation of civilian air-raid casualties. Numbered 1 to 34, each had 12 bogie vehicles – 9 brake vans equipped with brackets to carry stretcher cases, a passenger vehicle fitted with simple cooking facilities, and a bogie brake-third van at each end to accommodate staff and stores. Each could carry an additional 45 stretcher cases on the floor in an emergency.[42]

The Ministry of Health (MoH) was to inform the railway control officer at the earliest possible stage of the date on which the CETs should be ready, and the railway would have 96 hours to form them. CETs could be used to supplement the military ambulance trains, in which case the War Office would apply to the MoH for consent, and vice versa if military ambulance trains were needed by the MoH.

Fig 4.15
The way a bomb can twist rails like spaghetti is demonstrated in this 1940 scene at Abbey Mills Junction between Plaistow and Canning Town in east London.

CETs were controlled by the Movement Organisation of the MoH, and decisions would be based on vacant beds in receiving hospitals. The headquarters movement officer of the MoH would have direct control of CETs throughout the country (except Scotland) and might in consultation with the REC arrange such redistribution of CETs as the circumstances required. The initial allocation was London, 20; provinces and Scotland, 10; on temporary loan to the War Office, 4. In the event, London CETs were berthed at (1 at each unless numeral shown) Goodmayes (3), Cheshunt, New Barnet, Neasden, Reading (2), Slough (2), Watford, Walton-on-Thames (3), Bracknell, Streatham Eardley Carriage Sidings (2), Sevenoaks and Tubs Hill (2); provincial at Newcastle, Leeds, Manchester Longsight, Liverpool Edge Hill, Birmingham, Bristol, Exeter, Edinburgh Slateford carriage sidings, Glasgow Larkfield carriage sidings. The preliminary allocation of the 4 on loan to the War Office was Newhaven (2), Salisbury and York.

To avoid helping enemy pilots identify their location, an order was given in September 1940 that the height of station name-board letters in the open should be no larger than 3in, but so great was the zeal for obliterating station names that the policy had to be moderated within a fortnight.[43]

Bombing begins

The first bomb to fall on mainland Britain was at Wick, on 10 April 1940, the day after the invasion of Normandy. Before the end of May, the first town to suffer significant bomb damage was Middlesbrough, and the first raid on Hull took place on 1 July. On 10 July two lines at Swansea were severed and 11 people were killed. Until August 1940 bombing was only spasmodic, but that month heavy bombing commenced. The first fatality on the LMS occurred at Shoeburyness on 18 August 1940, when a bomb demolished the signal box and killed the signalman. During this raid, the homes of several railway staff were damaged, but almost every off-duty railwayman reported at the station to help restore traffic workings.[44]

The bombing of London began in earnest on 7 September, when four out of five SR London termini were closed. On one occasion, out of 14 lines into London only 1 was available.[45] On the night of 10–11 May 1941 at least 51 high-explosive and incendiary bombs and parachute mines hit Waterloo station, penetrating so deeply beneath the platforms that spirits stored in the arches ignited and burned for five days for want of water supplies to fight the fire. On the same night a 3,100lb landmine had been discovered dangling from Hungerford Bridge on the approach to Charing Cross, close to the signal box. A fire on Platform 4 was moving towards the mine, but the 67-year-old signalman, with 52 years' service, refused to leave his post. He had extinguished two incendiaries on the bridge, and by the time the fire was put out, it was just 12ft (3.6m) from the landmine. On the same night, bombs penetrated to the undercroft of St Pancras, closing the station for eight days.[46] The station in Britain with the dubious distinction of receiving the most bombs was Poplar.

Even deep-level stations were not immune to bomb damage. On 12 October 1940 a bomb penetrated to the Bakerloo Line station at Trafalgar Square, killing 7 people, and 19 died at Bounds Green the following day when part of the station tunnel caved in. The worst incident was at Balham on the Northern Line on 14 October 1940, when a fractured water main flooded the tunnels and swept gravel into the station, killing 4 staff and 68 civilians, and closing the line for

3 months. A high-explosive bomb going off at the top of the escalators at Bank on 11 January 1941 is thought to have killed 4 LT staff and 53 others. However, the greatest loss of life occurred at Bethnal Green on 3 March 1943, when 175 people were killed by suffocation and crushing after a woman tripped on a staircase.[47]

The use of Underground stations as bomb shelters reached its peak on the night of 27 September 1940, when 177,000 people took refuge. About 22,800 bunks were set up on platforms, and special trains delivered supplies to the 124 canteens set up in the stations. Admission was by free season ticket distributed by the local authority or nightly by station ticket offices if space permitted.

Railwaymen in provincial cities suffered similar experiences. Liverpool's worst nights were in May 1941 when it endured 7 nights of bombing by up to 800 planes. The roof of the LMS North Dock goods shed caved in when a bomb struck the bow of an ammunition ship which exploded in Huskisson No 2 dock, 2,500ft away.[48] The Exchange station was badly damaged, as was its namesake in Manchester. Birmingham was the third most bombed city, where New Street

Fig 4.16
St Pancras train shed after a raid in October 1940, almost certainly the one on the night of the 15th/16th when a landmine destroyed a large part of the roof, which required closure of the station for five days to clear the debris.

station lost Edward Cowper's magnificent roof over the former LNWR side – once the largest arched single-span iron and glass roof in the world.

The 'Baedeker raids' took their name from the German guidebooks and were aimed at destroying cultural heritage. Because the targets were generally smaller than industrial cities, they were more concentrated, and the GWR divisional superintendent at Exeter said the raid on 3–4 May 1942 was more intense than his experience of the London Blitz.

Fig 4.17
Damage to Platform 13 and the adjacent bar and grill room at London King's Cross station in 1941, again almost certainly the aftermath of a raid on 11 May when two chained-together 1,000lb bombs swept away part of the roof and exploded on the west side. They also damaged the general offices and wrecked the booking hall, but no trains were cancelled. Though the bombs fell in the small hours of a Sunday, 12 people were killed.

The most prominent railway casualty of wartime bombing was the LMS chairman Sir Josiah Stamp, who was killed together with his wife and eldest son at their home in Beckenham in April 1941. He had declined the position of Chancellor of the Exchequer the previous year.

During the Blitz, 'the life of the railway civil engineer was one long series of alarms and excursions. Gangs sometimes numbering 200 were assembled and put into action, and standby trains carried materials to damaged areas.'[49] Some relief was experienced when the attentions of the Luftwaffe were distracted by the invasion of Russia on 22 June 1941.

The most troublesome type of damage was the shattering of bridge abutments or when main and cross girders were destroyed, as at Alleyn Park Road in West Dulwich, when a 50ft-span bridge was destroyed. A bomb fell 60ft from the centre line of Penge Tunnel where there was only 20ft of cover. The concussion from the explosion caused the crown of the arch to collapse for a length of 35ft and a width of 16ft, causing soil to fall through until a hole showed at ground level. The line reopened 24 days later. Eight lines of track were severed when a bridge at Southwark Street was destroyed by a parachute mine. Between June 1940 and June 1941, there were about 1,800 instances of damage

Fig 4.18
Architecturally, one of the worst railway losses was the unusual roof covering three tracks at Middlesbrough in Yorkshire. Its deep end-screens reflected the most vertical proportions applied to a train shed in Britain. It was brought down by bombs in 1942 but William Peachey's magnificent station building with hammer-beam roof was spared.

to the SR from high-explosive bombs, and running lines were blocked on 750 occasions. 'Numerous cases have occurred where bridges have been so damaged that any reparation work has involved considerable risk to the men engaged thereon ... but in no case has there been any hesitation whatever on the part of any of the staff in doing what is necessary.'[50]

Delayed-action bombs often proved the most disruptive to traffic, requiring the area to be evacuated and cordoned off while the bomb-disposal teams worked to defuse them. Unexploded bombs (UXBs) had the same effect. To reduce risk to personnel defusing and removing bombs, a Government instruction of October 1940 stipulated that bombs should not be interfered with for 96 hours after they fell unless they were seriously impeding traffic. During November 1940 there were 30 UXBs on the LMS, 7 of which caused serious delay and were dealt with promptly by bomb-disposal squads. In a GWR report for autumn 1940 describing bomb damage from Ellesmere Port to Grampound Road, out of 1,170 incidents in October 1940, 141 were UXBs, and 88 of those caused damage affecting facilities for 'not more than one week'.[51]

Incendiary bombs were intended as markers for bombers following behind, so wherever an incendiary bomb fell, the nearest railwayman, whether shunter or footplate crew, had to try to smother it the moment it flared, using sacks, sand, stirrup pumps or wagon sheets. The large London goods yard at Globe Road and Devonshire Street was adjacent to Regent's Canal, and on one

Fig 4.19
A footbridge collapsed across the line at Hornsey on the LNER East Coast main line in 1940.

Fig 4.20
On 3 March 1943 a bomb fell on the LNER London Liverpool Street–Ipswich main line between Shenfield and Ingatestone, creating a large crater. Though the approaching 8.45 pm Liverpool Street to Harwich express was travelling at only 25mph (40km/h), it was too late to stop and the locomotive toppled into the hole, with the tender riding over the footplate and killing two Harwich men. Though one carriage fell down the embankment, only one passenger and the guard were slightly injured.

occasion when fires got a hold of wagons in the north yard, the only escape for the crew on the shunting locomotive was to jump into the canal.

Naval mines with a clockwork mechanism that would detonate 25 seconds after impact were dropped by parachute and could get caught up in wires and signal posts, calling for the defusing services of the Admiralty.

Fire-watchers were posted at strategic points, and daily logs kept. One for Broad Street, London, in September 1943 records that 21 loads of ammunition in transit from Tilbury Docks to Craven Arms in Shropshire had been held over because no locomotive was available, which would have caused great anxiety at the height of the Blitz.[52]

Inevitably it was the SR which bore the brunt of both bombing raids and more particularly the strafing of trains by fighter planes. Between 24 August 1940 and 10 May 1941, there were only two days when the SR was not bombed. Waterloo station closed completely for 12 days after the approach viaduct at Vauxhall was hit by a bomb on 7 September 1940, even though the Army helped the railway's own engineers. The most meticulous records to have survived are those kept by the SR in little more than school exercise books, detailing every loosened slate and broken signal-box windowpane. In contrast the LMS gave up daily reports, deciding in mid-September 1940 that 'about this time bombing throughout the country became intense, and it was therefore impracticable to enter details', relying on more general monthly reports about the 600 bombs that had fallen on LMS property in the previous month.[53] A two-day period in April gives a flavour of activity on the SR in the Plymouth area:

29 April 1941 – Devonport. Incendiary fell through signal box roof. Extinguished by signalman before causing further damage.

30 April 1941, 3am – Devonport area. Rail appears to have been worst ever. Lines being examined on foot starting from Bere Alston ... Patrol, which

started from Bere Alston, has reached St Budeaux. No additional damage to track. Signal box at St Budeaux damaged and 3 Co's cottages down. No knowledge of whereabouts of inhabitants and no station staff turned up for duty. Patrol now proceeding on to Devonport.

8.20am – German bomber crashed on the station alongside signal box [at St Budeaux] on the down embankment. Signal box demolished together with two cottages adjoining. Two trucks damaged and checker Boles has a lacerated face.

12.15pm – St Budeaux. Frame and top portion of signal box badly damaged. Basement apparently intact.

None of this could compare with the obliteration of the SR's terminus at Turnchapel near Plymouth. On 27 November 1940 a bomb ignited an oil storage tank: the fire raged for two days before adjacent tanks erupted and created rivers of fire that even crossed a 100ft channel to set a timber yard on fire. It took six days to extinguish the fires, with the water from hoses evaporating before it could have any effect. Station and signal box disappeared, and all that was left were contorted rails and lamp standards.

Opportunist attacks by fighter planes took place all over southern England. On 19 August 1940 the 4 pm Alton–Southampton train was machine-gunned when running between Ropley and Alresford but sustained no damage or casualties. When the train arrived at Alresford at 4.24 pm, bombs were dropped in the vicinity of the station, but the only impact on the company's property was slight damage by blast to the goods-shed roof. Trains even in Devon might be strafed: on 22 August 1940 the nine-coach 2.35 pm Exeter Central–Ilfracombe train was passing through Umberleigh station when an enemy plane attempted to machine-gun it. No damage was found on examination at Barnstaple Junction.[54] On 12 January 1941 a bomb on the Falmouth line derailed 2-6-2T No 4510 and two carriages.

Trains in the north did not escape such attacks, and on 11 November 1941 the northbound *Flying Scotsman* was strafed from end to end by two planes near Berwick-upon-Tweed. No passengers were hurt, but a bullet passed along the fireman's arm and emerged at the wrist. He still fired all the way to Edinburgh.

Footplate crews had to be resourceful in dealing with bullet damage to their locomotives; when class C 0-6-0 No 1054 was strafed between Greatstone and Lydd-on-Sea, the damage sustained was: 'Iron vacuum pipe broken. Holes in smokebox, splashers and boiler lagging. Cab plating and platform and casing of reversing gear damaged. Tender plating and tank pierced, water leaked out and driver had to plug holes. Buffer casting damaged. Lubricator steam and delivery pipes pierced.' The locomotive required 417 man hours to repair.

Consideration was given to providing trains with the means to fight back. On 14 July 1942 the SR's general manager, Sir Eustace Missenden, wrote to the REC's chairman, Sir Alan Anderson:

... towards the end of last year the South Eastern Command expressed a wish to consider the possibility of defending trains against low level air attack by anti-aircraft weapons mounted at the head and tail of trains, and tests have since been made on our Dungeness line with guns of various types, mounted in wagons or on the engine. A cardinal principle was that the arrangement should require the minimum of special equipment on the trains so that it could be readily applied in any part of the country or overseas.

As a result of the experiments the military have decided that the best positions for the guns (twin-Bren) would be a) on the engine tender, and b) at the rear of trains, in a suitable open wagon in the case of passenger services and on the platform of a brake van of freight trains.

The tests have been concluded, and it now remains for the military authorities to determine whether or not they consider it worth while making such provision.[55]

On 16 July 1942 Sir Alan replied from the Ministry of War Transport that 'I am told that our ships bristle with [anti-aircraft guns] now but I should have thought it was very doubtful policy to spend on trains all the artillery that would be needed to arm them. Probably the idea is simply to arm trains which are specially likely to attract air attacks.'[56] The idea seems to have gone no further, though in the same year the Air Ministry asked for analysis of machine-gun and cannon-shell damage in attacks on locomotives, coaches, track, chairs, signalling and so on, and an instruction was issued in October 1942 to space locomotives on shed as far apart from each other as possible.

Twelve trains of anti-aircraft guns were created using bogie-bolster wagons; three of them were manned by the Free Polish Army.[57]

The decision not to arm trains was certainly not for want of attacks continuing long after the Blitz. On 18 August 1942 SR class M7 0-4-4T No 48 was attacked between Ropley and Alresford: 'Tank bunker, coupling rod and wheels on right side of engine indented by impact of bullets.'[58] On 30 November 1942 the 10.10 am Plymouth to Brighton was machine-gunned between Broad Clyst and Whimple at 12.44 pm. The boiler and tender on Merchant Navy 21.C.4 *Cunard White Star* were pierced and four windows of the front coach splintered. The engine was taken out of service at Whimple and the train worked forward by an engine commandeered from a goods train. The driver suffered from shock and the fireman from slight leg injuries, but there were no injuries to passengers. There were bullet holes in the smokebox and the driver's seat, the left cab glass was broken, there was a cannon shell in the tender under the shovel plate and a lubricator oil pipe was severed.

Much worse was an incident on 30 November 1942 when class C3 0-6-0 No 2308 working the 12.05 pm Horsham to Steyning Special Freight was machine-gunned at West Grinstead at 12.50 pm. The driver was fatally injured. A bizarre incident occurred between Lydd and Appledore at 3.01 pm on 27 November 1942, when tank class D3 0-4-4T No 2365 was machine-gunned by two Focke-Wulf 190s. Bullets penetrated the boiler but it proved a Pyrrhic victory: the boiler exploded just as one of the planes was passing overhead, releasing a high-pressure jet of steam and causing the plane to crash. The fireman was badly scalded, the locomotive's main frames crumpled and the tanks were blown off.[59]

Protection for footplate crews was also considered, by fitting cabs with 2in plastic plates which broke up a projectile, whereas with steel plate a pellet

Fig 4.21
SR class D3 0-4-4T No
2365 at Lydd Town on 30
November 1942, three days
after its encounter with two
Focke-Wulf 190s.

was punched out and flew off with the same velocity as the projectile striking it.[60] Tunnels were the only possible sanctuary, and many a driver raced to a tunnel if an enemy aircraft showed interest in their train.

Steam locomotives are extraordinarily tough things. Only if the main frames were badly damaged was an engine condemned; of 484 locomotives damaged, just 8 were written off, most notably Gresley A4 Pacific No 4469 *Sir Ralph Wedgwood*, which was damaged beyond repair at York North shed in a 'Baedeker Raid' in April 1942.

Acts of courage

Railwaymen and firemen displayed extraordinary courage and resourcefulness in tackling fires following air raids. At Bordesley Junction in Birmingham, an 18-year-old GWR engine cleaner saved wagons from a blazing shed on 26 August 1940. He began by using hands and feet trying to extinguish incendiaries with ballast. A wagon examiner and a depot master's clerk approached and asked whether he could drive an engine: 'We want someone to take engine 7758 alongside the goods shed and get the wagons clear.' The cleaner volunteered and removed strings of wagons from three roads alongside the blazing shed.[61]

Incendiaries ignited a string of wagons in Temple Mills yard in London, so the firemen were lined up on the parapet of the Ruckholt Road overbridge with hoses between their knees while a locomotive propelled the wagons under them, stopped while each was doused and continued until all the fires were put out. The survival of Hull Paragon's station roof was thanks to the courage of four railwaymen who clambered and slithered over the roof putting out incendiaries, often by stamping on them. Risks that no foreman would have allowed were taken spontaneously.

Many acts of heroism went unrecorded or unrewarded, just part of someone's duty. Two unnamed naval officers attended a parachuted landmine wrapped around a signal at London Bridge on 9 December 1940. Having examined it, the more senior wrote down what he intended to do, so that someone else might know what not to do if he failed to come back. Happily he did.

But six men were decorated for their bravery at Tyne Dock near South Shields, four receiving the British Empire Medal and two the George Cross. The yard had 300 wagons of ammunition awaiting shipment, and 10 of them were set alight during a raid on 10 April 1941. Driver J Steel hooked a locomotive to the 10 wagons and drew them in turn under a water column until the fires were out.

The George Cross was also won by Norman Tunna, a GWR shunter from Birkenhead, who during a raid on Liverpool Docks discovered two incendiary bombs burning in a wagonload of 250lb bombs. The top layer of bombs was already hot but he tore off the sheet covering them, hoping to take the incendiaries with it. One fell outside the wagon but the other fell between two bombs. Water from a stirrup pump brought up by the locomotive's driver and fireman had no effect on the incendiary but it did cool the bombs. Tunna managed to prise the bombs apart to release the incendiary, which he threw out of the wagon, and continued to water-cool the bombs until they were judged safe.[62]

Besides the formal evacuation of children, many adults also used the railways to escape the bombing, even on a daily basis. A nightly exodus from London headed to Bromley for Chislehurst Caves – 22 miles of intersecting tunnels hewn out for flint and chalk since the mid-13th century – which sheltered up to 15,000 people at a time, with a chapel and a hospital. When the bombing of Hull was at its worst in the summer of 1941, evening trains out of Paragon would be swamped with adults preferring to spend the night in fields around Beverley than their homes or bomb shelters. A similar migration took place by train from Plymouth to Bere Alston in search of a billet, barn, village hall or even a hedge.

One of the impacts of bombing was naturally the disruption of public transport, which meant that shifts could last until someone arrived to relieve you. Nor was sleep always possible even for those away from target areas, with the sound of air-raid sirens and distant explosions. Still worse was the plight of railwaymen whose homes were destroyed or damaged. Their distress was eased by the work of Women Welfare Officers, some of whom were attached to a large depot and helped to secure leave.

By 1944 bombing raids had become sporadic, and one of the last recorded by the SR before the onslaught of V-1 and V-2 rockets was on 15 May, when the gatehouse at Burton Common Crossing between Wool and Moreton in Dorset was demolished and Mrs Ricketts, the crossing keeper, was killed.

Parts of Kent were in range of German guns in France, and as late as September 1944 the south coast between Folkestone and Ramsgate was still suffering from daily shelling. During the war, the Dover area was hit by 3,000–4,000 shells, and on a clear day the gun flashes allowed people exactly 53 seconds to find shelter. Dover Priory's station master received the British Empire Medal.

Railwaymen raised funds to procure the means to fight back. The railways, in common with many towns, had Spitfire funds; the LNER's Spitfire was named *Flying Scotsman* and the SR's *Invicta* after the Canterbury & Whitstable Railway locomotive of 1829.

Taking all damage, the SR had 170 'incidents' per 100 route miles, the GWR 33, LMS 29 and LNER 28. During the war enemy action killed 893 railway employees and injured 2,444; 118 passengers were killed and 1,078 injured; and 387 other persons were killed and 929 injured on the railway. The breakdown between companies of those killed was: SR 300; London Passenger Transport Board 225; LNER 170; GWR 126; and LMS 72. Eight locomotives were destroyed and 484 damaged; 637 carriages were destroyed and 13,487 damaged.[63]

Resilience of railways

The forethought given to recovery from bomb damage was evident from the extraordinary speed with which railwaymen brought damaged lines back into use. Nor was the responsiveness confined to urban areas where resources were greatest. At 8.25 pm on 31 March 1941 a bomb blew a crater 30ft deep and 30ft wide on the up line between Barnstaple Town and Wrafton on the line to Ilfracombe, and a second smaller crater was thought to contain a delayed-action bomb. Yet the up line was back in use by about 10 am on 2 April.

Nonetheless, the delays caused to services didn't stop ill-informed and unthinking journalists complaining about them in the press, and one instance illustrates the difficulties faced by the railways. On 17 November 1940 the *Sunday Express* published an account of an express journey to London that took 10 hours instead of the scheduled 4. Restrictions on the railways' freedom to respond to such criticism cannot have helped morale, and the frustration is palpable in an LMS paper:

> Though not stated in the article, it was the 9.45 am from Manchester (London Road) to London Euston on 15 November 1940. The lazy journalist had not bothered to discover any of the facts that caused delays to the train. Two unexploded bombs between Nuneaton and Rugby had stopped all traffic. It was the day after the notorious raid on Coventry so diversion through that city was impossible, and two unexploded mines had been dropped on the intended diversionary route between Nuneaton and Leicester, which caused the train to be halted at Stone, after its last scheduled stop at Stoke-on-Trent. To reach the Midland main line via Uttoxeter, Tutbury and Burton, the locomotive had to run round its train at Stone and return to Stoke where a locomotive change was necessary because of weight restrictions between Burton and Leicester. The train travelled down the Midland as far as Market Harborough where it took the Northampton line to rejoin the West Coast main line at Roade. Finally while running between Tring and Watford an air raid began on London and the driver was instructed to proceed at 15mph all the way to Euston.[64]

To increase capacity and alternative routes, many new works were carried out during the war, which could not be reported in the railway press. They ranged in scale from simple curves at places where lines crossed without connection, to major widening work, such as the quadrupling of York–Northallerton, Severn Tunnel Junction–Newport and the 6 miles between Landsdown Junction at Cheltenham and Engine Shed Junction, Gloucester, from 24 August 1942. The last was a jointly owned line, so the LMS carried out the construction work while the GWR laid the track and installed the signalling. New loops were provided for slow-moving trains to be overtaken, and new marshalling yards created at such places as Woodford Halse and Banbury. They were financed by the Government and remained its property until the end of the Railway Control Agreement.

The huge increase in demand on the railways could not be matched by a corresponding rise in the number of locomotives or rolling stock. Steel for new construction was at a premium, so the railways had to keep running locomotives that would have been scrapped as obsolescent in peacetime. Nonetheless new locomotives were built: 587 between the outbreak of war and the end of 1942. The position was relieved in the run-up to D-Day as about 400 US-built locomotives were able to share duties on Britain's railways before being shipped to the Continent. Time for locomotive repairs was reduced by the demands of the War Office for non-railway work.

Fortunately for Britain, the reckless line closures of the post-war years had not begun, so diversionary routes were often available when bomb damage closed a section. Between 21 April and 7 May 1941, 42 SR trains ran over the GWR in the South West.[65] The following year on 4 May two delayed-action bombs buried themselves near City Basin Junction in Exeter. For the two days it took to extract them and reopen the line, all GWR traffic was diverted over the SR, entailing much reversal at St David's.[66]

Locomotive crews were commonly presented with some tough challenges. Even before the end of 1939, an LNER V2 locomotive had arrived at King's Cross with a train of 20 bogie carriages and 4 vans totalling at least 750 tons gross weight, and the crew had managed to keep time from Peterborough. It was not only the weight of trains that stretched footplate crews; where they could be spared, locomotives were transferred to places of greater need, which led crews having to adapt to the different firing and driving methods required by each design. A pair of SR Marsh class I3 4-4-2 tanks was assigned to Worcester shed, and one was recorded making a creditable ascent of Hatton bank with six bogie coaches. An SR 0-8-0 heavy shunting tank was transferred to Stranraer, but perhaps the longest peregrination was a diminutive SR Stroudley D1 tank posted to Wick.

Given the pressures, it is astonishing that during the war less than 1 per cent of trains serving Ministry of Supply ordnance depots arrived more than 10 minutes late.

The railways' resilience during the war was praised by Winston Churchill at a luncheon held at the Dorchester in 1943 to mark the 21st birthday of the post-grouping companies:

> Throughout the period of the heavy German raids on this country the arteries of the nation – the railways – with their extensive dock undertakings, were subjected to intensive attacks. Yet the grim determination, unwavering courage and constant resourcefulness of the railwaymen of all ranks have enabled the results of the damage to be overcome very speedily and communication restored ... Results such as the railways have achieved are only won by blood and sweat, and on behalf of the nation I express gratitude to every railwayman who has participated in this great transport effort which is contributing so largely towards final victory.

Churchill's words were echoed the following year by Sir Alan Mount, the chief inspecting officer of railways: the year was an 'eloquent tribute to their efficiency, standard of maintenance, and on the high factor of safety attained, all of which reflects the greatest credit on every railwayman and woman for the part they played in this historic year'.[67]

Distant campaigns

After the dispatch of the BEF, the second major exodus of troops to fight Germany took place in April 1940 with the sending of the expeditionary force to Norway entailing 202 trains, mainly to Glasgow and Leith.

After soldiers rescued from Dunkirk had been dispersed, major troop movements were for training exercises. The detail of an exercise in fen country requiring 61 trains from the LNER survives. They were:

> ... run from Newmarket via St Ives to March, the Higher Command in their wisdom having decided that Ely was 'blocked by the enemy'. From March they went to King's Lynn where they unloaded. Then to East Winch, Narborough and Swaffham, and back by Watton and Brandon to Ely (which by this time had been mercifully cleared of the enemy). From Ely they returned to Newmarket, and there they loaded up again, and set out on a second trip round the whole circle. Round and round those sixty trains went, until each train had completed two or three circuits.[68]

It wasn't always possible to predict where such exercises would end up. Moving the two forces and all their tanks and motorised equipment for a major exercise in March 1943 in the south of England between 'Eastland' (the 'enemy') and 'Southland' (actually mostly Canadian troops) required 221 specials between 24 February and 2 March. Staff set up a central office in Oxford from 7 March, but only on the 11th was a ceasefire declared and the main dispersal point revealed as the Bletchley area. Dispersal took place over 13–17 March in 211 special trains.[69]

Some unit moves entailed unusual resources. The movement of the 1st Mountain Regiment of the Royal Artillery from Abergavenny in autumn 1941, part to Scotland and part to Cornwall, required cattle trucks for the track mules as well as horseboxes.

Notice was required for groups of more than 20 travelling to training establishments so that 'Not for public use' labels could be applied to some carriages or special through-carriages laid on. Up to a thousand parties a day might travel under these arrangements. Leave for servicemen was especially difficult to plan for unless the unit had liaised with the railway. The policy was, whenever possible, to grant a week's leave every three months in addition to the weekend leaves.

The proximity of a training camp could be a mixed blessing. An epidemic of failed communication between the single-line instruments at Sheringham West and Weybourne signal boxes was caused by 'strays' or potshots at the wires by soldiers on the adjacent rifle range.[70]

Not all the campaign movements entailed south-coast ports. The build-up of forces in the Middle East and the movement of the 1st Army for the North African campaign in October 1942 were largely through Merseyside and the Clyde, supplemented by Avonmouth. The First Army movement of 185,000 men, 20,000 vehicles and 220,000 tons of stores required 440 special troop trains and 680 special freight trains between October and December 1942. Each train would have been planned in shadow form and given a code, so that a telephoned code was all that was required for the railway to operate a train of predetermined make-up and schedule. It was imperative that trains arrived at the docks in correct sequence – tanks and artillery as bottom cargo before lighter stores for top loading, for example. It requires little imagination to conceive the strain that a delayed ship for such outbound cargoes might cause to such meticulous plans.

Regular supplies for campaigns came under the Stores Shipment Programme. It remained modest while the BEF was in France at a few trainloads a week, but expanded as forces in the Middle East built up. By summer 1942 the programme provided for 8,000 standard journey times from depots all over the country to most of the ports. Each train had a code, running time, detailed route and maximum number of wagons. Problems arose when train arrivals exceeded the ability of the docks to load ships, forcing trains to be held in the hinterland and called forward. Aid to Russia began to flow early in August 1941 through a variety of eastern and southern ports.[71]

The pressures of rising traffic

The demands placed on the railway fluctuated according to individual events such as evacuation and Dunkirk, and to the progress of campaigns such as North Africa and Italy, but the general trend rose sharply. The war greatly added to the burden on the railways, while diminishing the means to carry it. By 1942 passenger numbers compared with 1938 had risen by 50 per cent, using 28 per cent fewer trains, and by 1943 the railways were forwarding 3 million loaded wagons a month.[72] The passenger increase was partly generated by the constant coming and going of troops on leave, on exercises or training courses and being reposted. In addition to the millions getting to their normal work each day, there were the wartime government factories, which alone required 7,000 daily special trains.

Adoption of the convoy system imposed surges of traffic with pressure to clear unloaded supplies from the docks quickly to reduce the turn-round time of ships. Moreover military traffic meant much unbalanced working of locomotives, and by October 1941 the REC was looking at ways of increasing through working across company boundaries. The reduction in passenger timetables had allowed more passenger locomotives to be used on freight, and consideration was being given to new locomotive construction that would allow operation over all main lines; GWR locomotives with a width over cylinders of 8ft 11in naturally could not work over LMS lines with a clearance for 8ft 7 11/16in. Locomotive maintenance was already being hampered by the loss of skilled men because the railways were not covered by the Essential Works Order limiting the freedom to enlist.

As in the First World War, wagons were at a premium, though construction had been accelerated; at an early stage in the war 5,788 were in the programme, which would produce a net increase of 4,646 after breaking up life-expired wagons.[73] Wagons were again pooled, including the 600,000 wagons owned by 4,000 different private owners. From 1941 the Inter-Company Freight Rolling Stock Control at Amersham monitored the moves of 1,250,000 wagons, 408,000 wagon sheets, 219,000 lashing ropes and 17,318 containers,[74] as well as allocating them to meet needs. The weekly exchange of wagons between companies was abandoned as part of the drive to improve wagon utilisation and minimise turn-round times, and the practice of RCH number-takers recording the details of wagons at inter-company exchange points was stopped as soon as the Government assumed control.

History also repeated itself in general war-weariness and the impact of working long hours through shortage of men. The LMS had to increase the hours of duty for fitters from 47 to 56 per week to cover the loss of trained men. Rates of absenteeism, especially on Sundays, had reached such a crisis that a special meeting between the LMS and the two unions was held on 24 February 1942. No improvement followed, so a full meeting between the Railways Staff Conference and the two unions was held in London on 19 March with G L Darbyshire, chief officer for labour and establishment at the LMS, in the chair.

The discussion hinged around long hours – or what constituted long hours when on a war footing. At York on Sunday 8 March 1942, 156 men were unwilling to work, yet 97 of them had worked less than 50 hours in the previous six days, Darbyshire argued. On a recent Sunday, at the 23 principal LMS depots 809 trainmen failed to turn up for duty. There were cases of guards leaving their trains when 'in many cases they had only been on duty 8½, 9 or 9½ hours'. On a Sunday in March, 41 drivers and firemen had refused to attend for duty even though 31 had worked less than 60 hours the previous week.[75]

The General Secretary of the NUR, John Marchbank, spoke for unions and cited long hours as the main reason for such refusals, caused by lines being completely blocked by the density of traffic in many districts. Requests for relief had been ignored by Control even when relief was available. It was recognised that performance of the railway had slowed because of wartime conditions, and especially reduced lighting. It was agreed to spread Sunday duties, though local negotiation and problem resolution were seen as the best solution. Consideration would be given to a proposal to extend shunting duties to 10 hours under certain local agreements.

There is little doubt that wartime tiredness and worry played a part in some accidents, such as the derailment on trap points of an overnight westbound express at Norton Fitzwarren in Somerset in November 1940, when the driver misread signals. His house had been damaged by bombs two days previously.

As in the First World War, the number and quality of services declined. Public dismay with standards during the war was the more pronounced because of the quality of service by 1938, when accelerated freight trains meant next-day delivery between most principal cities and towns, and passenger train punctuality was at 91 per cent. On 15 March 1940 Lord Stamp said at the LMS AGM: 'During the summer [of 1939] the claim was confidently made that efficiency of working on the LMS had reached its highest point since amalgamation. I examined this claim by every available test and came to the conclusion that it was completely justified.'[76]

Punctuality suffered for a variety of reasons, foremost being the blackout (see p 106). Others included the increased proportion of passengers travelling with luggage, the lack of strong younger men to load parcels and newspapers expeditiously, lack of relief men, reduced line speeds and locomotives loaded to their maximum allowance, thereby reducing their ability to recover time. Longer trains meant drawing up a second time at platforms shorter than the train, but this necessity was not always understood by passengers, and the experience of an army private ending up in the River Avon at Bath was not unique. The locomotives themselves were less well maintained, as overhauls were postponed and locomotive depots took over minor repair work within their competence to relieve pressure on the main workshops. Before the war the GWR claimed a locomotive failure figure of one every 126,000 miles; immediately after the war it was every 40,000 miles.[77]

After their initial withdrawal, daily restaurant car services had risen by the end of 1941 to 426, but after Whitsun weekend 1942, during which restaurant cars ceased operation, the total number of dining and Pullman car services on all railways numbered just 72.[78] The LMS had such acute difficulty in staffing dining cars due to men being called up that from October 1941 only 57 dining-car services remained, compared with pre-war totals of 234 in summer and 207 in winter. In May 1942 dining cars were withdrawn from all but 28 LMS trains, and even those were withdrawn from April 1944.[79] Ironically this sometimes meant a return to pre-1880s travel, when long-distance trains stopped for passengers to bolt down some sustenance in about 20 minutes; the LNER instituted stops at Grantham and Peterborough until restaurant and buffet cars were partially reinstated.

The decision to axe dining cars was partly based on the 'need for diverting powerful passenger locomotives to hauling important freight trains and the increased demand for service travel on the limited number of long-distance trains that can be run'. The Minister of War Transport 'strongly endorses the railway companies' advice to the public to carry their own food with them, and if possible a water bottle or thermos flask as well. They may, indeed, find it necessary before long to carry their own tin mugs as the companies are running short of cups.'[80] By 1942 an appeal had gone out for the public to carry their own cups, so high was the level of breakages.

Feeding railway travellers therefore fell to station refreshment rooms, which numbered 767 at the beginning of the war, but a need for the space they occupied or the staff who ran them reduced the number to 595 by 1944.[81]

Yet astonishingly horse racing was considered a valid use of resources. Not until September 1942 did the Ministry of War Transport issue an instruction that horses for race meetings should be refused, and that was moderated the following year to allow specified meetings at Newmarket to be held. In 1944 meetings at selected courses could be held providing they did not require rail transport of horses. Even the vans run for pigeon fanciers continued, albeit roughly halved, so that birds could continue to be trained for use by the forces.[82]

Echoing heating arrangements in medieval monasteries, steam-heating of trains was ordained by date rather than weather. Heating of LMS long-distance expresses in 1942 did not begin until 18 September, for example, and was withdrawn the following 4 May. On other trains heat was not provided until 1 November and discontinued after 31 March, as part of efforts to save coal. Passengers became accustomed to dressing warmly.

The source of power behind most trains declined in quality: some coal consignments were so small and dusty that some coalmen refused to handle it, and it was confined to sheds with mechanical coaling plants. It was a particular problem on the GWR, whose locomotives were designed on the assumption that only the best Welsh steam coal would be shovelled into the firebox. Periodic shortages added to the worry. The LMS estimated that coal deliveries were insufficient to see it through the winter of 1944–5; during the week ending 27 January, for example, it received only 95,000 tons against a requirement of 124,000 tons for its motive power depots.[83] Even the quality of locomotive lubricating oil deteriorated, which did nothing to help footplate crews expected to work their charges to the limit.

Travel was discouraged with such familiar campaigns as 'Is your journey really necessary?' Overwhelmingly people thought it was, and entreaties by radio, poster and press advertising to travel less met with failure. Quite apart from servicemen travelling on duty or leave, countless families had been separated by work or concern for safety and wanted to see one another. Others simply wanted a break. On Saturday, 29 July 1944, Paddington station had to be closed for three hours because the concourse and platforms could accept no more people, and colossal queues built up along both sides of Eastbourne Terrace. Part of the problem was the restriction in services, limiting the railways' ability to meet demand. On that summer Saturday, it took three phone calls from

IS YOUR JOURNEY REALLY NECESSARY?

TICKETS

IS YOUR JOURNEY REALLY NECESSARY?

RAILWAY EXECUTIVE COMMITTEE

Fig 4.22
This REC poster and others like it intended to discourage train travel did not have the hoped-for impact. As with many similar 'nudge' campaigns, it was widely felt that it was other people's journeys that should be sacrificed. The poster was designed by Bert Thomas (1883–1966), who contributed to *Punch* for 30 years.

Sir James Milne, the GWR's general manager, to the Ministry of War Transport to extract a relaxation of restrictions and order up extra trains from Old Oak Common. Though it is impossible to segment the reasons for passenger travel, passenger traffic on the LMS between May and September 1942 was 74 per cent higher than in 1938.[84] On the GWR the number of originating passenger journeys in 1938 was 129 million; in 1944 it was 190 million. Overcrowding of trains became the norm on principal routes.

This was made worse by the cuts needed on the approach to D-Day. Service withdrawals began in April to save 12,000 train miles per week. By 21 May the cuts saved 60,000 miles a week and these were raised to 264,000 miles a week on 22 May and almost 290,000 miles by July. This was too severe. On 31 July 1944 the 10.05 am train from Euston to Glasgow left with an estimated 800 people standing, while 100 passengers were left behind when the 10.28 from Birmingham to Newcastle left with some 1,200 passengers. Relief trains had to be laid on.

Journeys on the LNER rose by 188 per cent between 1939 and 1945. Trains of 20 coaches on the East Coast main line were common, calling for skill and stamina on the northbound climbs to Potters Bar and Stoke summit. Southbound trains posed a particular operating difficulty as 20 coaches exceeded platform lengths at King's Cross; a pilot had to be placed in the engine siding at Belle Isle north of Gasworks Tunnel. Once the incoming train had arrived, the pilot followed it into the station and hauled the uncoupled excess carriages back into the tunnel and into a vacant platform.

The royal family eschewed even the idea of leaving London during the Blitz, and tours by members of the royal family were considered good for morale. By the end of 1944, 57 tours had been made on the LMS, 44 on the LNER, 13 on the GWR and 6 on the SR. Few railwaymen were notified in advance of the train's itinerary, and overnight locations were carefully chosen, often close to a tunnel in which the train could take refuge.

Loss of staff and equipment

As in the First World War, the railways gave a commitment to staff to find positions for returning servicemen. As the LMS put it: 'Staff serving with the Forces or giving whole time service with Civilian Defence Services (in either case with the permission of the Company) will be treated as absent from duty with leave from the Company, and on their return, subject to being physically and otherwise fit will be reinstated in positions as nearly as possible similar to those vacated by them.'[85] In marked contrast to the First World War, there was no immediate exodus of staff in response to the call for volunteers. The eagerness to join up of the earlier conflict was absent. Only the 12,000 men who had joined Territorial and Reserve units at the encouragement of the railways were automatically called up.

But as staff gradually enlisted, shortages of skilled staff hampered the railways as they had during the First World War. Railway staffing levels had contracted between the wars because of the Depression, making the release of almost 110,000 staff during the war even more keenly felt. Moreover, the first three winters of the war were especially bad. Quite apart from the extra demands that snow and ice clearance placed on staff, many railwaymen contracted influenza – at one point 9 per cent of LMS drivers and 13 per cent of guards were off work – but despite staff shortages on this scale, in only one of the first eight weeks of 1940 was the movement of freight smaller than the same period of 1939.

Staff shortages were so severe by May 1942 that the REC warned the Ministry of Transport that operating manpower was 'dangerously weak'.[86] It was agreed that men would not be released without the company's consent, and men would relinquish positions suited to women and move to ones that weren't.

The third Report from the Select Committee on National Expenditure 1943–4, published in March 1944, recommended 'that not only should there be a cessation in the call up of railway workers, but that a steady influx of labour should be directed to the railways'.[87] Nonetheless staff numbers on the LMS actually increased during the war, from 122,843 on 3 September 1939 to 137,045 at 23 December 1944, with the number of drivers, firemen and cleaners increasing by 3,600 or 12 per cent in the year following February 1940.

More staff were needed partly because of the inefficiencies created by air raids, especially in train operation; a train normally covered by a single shift sometimes required three sets of men before it reached its destination. Comparing a three-month period during the height of the Blitz in 1940 and the same period the previous year, the number of instances when drivers worked over 10 hours rose from 2,997 a week to 15,780, and those working over 14 hours rose from 18 a week to 2,341. Guards working over 10 hours went from 2,230 to 12,096 and over 14 hours from 16 to 2,018.[88] A corollary of long shifts was the difficulty of keeping train crew fed. Those railway-owned hotels still open helped, but permission had to be obtained from the Ministry of Food for arrowroot biscuits and tinned meat roll to be available for purchase by trainmen before commencing duty at enginemen's and guards' depots employing 10 or more men.[89]

What could not be replaced quickly was experience. Owing to the release of men to the forces, the LMS found it necessary for youths aged 17, after a comparatively short time on the shed, to be sent out on firing duties on shunting engines and within shed yard limits. During 1943 this was lowered to 16 by agreement with the unions, and from 1943 the minimum age for a signalman was lowered to 18.

During 1943 some Euston expresses left late for want of footplate staff. The difficulty in finding volunteers to train for key grades led to the railways securing authority from the National Service Officer to make transfers, mostly recruited through labour exchanges, but the LMS intake still fell short of requirements by 2,667. By 1944 the situation was so bad that authorisation was given for 451 men to be released from the services from June to work in the LMS motive power department, and 206 of those were soon passed for firing duties.

Paid voluntary part-time workers were recruited from July 1943 by the LMS to clean engines in their spare time at weekends; by this time 'the amount of cleaning ... was infinitesimal compared with pre-war standards ... During a period of 28 weeks, mainly at weekends, a total of 47,687 volunteers worked 373,991 hours and cleaned an equivalent of 21,592 engines.'[90] Operations began on a small scale, with volunteers from members of the staff and their families as well as a number provided by the Ministry of Labour, and following the success of the experiment, the arrangements were extended throughout the system. On the GWR volunteer paid labour was used to unload wagons, and over a weekend in October 1943 the greenhorns managed to unload 27,000 wagons. The volunteers came from many walks of life – butchers, insurance agents, university students, women clerks and housewives.[91]

As in the First World War, rising prices prompted demands for wage increases. An advance of 4s a week to railway workers and £10 a year to salaried staff was awarded in February 1940 by the Railway Staff National Tribunal. In May 1941 railway workers were awarded a further 4s, raised to 7s, a week, and £18 a year to salaried staff, backdated to 6 January 1941, so by May 1941 wages had risen by 11s a week and salaries by £28 a year since the war began. Yet by October the NUR demanded 60s a week minimum wage, as the basic income on which a family could be maintained in health and decency. According to the NUR, about 150,000–160,000 railway workers were on less than 60s a week.[92] By 1943 the total staff employed by British railways and LT was 668,145, of whom 114,000 were women. Over 110,000 former railway staff were serving in the forces and full-time civil defence.[93]

Railway staff who had been taken prisoner were not forgotten. The LMS Prisoners of War Comforts Fund was established in 1942 and within two years had sent over 3,000 quarterly parcels to colleagues who were POWs. Among other articles they contained 20,000 razor blades, 5,000 pairs of socks, 8,000 other articles of clothing, 2,500 towels, 2 tons of chocolate and 1 ton of soap. Cigarettes were supplied as well as requested books, records, watercolour paints and games. The number of known LMS POWs increased from 360 when the fund was established to 860 by July 1944; 200 of these were in Japanese hands and to them 'so far it has unfortunately not been possible to afford any material assistance'.[94] The fund was primed with £250 from the company and augmented by the agreed deduction of 1d a week from staff pay.

As in the First World War, the railways had to relinquish locomotives to supplement those being built for service overseas. In 1917 the GWR had supplied new 2-6-0s for the ROD, so some must have been surprised by the WD requisitioning 100 'Dean goods', the earliest dating from 1883. They had the attribute of a light axle loading and were reconditioned at Swindon and Eastleigh and fitted with Westinghouse brake equipment before shipment.

The role of women

At the outbreak of the war, almost 25,253 women and girls (compared to 563,264 men and youths) were employed on the railways, mostly in clerical grades as shorthand typists and as machine, telegraph and telephone operators. Small numbers were employed as carriage cleaners, waiting-room attendants, cooks and mess-room attendants, crossing keepers and office cleaners. The range of tasks became much greater in the Second World War, as reflected in the paintings of war artist Laura Knight showing women operating sophisticated machine tools and electric and oxy-acetylene welding.

Their activities spread to many other roles: ticket duties, porters, announcers, carters looking after horses, and locomotive and rolling stock maintenance. The SR's depot producing sleepers at Redbridge near Southampton was largely staffed by women, who accounted for 70 per cent of the workforce, and there were women architects, draughtswomen, motor-van drivers, woodworkers and metalworkers, crane operators, fog signallers and gas fitters. Over 1,200 women

Fig 4.23
The range of tasks under-
taken by women on the
railways during the Second
World War was wider than
in the First. One of these was
trackwork, which seems not
to have been one of their
roles during the earlier
conflict. Here a group of
women oil the moving parts
of a single slip point at
Reading Central goods depot
on 20 April 1943.

Fig 4.24
The 30-year-old Mrs Millie
Young of the Gray's Inn
Road, London, driving the
only railway pair-horse van
in Britain which had an all-
female team. The picture was
taken on 10 September 1942.

Fig 4.25
Locomotive cleaning was
an occupation common to
women in both wars. These
women were photographed
at a northern LNER depot in
June 1941.

Fig 4.26
An obviously posed wartime
propaganda photograph at
the LNER's Doncaster Works
on 14 August 1943. Black
women on the railways were
uncommon at that time, and
this woman looks a little less
than fully confident in her
stance as the striker. The
component being made looks
to be a smokebox door-hinge
strap. The smith is holding
a set chisel used for cutting
down the red-hot metal.

were trained to take over signal boxes. Training for signalling and passenger guard duties took time, but by the end of 1944 the LMS employed 377 women guards and 623 signalwomen. The LMS employed about 39,000 women in 250 grades, some 17 per cent of the total staff.

By 30 September 1942 the railways had 105,656 women in their employment,[95] and women worked in so many roles that almost the only place they could not be found was driving or firing a steam locomotive. A female booking clerk had been an ichthyologist, a gas fitter had been a cow-puncher in Mexico, a railway policewoman an opera singer and one grandmother drove a 50-ton crane at Gorton. By the war's end the total of women employed on the railways had risen to 124,000.[96]

Less opposition from the unions was encountered than in 1914–18, partly because times had moved on and the objections of the previous conflict already looked antediluvian. The honouring of the commitment to give returning servicemen back their jobs in the First World War must also have played a part. As in the First World War, women in the role of guards suffered the greatest hostility, though the SR had a female guard as young as 19 on trains to Tattenham Corner. The largest increases were in the railway workshops, partly due to the low figure at the beginning of the war; the number of women in the works at Brighton and Lancing was just 8 in 1939, and rose to 549.[97] The induction of so many women into the railways required training facilities to be established. The SR set up schools at London Victoria, Chislehurst and East Croydon.

A number of women displayed exceptional bravery during the war. When a 77-year-old man fell on the track at Walsden (LMS), Porter Nellie Bentley ran along the line waving a red light to help the train stop 8yds short of the man. Following the attack on a Guildford–Horsham train near Bramley station on 16 December 1942, Porter Violet Wisdom locked the booking office and ran along the track to help, finding the driver, guard and eight passengers had been killed. The fireman was adept at first aid and had done all he could on his own, before six Canadian soldiers arrived to help. The only woman railway employee to receive the George Medal was stewardess Elizabeth May Owen on the GWR's *St Patrick*. On 13 June 1941 she saved six women, one of them hysterical, by negotiating tilting cabins and companionways as the vessel sank after being dive-bombed en route to Rosslare.[98] She held up one of the women in the sea for two hours – without a lifebelt – before they were rescued.

Special trains and rail-mounted guns

Special trains were created for key individuals such as the Prime Minister, Commander-in-Chief (Home Forces) and C-in-C (US Forces in Europe), and each train was given a code name. These trains were travelling hotels with office, sleeping, dining and bathroom accommodation. Suitably quiet and safe sites were chosen for conferences or a good night's sleep. The LNER provided the Prime Minister's train, though an LMS saloon was also adapted for his use and the LMS then took over the role, providing LMS staff wherever it went. The LNER also provided the train for the C-in-C (Home Forces) and the GWR a train for the C-in-C (US).[99]

An LNER sleeping car was clad in armour plating and fitted with armour-plate glass for the use of General Eisenhower on the Continent. Six of the berths were converted into a conference room and a combined sleeping and dressing compartment, and a roof aerial was fitted.

Various rail-mounted guns were sited around Kent to lob shells across the Channel: three 13½in guns were located around Shepherdswell on the East Kent Railway; 9.2in guns were stationed near Hythe and Canterbury; and 12in howitzers were sited around Guston Tunnel between Dover and Walmer. An 18in howitzer named 'Boche Buster' was kept in Bourne Park Tunnel at Bishopsbourne on the Eltham Valley line between Folkestone and Canterbury, but since its limited range confined it to defence against invasion, it was never fired in anger.

Sustaining the war effort

Fig 4.27
This 250-ton 18in gun was photographed at Catterick on 12 December 1940. It left Catterick on 2 February 1941 for Bishopsbourne on the Folkestone–Canterbury line, which was taken over by the Army.

As in the First World War, responsibility for supplying factories with raw materials, moving their products to where they were needed and supplying the basic needs of the population devolved almost entirely on the railways. The railways already carried most freight in Britain, and the tonnages involved were prodigious, especially in raw materials. Roughly 80 per cent of coal mined was moved by train, and in 1942 this amounted to 160.7 million tons. The busiest year during the war was 1943 when the railways moved 300,858,000 tons of freight.[100] Practically all 4.5 million tons of the grain harvest went by rail to mills and storage depots.

Government department requirements for rail transport were channelled through 900 railway liaison officers. Each morning, special movements and operating difficulties were discussed by telephone for a maximum of 30 minutes at the Central Operating Conference.[101]

Once again railway ports were crucial, with 95 miles of railway-owned dockside quay at 77 harbours. Some small ports were revived because of their safe location, such as the LNER port of Silloth, which received US imports and participated in supplying the North Africa campaign. Railway vessels were also taken over for war work; of the 139 ships owned by the railways in 1939, 31 were lost.

New ports were developed and lines built to serve them. One of the most secluded was Faslane on Gare Loch, reached by a steeply graded WD-operated double-track line from Faslane Junction near Rhu on the West Highland line. Built from December 1940, the port had accommodation for 3,000 people and sidings for 1,700 wagons. It became the embarkation point for many of the troops and much of the equipment bound for the North African landings of autumn 1942. Further south, Cairnryan near Stranraer became Military Port No 2; it was begun in January 1941 and completed in 1943, and helped to build Mulberry harbours.

The railways' fleets of special wagons for such loads as plate glass, theatrical scenery, circuses and girders proved invaluable in moving aircraft parts, guns and tanks. Many of these were 'out of gauge' loads which entailed circuitous and slow journeys. Special wagons were required for the hydrogen gas that filled the barrage balloons made at Cardington in Bedfordshire and stationed around Britain under Balloon Command, with 52 balloon squadrons. High numbers of

Fig 4.28
Ordnance BL 12in Mk V (foreground) and two Mk III howitzers at Catterick in Yorkshire on 12 December 1940. All three dated from the First World War and were made at Armstrong Whitworth's Elswick Works on Tyneside.

trains were required for unfamiliar cargoes: by June 1942 the LMS had handled 760 special trains carrying 5 million coils of barbed wire from a single factory in the north-west.[102]

As in the First World War, movement of matériel added colossal tonnages to the railway's carryings. The total volume of wagonloads hovered around a million a week in the busiest months, overseen by Central Wagon Control, which assigned freight vehicles to movements. The inevitable volatility of wartime traffic made this exceptionally challenging, and it was made even more so by the shortage of manpower which often delayed unloading; a 1943–4 analysis showed that 87,000 wagons a day were being lost through wagons having to wait more than 48 hours to be unloaded.

Adding to the pressure was the diversion of traffic from coastal steamers to the less vulnerable railway, which increased the already immense tonnages of coal carried. During the peak year of 1941, 10,034 coal trains trundled south from the Midlands and north-east coalfields. The inability to import raw materials created some long-distance flows. The blast furnaces of Scotland had relied on previously imported high-grade iron ores, but had to switch to low-grade ore from domestic sources such as Northamptonshire. Even though new wagon construction was severely rationed, 3,500 new iron-ore hoppers had to be built to meet the higher demand.

Two examples can stand for the numerous rural stations whose quiet pre-war existence was transformed by a new role. At Dunbridge, between Salisbury and Romsey, the goods yard handled 182 wagons in June 1938; in June 1944 it handled 5,246. Further north, Tanfield was the single intermediate station on the LNER branch between Melmerby and Masham in Yorkshire. In 1941 Tanfield was chosen as a suitably safe place to create an ammunition sub-depot, perhaps helped by closure of the branch to passenger traffic in 1931. The Royal Army Ordnance Corps built a training camp opposite the station which received explosives from factories liable to air attack; the ordnance was stored beside lanes around Tanfield and Masham. Besides Tanfield's yearly wartime average of 3,000 tons of grain, 3,000 tons of potatoes and 2000 tons of sugar beet, the small goods yard, capable of holding 34 wagons, was called on to handle up to 76,000 tons of military traffic in the busiest year of 1944. Army staff supplemented the railway staff of two male porters, a lad porter and a female clerk. The station was open every Sunday for five years, and work often went on throughout the night. Shunting was a challenge when trains of 40–50 wagons were received. During the 6 weeks before D-Day, 42 special trains were run over the branch. The risks attached to the traffic are obvious and became manifest when there was an explosion at Catterick Bridge, which killed the stationmaster. Even when the war had ended, the thousands of tons of explosives still stored around Tanfield required numerous trainloads to remove them – 17 trains to remove ¾ million landmines alone.[103]

In repetition of the First World War, the area north and west of Inverness was made a Protected Area, from 1 April 1940. Mines were again brought in through Kyle of Lochalsh, and the naval bases at Scapa Flow and Invergordon generated huge increases in traffic. Following the sinking of HMS *Royal Oak* by a U-boat in Scapa Flow in October 1939 and repeated air attacks encouraged by the base's lack of anti-aircraft guns and searchlights, the fleet largely abandoned Scapa Flow until March 1940 while defences were strengthened. This work required special trains for Heavy Anti-Aircraft and Searchlight regiments and matériel. Some of the fleet went to Loch Ewe in Wester Ross while this work was in progress, and the decision was taken to create an alternative base there in case Scapa Flow should again be rendered unserviceable. Achnasheen became the railhead for construction work which entailed anti-aircraft batteries.

Fears of invasion following the capitulation of France and Norway led to a brigade and auxiliary troops being stationed in each of Caithness, Orkney and Shetland. The large numbers quickly overwhelmed service trains, so from 16 April 1940 a services special with capacity for 530 was run from London Euston serving Crewe, Carlisle, Perth and Thurso, echoing the Jellicoe specials of the First World War and perpetuating the name. From the same date, a return train was operated for those on leave, with both operating six days a week.

The LMS stock used on the trains brought immediate protest. The Commander-in-Chief of the Home Fleet wrote to the Admiralty: 'The carriages provided for Thurso are usually of a very old and uncomfortable pattern and frequently not even cleaned. The lavatory accommodation has been described as beastly. There are often women (nursing sisters, members of the WRNS [Women's Royal Naval Service], etc) travelling in the train. The imposition of such conditions is scandalous.'[104]

Additional trains had to be laid on as demand grew. Some trains were provided with sleeping-car accommodation for officers from May 1942, and an August 1942 meeting agreed to increase some trains to 15 carriages, requiring two locomotives. Over the two years ending 31 May 1944, about 621,000 people arrived at or left Thurso aboard Jellicoe specials. To begin with, no refreshment facilities were provided on the train north of Crewe, and north of Perth the only chance for a bun and cup of tea was during the nine-minute water stop at Helmsdale, thanks to the Women's Voluntary Service, who served 104,000 northbound Jellicoe passengers in 1942.[105] However, one service gained a canteen car staffed by the Salvation Army from 12 November 1940.[106]

Besides the scheduled public and services trains, special trains were run over Highland lines, most poignantly to carry the 400 survivors of the *Royal Oak*. After Dunkirk, Highland regiments were re-formed in the region, such as the Seaforths at Strathpeffer, using the former HR hotel and others. Beauly was chosen as the destination for 20 trainloads of Norwegian troops after the fall of their country.

Occasional special trains took Winston Churchill to Thurso, most significantly on 4 August 1941 on his way to the momentous meeting with Roosevelt in Newfoundland which produced the Atlantic Charter. Churchill had left Chequers on the 3rd 'with a retinue which Cardinal Wolsey would have envied', as John Colville put it.[107] Preparations for D-Day included units practising landing with tanks along the coast of Nairnshire and Moray and in Easter Ross, for which the civilian populations had to be evacuated. General Bernard Montgomery used his train named 'Rapier' to visit naval and military establishments in the run-up to D-Day, and paused his southbound journey from Inverness for four nights at Dalwhinnie to visit troops and refine the invasion plans.

Airfields and air-gunnery ranges at Castletown, Dalcross, Evanton, Alness, Kinloss, Tain and Wick added to the pressure on the Highland's limited capacity. A secretive POW camp was built in 1945 at Watten in Caithness, where the prisoners eventually numbered 2,800; they included some prominent Nazis, among them the U-boat captain Otto Kretschmer. Italian prisoners of war passed through Invergordon – 588 of them on 14 July 1942 – which would almost certainly have required a special train,[108] and U-boat crews were taken by special train from Kyle of Lochalsh to the interrogation centre at Kempton Park in Surrey.

Whole forests were felled in Ross and Cromarty to supply the pit props that had previously come from Norway, and timber traffic increased to such an extent that a report into the working of trains over the Highland section was commissioned to identify how delays might be reduced. Dated 23 November 1942, the report blamed congestion between the Inverness signal boxes at Welsh's Bridge and Millburn for causing operational difficulties as far afield as Aviemore. It itemised the source of 202 wagons of timber forwarded on a single day in October, and gave the number of wagons detached in Inverness yards that month as 14,949.[109]

The timber being felled by lumbermen from Canada and British Honduras had required new sidings at Beauly and light railways at Invershin and Achnashellach, and by 1942 327,843 tons of wood was dispatched by train.[110] The report cited the complaint by Mr Peterson, Ministry of Supply transportation officer at Glasgow, that 'a large number of forestry personnel had already arrived in this area [Carr Bridge] without any prior consultation with him as to whether transportation was available for the increased amount of timber to be forwarded from Carr Bridge'.[111]

The increase from 1938 to 1942 was 87.79 per cent in freight train miles, 76.81 per cent in total wagon miles and 135.07 per cent in total engine hours. Eleven Stanier 8F 2-8-0s were transferred to the Highland section to help. There was a reduction in ordinary passenger traffic, but the number of passenger train miles was equal to the pre-war figure because of the number of special service personnel trains which were required, usually double-headed. To cope with all this extra traffic, five new crossing places were brought into use during 1942, two new block posts on the double-track sections were inserted and a third was repositioned, and new sidings were created at Perth, Aviemore, Georgemas and elsewhere. Bad weather impeded services, notably in January 1942, when one Jellicoe took four days between Inverness and Thurso after it became stuck fast between Kinbrace and Forsinard. When the heating ceased to function, doors and tables were burned, and blankets and food had to be dropped from planes.[112]

The large increase in population in the Highlands – the population of Inverness doubled – outstripped the production of local dairy cows and required the import of 290,000 gallons of milk by rail in 1942. Larger quantities of herrings from Stornoway overwhelmed the facilities at Kyle of Lochalsh, because the Admiralty had requisitioned half the pier's capacity. The alternative port of Mallaig was beyond the reach of smaller vessels, so they took to unloading their catches at Gairloch and Ullapool for transfer by road to the railway at Achnasheen and Garve, two stations that had barely had to deal with fish.

Operations were not helped by the first three winters of the war being particularly severe, the winter months of 1939–40 being the worst in living memory. During the first months of 1940, there were 313 instances of lines being blocked for an aggregate of 47,757 hours and drifts up to 20ft deep, with 90 passenger, 88 freight and 40 light engines stuck in drifts. At one hump yard, wagons were processed at just 50 per hour instead of 150–200, and at docks the contents of coal wagons had to be hacked out instead of being tipped. Though the following winter was not as bad, in January 1941 food had to be dropped by RAF plane to a permanent-way inspector and about 20 men who were snowbound between Forsinard and Altnabraec in the Highlands, and again the following month to 90 passengers and 62 permanent-way men isolated at three places on the same section of line.[113]

A major contribution to maintaining morale was letters from home, symbolised by the GWR's First World War memorial (*see* p 181). The headquarters of the Army Postal Service was in Nottingham and the city's Victoria station became its fulcrum. The LNER station's constrained layout between two tunnels forced some postal traffic to be taken by road to outlying stations and the postal vans were then marshalled into trainloads.[114] After D-Day a daily train ran from Nottingham to Tilbury until November 1944, when it switched to Dover. Sutton Park goods depot in Birmingham became the main US Army Post Office from July 1942, and by the end of 1944 it had received and dispatched 1,182 special mail trains. Canadian mail was dealt with at Manchester (Mayfield) until July 1943, when it was transferred to Kensington (Addison Road). Parcels for the forces abroad were sent to a central depot at Bournemouth for customs scrutiny.

A recurrent problem exacerbated by shortages and rationing was the extent of theft. Between 1938 and 1942, prosecutions for theft on the railway rose by 300 per cent, accompanied by rising levels of vandalism. It had become so serious by March 1944 that the Select Committee on National Expenditure 1943–4 warned 'that in the interests of the conservation of national resources drastic action should be taken by the authorities to deal with the alarming extent to which thieving has increased'.[115] The shortage of railway police reduced the risk and the blackout increased the opportunity for theft. In February 1945 John Stourton MP told the Commons that 'thefts from the railway companies' premises and vehicles has become an organised industry', a claim borne out by the figures: total claims paid by the railways in 1939 amounted to £161,000; for the first nine months of 1944 it was £1,776,192.[116] LMS claims were almost double those of the LNER, which paid out twice as much as the GWR and four times the SR's figure.

The role of railway workshops

Though the grouping of 1922 had led to a reduction in the number of railway-owned heavy engineering workshops, there were still dozens in 1939, ranging in scale from the township of Crewe to the modest facility of Melton Constable. Many locomotive sheds also had substantial repair facilities, such as the GWR sheds at Newton Abbot, Tyseley and Worcester, the LMS depot at Bristol Barrow Road or the LNER's Colwick. They employed tens of thousands of highly skilled men and women and represented some of the best engineering facilities in the country. Some of the works which had been scaled back following the grouping into the 'Big Four' companies in 1922 were brought out of semi-retirement, such as Brighton, which even resumed locomotive manufacture. The railway companies' works were supplemented by the independent locomotive and carriage workshops producing to order, though the Depression had hit them hard: capable of building 600 locomotives a year, the North British Locomotive Co produced just 16 in 1933. Some had closed altogether; others amalgamated. It was fortunate that the workshops were little affected by bombing, though delivery of raw materials was periodically interrupted.

Though the first recorded order from the War Office was placed with the LMS in 1937, for tanks, surprisingly the railways received few orders from the Government before April 1940, by which time they had already lost more skilled men to the forces than they could spare, and it was to staunch this loss that the REC met the Government and urged full use of the railway workshops. This led to the creation of a committee with representatives of the ministries of War Transport, Supply, Aircraft Production and Labour, the Admiralty and the REC to decide what to produce and the allocation of work to absorb spare capacity.

As in the First World War, the railway workshops were called on to help produce weapons and ammunition, but made a much wider range of items, reflecting the development of air power in particular during the intervening years. Consequently the technical sophistication of the work carried out by railway workshops during the Second World War far exceeded the First. As noted, the first request from Government came in June 1937 to the LMS, which produced designs for the Covenanter tank at its Locomotive Drawing Office at Derby, requiring 5,000 drawings.[117]

The LMS works at Crewe made 161 Covenanter tanks, part of its wartime total of 1,771 tanks. Derby Carriage and Wagon Works began the Second World War renovating 23 12in howitzers mounted on bogie-bolster wagons which had been completed in 1918 too late to see service. The LMS's Horwich Works made 481 Cruiser, 406 Matilda and an unknown number of Centaur tanks, as well as numerous artillery components and shells, and kit wagons for assembly in Turkey and Egypt.[118]

The GWR produced parts for nine types of plane, and Swindon equipped dozens of new or converted munition factories from the beginning of the war. It made items as delicate as a Sperry Gryro Pivot, which required the use of a watchmaker's glass, and, unofficially, objects as crude as 2,000 cudgels from old boiler tubes for the Home Guard. Whimsically it made roller skates for the recreation of neighbouring troops and sewing-machine parts for a local American Hospital Group.[119]

Aircraft body and wing repairs were a natural fit for the skills found at carriage and wagon works. The LMS produced wings for Hurricanes and 1,000 Typhoons, and repaired aircraft such as Hampdens, Lancasters, Whitleys (at Wolverton) and Spitfires. A runway was devised on the golf course at Troon beside the former GSWR wagon works at Barassie in Ayrshire, so that repaired Spitfires could fly back to their airfields. Horsa gliders were a collaboration between Lancing, York and Doncaster. The skills within the railway were utilised by collaborative work on projects: in late 1938 the SR's Eastleigh Works carried out research with the Royal Aircraft Establishment at Farnborough into the best way to convert Blenheim bombers into fighters, before going on to make 1,475 conversion sets. Railway skills found an outlet in new areas: railway air-brake fitters, for example, applied their knowledge to power-operated gun turrets.

Besides tanks, guns, shells and aircraft parts, railway workshops produced landing craft, Horsa gliders, Bailey bridge parts, radio transmitting cabins, submarine detection devices and parts of two-men midget submarines, but a catalogue of each works' output soon becomes repetitive.

There was also a greater degree of cooperation between the four companies in meeting urgent demands. To meet an order for Iran, 1,600 12-ton wagons were built in three months during 1941 by the SR's Ashford Works. The LMS and LNER supplied some of the 1,792 component parts to the SR, which assembled them at the rate of 1 every 37 minutes. The 130 men, 22 women and 19 boys each averaged 67 hours a week.[120] Ashford Works achieved astonishing levels of productivity, even though it received 2,881 red warnings of imminent attack and had only a rooftop anti-aircraft gun manned by the Home Guard as defence.

Both workshop employment numbers and hours increased. The Brighton workforce rose from 253 men in 1939 to 755 men and 214 women working full-time and 38 part-time by the end of 1943.[121] The working week in LMS workshops was raised to 66 hours in 1940 and it was not unknown for men to work 88 hours a week.

Railway-owned maritime workshops also undertook contract work, with the LNER facility at Parkeston Quay carrying out £1 million worth of work for the Navy. The SR marine workshops at Southampton repaired 184 warships and 723 merchant ships and maintained water ambulances. Newhaven handled 603 warships, 140 merchant ships, 10 hospital carriers and 21 RAF high-speed launches.

One of the more unusual railway facilities turned over to war production was the car-cleaning sheds at Aldenham near Elstree, which was built for the extension of the Northern Line under the New Works Programme of 1935–40. Though work on the extension was never to resume, it was decided to complete the building so that the London Aircraft Production Group could use it to build aircraft. Besides producing 710 Halifax bombers for the RAF, the building was used to assemble Mosquito fuselages, and the workforce numbered 967 by the end of September 1942. Production ended in February 1945 and the building became an LT bus overhaul works in 1956.[122]

Commercial railway workshops too carried out impressive work, much of which became 'essential undertakings', which meant they had to cancel contracts in progress and postpone ones not begun. Beyer Peacock of Manchester received its Essential Works Order on 13 May 1941 which stipulated that no workman could leave or management discharge an employee without agreement of the Ministry of Labour. 'With a stroke of the pen the whole practice of management in Great Britain was revolutionised. Speaking very broadly, management prior

Fig 4.29
The freight traffic work-horse built during the Second World War was Riddles's 2-8-0 design. They were rough-and-ready locomotives, but lasted into the 1960s.

to 13 May 1941 was 10% leadership, 90% discipline. On and after that date the position was reversed, and management willy-nilly had to be 90% leadership and 10% discipline.'[123]

Beyer Peacock was one of a number of companies which continued to build steam locomotives during the war, some unconnected with the war effort, in order to earn foreign currency, supplying locomotives to Brazil, the Burma front, Ceylon, France, French Equatorial Africa, the Gold Coast, India, Iran, Kenya, the Near East, Nigeria, Northern Ireland, Sierra Leone and South Africa. Priority over all others was given to the order for Burma, which needed locomotives for the Ghat section of line between Mandalay and Lashio with gradients of 1 in 25. To deliver the locomotives in time for the 14th Army's attack on Burma in 1944, Beyer Peacock condensed production from the date of order to steaming to 118 days. The War Office wrote: 'This accomplishment, in face of all the difficulties of changing programmes and supply of materials urges me to send my heartiest congratulations to you, your staff and all your workpeople for this magnificent effort.'[124]

The largest class of locomotive constructed during the war was the WD Austerity 2-8-0, of which 935 were built by Vulcan Foundry in Newton-le-Willows and the North British Locomotive Co in Glasgow in 1943–5. Though based on Stanier's LMS 8F, it was modified to reduce construction costs by Robert Riddles, who had left the LMS at the start of the war to become director of transportation equipment at the Ministry of Supply. His brief from the WD was for a locomotive that could haul a 1,000-ton train at 40mph, and design work on 2-8-0 and 2-10-0 wheel configurations began in mid-1942. Before cranking out the Austerities, Vulcan Foundry had designed the Matilda tank. The Austerity 2-8-0s were intended to serve on the Continent after D-Day, and all but three did. The North British built all 150 2-10-0s, of which 103 went to the Continent and 20 to the Middle East. The former were concentrated in Holland and were later bought by Netherlands Railways after the end of the war.

Building and supplying new factories and airfields

Even before hostilities started, factories were being created in places considered comparatively immune to bombing, spreading munition factories, warehouses and storage facilities around the country, with camps and airfields often set up in far-flung districts. Rural goods yards accustomed to dealing with a dozen or two wagons a week were often overwhelmed by the demands placed on them. Barnham on the Thetford–Bury St Edmunds line went from handling 2,000 loaded wagons in 1938 to a wartime annual average of over 22,000.

As in the First World War, ordnance factories became some of the largest employers. Sixteen Royal Ordnance factories were set up to fill munitions. The largest was built at Bridgend in South Wales, covering 4 sq miles and flanking the GWR line, with a warren of underground magazines and an internal railway of 24 miles. The exchange sidings could hold 600 wagons. Construction took three years and required 145,000 tons of concrete and delivery of 496,000 tons of equipment. Most of the 37,000 workers at what is thought to have been Britain's largest factory had to be brought in by train, so Tremains Halt, a four-platformed halt with platform loops, was constructed to the east of Bridgend.

Production began in May 1940 when five special trains a day each way carried the workforce; by 1945, 58 trains a day were needed for the country's largest single-site employer.

One of the largest munitions plants on the LNER was at Thorp Arch on the Harrogate–Church Fenton line. The impossibility of blocking such a busy line while up to 18,000 workers alighted or boarded trains over a 24-hour period forced the construction of a 6½-mile circuit around the factory serving four stations. From a triangular junction with the main line, trains ran clockwise around the loop under the control of colour-light signals.

Another Royal Ordnance factory was built at Glascoed on the Pontypool Road–Monmouth branch; it opened in April 1940 and covered 1,000 acres. The rail link allowed the thrice-daily movement of up to 13,000 workers, as well as delivery of raw materials and dispatch of bombs, including Barnes Wallis's famous bouncing bombs. A halt created in 1938 for the Royal Arsenal factory at Chorley in Lancashire received nearly 16,000 workers each day, requiring 426 trains a week.

Fig 4.30
The afternoon shift changeover at the Royal Ordnance Factory Bridgend fills the up platform at Tremains Halt on 3 June 1942. This four-platformed temporary station was built specifically to serve the munitions factories at the ordnance depot.

Fig 4.31
An industrial 'pug' shunter at the Woolwich arsenal. A pug was a generic diminutive for a four-coupled industrial shunting engine. At its greatest extent, the railway system at Woolwich amounted to 147 miles, some of it dual gauge.

Once manufactured, the munitions had to be moved to storage sites. Among rural sites for ammunition created before the war was the worked-out Bath-stone quarry at the Ridge near Corsham in Wiltshire, where 6 acres of storage space were available, half of which had been used for the purpose in the First World War. Siding accommodation for 21 wagons and a specially adapted loading platform for handling ammunition were provided at Corsham station, linked to the quarry by a 2ft (600mm) gauge line. Even larger was the 45 acres of storage space at nearby Tunnel Quarry, accessed by a siding entering the maze of tunnels through a side tunnel at the eastern end of Box Tunnel.[125] Ammunition from Corsham supplied many of the British campaigns during the war, including the Normandy landings, and by June 1944 over 10,000 tons of ammunition per week were being moved.[126]

Training facilities too were set up in equally remote locations. Major training centres and grounds were located near Dalmally on the Oban line, Warcop between Penrith and Kirkby Stephen, and Kirkcudbright. Anti-aircraft practice camps were established at Weybourne in 1936 and later Stiffkey on the M&GNJR, which also required deliveries of steel and cement.

During summer 1942 plans were drawn up for a major bomber offensive against Germany which would require almost 150 new airfields to be built in East Anglia, principally for bombers, with additional supporting airfields for fighters in Kent and Sussex. More than three-quarters of Britain's bomber aerodromes were served by the LNER. Most of the stations called upon to handle construction materials had coped with little more than local agricultural and domestic coal traffic. At one station the tonnage dealt with in the first six months of 1943 was 2,600 per cent up on the whole of 1940, mostly bricks, tarmac, cement, slag and rubble. Flows of rubble from bombed sites in London began in November 1942 at the rate of six a day, rising to nine, and similar flows developed from Birmingham and Portsmouth. East Anglian sidings received ¾ million tons of rubble over nine months.

After the foundations were laid, cement was required – over 500,000 tons of it. Each 150ft-wide runway required 640,000 sq yds of concrete, and between August 1943 and March 1944, 900 trains of cement were run to distribution centres, from which daily requirements would be dispatched. That was followed in July 1943 by 40 special trains carrying 14 million bricks from Bedfordshire to the airfield sites, and finally 3,000 tons of tarmac a day were taken from the Midlands to East Anglian airfields.

By the time the bomber airfields were built and equipped with hangars, Nissen huts, petrol tanks and electricity and water supplies, about 20 million tons of materials had been delivered. Construction teams and then ground staff were conveyed to the East Anglian airfields; within two years from the autumn of 1942, the LNER ran 460 special trains for 167,000 personnel.

The next demand on the railways was the means to carry out a bombing raid. Whole trains of bombs became the norm as the number of aircraft in a raid increased, and in the three months after D-Day 30,000 wagons in 600 trains delivered 250,000 tons of bombs to just three centres. One of them cleared 626 wagons in a day. A 1,000-bomber strike required 28 trains of petrol and 8 trains delivering 2,900 tons of bombs in 362 wagons. The heaviest raid by Bomber Command saw 10,300 tons of bombs dropped in 24 hours.

Probably the most remarkable wartime act of heroism by railwaymen occurred at Soham in Cambridgeshire on 2 June 1944, when the wagon next to the locomotive on a March to White Colne goods train via Ipswich and Marks Tey caught fire; the train was made up of 51 wagons of bombs, and they had passed the Soham distant signal when fireman James W Nightall first noticed the flames, probably caused by a hot axle-box. He uncoupled the wagon from the rest of the train and driver Ben Gimbert drew forward to the signal box to see if it was safe to proceed on to the single-line section on to Fordham and take the wagon clear of the town. As the driver and signalman were talking, the wagon of 40 500lb bombs exploded, creating a crater 64ft wide and 15ft deep.

Fig 4.32
A WD/GWR Dean Goods shunts wagons on to a US transport ship at an unknown location on the south coast. During the First World War, of the 62 Dean Goods taken over by the WD, one was fitted with pannier tanks and condensing gear. In the early days of the Second World War, the WD requisitioned 100 and then another 8 in December 1940 after the fall of France and the loss of the 79 engines which had already been shipped to France. No 179 (GWR No 2466) was 1 of 10 fitted with pannier tanks and condensing gear, and it may have been 1 of 4 sent to China under the United Nations Relief and Rehabilitation Administration programme.

The signal box and stationmaster's house were destroyed and 700 buildings in Soham damaged. Nightall was killed and Gimbert badly injured, but their action had saved the entire train from exploding, which would almost certainly have destroyed the town. Both men were awarded the George Cross, and Nightall's medal is on display at Soham Museum.

By September 1943 the LMS was running 908 trains of petroleum a month to the airfields from the Mersey and Severn ports through which most fuel was imported. The following month a pipeline from the Mersey opened as part of an 504-mile network of pipelines, reducing rail-borne traffic, though a record 1,579 trains of petroleum operated in the four weeks following D-Day.[127]

Military railways

Censorship prevented any mention during the war of the railways created for training or storage, though their size and the volume of traffic they generated must have made them common knowledge to local residents.

Longmoor continued its dominant role for the RE. Before the war the LMR had been extended: in 1933 a new line was built to join the SR at Liss. This helped cope with the rapid build-up of traffic through the creation of the large enclave around the Longmoor–Bordon area. At Longmoor alone 126 new units were formed, trained and dispatched to all parts of the globe. Track distance grew from 18 miles in 1939 to 71 miles in 1945. Thirty wagons a day would arrive at Bordon soon after the beginning of the war, rising to 74 a day by July 1942 and 184 at the year's end. Congestion prompted construction of the Liss interchange to create a north to south flow of wagons. By 1943 there were 275 external and 300 internal wagon movements a day, requiring up to 27 locomotives in steam.

By the end of the war more than one-third of the Royal Engineers were transportation troops, and most of those 76,000 had been trained at Longmoor and dispatched to all parts of the globe. Longmoor also saw contingents from Canada and the US and recruits from Poland, Czechoslovakia, Norway, the Netherlands and France. Paratroopers also came to Longmoor prior to railway wrecking assignments on the Continent, learning where best to place explosives on a locomotive. During the peak years of 1943–4, 42 trade training courses were run simultaneously, with as many as 900 people under training. A frequent comment by unit commanders was said to be: 'You can tell a Longmoor-trained sapper anywhere, but you can't tell him much.'

In the East Midlands, the Melbourne Military Railway was created out of the former Midland Railway branch from Chellaston Junction to Ashby-de-la-Zouch as an alternative training centre to the LMR. The branch was taken over from midnight on 19 November 1939. Initially goods services over the line continued to be operated by LMS staff, but the WD took over, working from exchange sidings at Chellaston. Six 1F 0-6-0 tanks were loaned by the LMS, supplemented by 16 other locomotives and a diesel. The branch and locomotives were handed back to the LMS on 1 January 1945.

Construction of the still-functioning Bicester Military Railway in Oxfordshire began in 1941 to serve a number of ordnance depots, and it took on the role of the main support base for operations on the Continent from 1943. Covering 12½ sq miles, its 40 miles of track were connected to the LMS Oxford–Cambridge line.

The Shropshire & Montgomeryshire Railway was taken over by the Government from June 1941 to serve the newly built Central Ammunition Depot Nesscliffe, constructed on four separate sites to reduce the risk of total catastrophe if an accidental explosion occurred. Each site could store around 50,000 tons of ammunition. The SMR was operated by the WD with a detachment of 193 Railway Operating Company, and its first task was to improve the track, which was described as being in a 'deplorable condition'.[128] The remedial work required up to five locomotives and a large number of ballast trains, which impeded military traffic. Passenger services for ordnance personnel were operated using the 16 passenger vehicles, and traffic was sufficiently heavy to require a night shift. US Army Transport Corps 2-8-0s were used on the line; No 1616 worked a Hookagate to Cardiff Docks train on 5 May 1943.

Some railways were taken over for training purposes. The Letterston Junction–Trecwn section of the North Pembrokeshire & Fishguard line was used to practise aircraft train-busting shoots. Maenclochog Tunnel on the same line was used to test a modified version of Wallis's bouncing bomb on 7 October 1943 with the inventor in attendance. It was intended to use it to penetrate tunnels and collapse the structure.

Prisoners of war

The first train carrying enemy prisoners is thought to have run in September 1939 from Thurso with the captured crew of a U-boat. At the beginning of the war, most prisoners were airmen; officers were taken to Windermere for the officers' camp at Grizedale Hall, while other ranks were taken to Oldham for Glen Mill camp.

In July 1941, after the first successes in the North African campaign, four trainloads of Italian POWs were distributed around the Midlands for agricultural work. Special vestibule-type coaches were used so that an armed escort could stand at the end of each coach to prevent escape.[129] Italian POWs were also used at large LMS goods depots within 25 miles of a prison camp or hospital, though the regular staff at London, Birmingham, Crewe and Manchester strongly protested against working alongside POWs, and the practice was not enforced at those depots.[130] So many POWs arrived following successes in North Africa in June 1943 that 42 trains were required over three days from Clyde and Mersey ports.[131]

Between D-Day and the end of 1944, 765 loaded trains ran between ports and transit camps from where prisoners were dispatched for internment in Britain or overseas.[132]

After D-Day the main receiving port was Southampton, supplemented by Newhaven, Gosport, Tilbury, Purfleet and Portland. POWs were sent on to transit camps for initial sorting and cleansing, the main ones being at Kempton Park in Surrey for prisoners captured by British forces and Devizes for those captured by US forces. Another was later added at Moreton-in-Marsh. Prisoners were cleaned up before being sent on to internment camps, which required 683 special trains between D-Day and the end of 1944.

Following the surrender of 33 U-boat crews in the fjord of Loch Eriboll in Sutherland in May 1945, several trains were run to take the crews from Kyle of Lochalsh to Kempton Park.

Fig 4.33
German prisoners entraining
at a London station on
8 September 1943.

In October 1945, when evidence was being compiled for the trial of leading Nazis at Nuremberg, a party of 42 German generals travelled from London to Windermere, in first-class accommodation at the request of the War Office.[133]

Allied troop arrivals

The first Canadian troops arrived in December 1939 on the Clyde, requiring 17 trains to the south of England. The Clyde remained the principal port of entry until May 1940, when Liverpool was also used. Often the railway was not told which port a ship would use until it was in British waters, which required much long-distance empty-stock working despite the huge fleets of carriages then available.

But it was with the entry of the US into the war in December 1941 and the arrival of the first US troops from May 1942 that the burden on the railways steadily rose to the climax of D-Day. The Mersey ports were the main gateway, followed by the Bristol Channel and the Clyde, and from the beginning of 1943 the LMS ran about 30 trains a month from the docks. To help organise the routing of supplies from the US, railway officials were sent to America to advise on how to minimise land movements from the ports.

The first big convoy arrived in July 1943 and required 86 trains over three days to clear the personnel – 32 from the Mersey and 54 from the Clyde. The largest convoy was in October: over six days it required 86 trains from the Clyde, 88 from the Mersey and 35 from the Bristol Channel. Particular problems were experienced on the Mersey: ships had to wait at the mouth of the river for high tide, and gales and frequent fogs often hampered berthing.[134]

The LNER supplied 12 ambulance trains for the use of American forces in Britain. Each was hauled by a B12/3 4-6-0 locomotive, and two engine crews and a fitter were assigned to each train; they lived on the train and had 48 hours' leave each month. The trains were based at various depots on the GWR and SR and operated under US orders.[135] Drivers received 12 guineas a week and firemen 10 guineas, irrespective of the number of hours worked. A free pass was provided from the point at which the train was stationed to the crew's home depot. The trains were moving hospitals capable of carrying out operations, and the volunteer staff were fed by the American authorities and lived on the train.[136]

Besides troops and their equipment, locomotives also came across the Atlantic to docks at Cardiff, Birkenhead, Manchester, Glasgow, Hull and London, initially to augment the numbers in Britain and later to be deployed in France and elsewhere. Of 2,120 US Army Transportation Corps S160 class 2-8-0s, about 800 were shipped to Britain. The modifications required on arrival were supervised by the LMS but undertaken by all four railways. And all four railways received some of the 398 S160s put to work in Britain: GWR, 174; LNER, 168; LMS, 50; and SR, 6. A second batch of 358 came through western ports and were moved to the GWR's large shed at Ebbw Junction in Newport for both preparation and storage, though 43 were also dealt with at Doncaster Works. Similarly, 382 S100 0-6-0Ts were brought over for use on the Continent, but 24 were modified by a private contractor in space provided at Worcester shed. To replace some of its ageing shunting engines after the war, the SR bought 14 of them plus one for spares after some barely used S100s had been stored in sidings at Newbury Racecourse.

As D-Day approached, resources were even more heavily taxed. April 1944 was the heaviest month, when 559 trains were required. Gales sometimes delayed arrival, or ships had to wait for the tide, so timetables were frequently revised; one programme of 87 trains meeting a convoy split between the Clyde and Mersey was adjusted eight times. The largest 1944 convoy entailed 217 special trains split between the Clyde, Mersey and Bristol Channel on 21–6 February and required 334 locomotives, 447 sets of enginemen and 415 guards. The longest of the journeys was from Greenock to Blandford and involved five engines, eight sets of enginemen and five guards.[137]

An SR driver remembered going through the carriages of a US troop train they had just worked in search of half-consumed ration boxes, which often contained chewing gum and chocolate.

Overlord/D-Day

The transport requirements of the expeditionary force to North Africa in October 1942 were a rehearsal for the much greater demands of D-Day. A trial landing on the coast of South Wales in the summer of 1943 informed the loading requirements for ships as well as the supplies themselves. Training exercises for the invasion added to the railways' traffic, such as the catastrophic practice landings at Slapton Sands in Devon in April 1944, when Operation Tiger required removal of the civilian population and livestock and placed a major burden on the Kingsbridge branch.

The railways had to be made privy to the plans for the invasion of France, so that detailed planning and even testing of the logistics could take place. The four companies began planning under strict secrecy to coordinate the movements required, their sequence and the tonnages from depots to ports along the south coast, from Falmouth to Tilbury. Though D-Day was 6 June 1944, the official date on which concentration of troops began was 26 March, from as far afield as the Highlands. From that day until 24 June, the LMS alone ran 13,729 trains in conjunction with D-Day and other military traffic. An LMS district controller at a key point handling 150 extra specials a day acknowledged with characteristically British understatement that 'we were nicely busy'.[138]

Complete trains of coaches were assembled at strategic locations for the process of moving troops to invasion marshalling centres near the coast. From 26 March 1944 the railways ran 24,439 special trains of troops, ammunition and equipment, largely for D-Day. Planning was complicated by the US forces having a separate command.

South Wales ports were fed with 33,000 tons of steel for fabrication of Mulberry harbours. After testing between Swansea and Watermouth in Devon the concept of an oil pipeline, construction of Pluto (Pipe-Line Underwater Transportation of Oil/Pipe-Line Under The Ocean) added to traffic on the SR. Several pipelines were built, from Shanklin Chine on the Isle of Wight to Cherbourg, Walton-on-Thames to Lydd and Dungeness, where the pumping station masqueraded as a cottage, and Paddock Wood to Port Victoria.

Movement of stores and equipment began on 10 May 1944, in sequence for landing craft, followed by coasters and finally cargo ships, requiring 800 special trains carrying 7,000 vehicles, as well as 6,000 wagons by scheduled trains. Being out of gauge, tanks required special arrangements. Traffic grew to a crescendo in the weeks prior to 6 June, at 3,636 special trains in a single week, though the use of tarpaulins prevented many being aware of their cargoes. Huge stores were assembled around stations at Brockenhurst, Beaulieu Road and Lyndhurst, waiting to be loaded at the military port at Marchwood. Before the war, Dunbridge station between Salisbury and Southampton was accustomed to handling a heavy traffic in strawberries and about 180 wagons a month; having become the access point to the US Army depot at Lockerley with its 15 miles of sidings and 134 sheds, it handled 5,246 wagons in June 1944. Lydford on Dartmoor gained extra sidings to store supplies that would be shipped through Plymouth. The flexibility of routing trains over the GWR and SR lines through Devon was increased by three new connections put in at Launceston, Lydford and St Budeaux near Plymouth, specifically to help with D-Day traffic. Tunnels on the Chichester–Midhurst line, which had lost its passenger service in 1935, were used to stable ammunition trains. Around Southampton alone there were 499,000 British and 2,340,000 US soldiers and 1,412,000 tons of stores.[139]

D-Day (6 June 1944) marked the start of the busiest four weeks in the history of Britain's railways, when 17,500 special trains for troops and stores were operated. Between D-Day and 31 December, 14,763 special freight trains were run over British railways, according to War Office figures. Sometimes whole trains had to be stabled for a day before they could be received at a port. Between D-Day and VE Day (8 May 1945), Southampton Docks saw the passage of 364,350 British and 2,165,883 American troops and 310,113 POWs.[140] Others left for France through Newhaven and Lymington. Littlehampton concentrated on ammunition, Poole on petrol for the US forces, and Hamworthy on fuel for British troops.

Until all forces had returned home after the liberation of the Continent, there was a constant stream of supplies to the 15 ports channelling matériel to

US forces and the 10 different ports supplying British and Empire forces. Each week a programme of stores trains was drawn up at a War Office conference attended by all four railways. Every evening at 7 pm adjustments were made to the next day's schedules. A growing number of trains were devoted to foodstuffs for liberated populations; from D-Day to VE Day the LNER ran 650 special trains of potatoes for the Ministry of Food and the military authorities. Some of the food was dropped from planes as supplies for paratroopers.

Supply ships returned with more traffic for the railway. Many of the wounded came through Southampton, enough to warrant 104 ambulance trains in June and 115 the following month. They also came through Tilbury, where hospital ships were usually met by four ambulance trains, two at Riverside station and two at Shoeburyness. Though notionally running non-stop to the base hospitals, the officer-in-charge sometimes required water en route, which caused inevitable delays to other services. As a 17-year-old railwayman, Cyril Powell remembered:

> ... hospital trains used to come into [Manchester] Victoria Station at around 1am and 2am on the long platform, No 11, which connected Manchester Victoria and Manchester Exchange. The trains were around 12 coaches long and had been specially adapted for stretchers. The wounded were taken off the trains and lined up on the platform. Ambulances would drive onto the platform and load up. Single-decker buses would take the walking wounded. They would then drive along the No 11 platform and go out at Manchester Exchange. By 4am, you wouldn't know anything had ever been there.[141]

Soldiers on leave began returning in December, the British through Dover, Folkestone and Harwich, and US troops through Southampton. By VE Day, 1,881 leave trains had been run.

The first liberated British POWs arrived in the Clyde on 15 September 1944, to be forwarded in four ambulance trains and one ordinary train to different reception camps. This was the start of a steady stream, though most were brought home by air before distribution by train. Some arrived in the Mersey in February 1945, 'most of them in sorry plight', and were taken by ambulance train to Watford, Oxford and Aldershot. One reception camp for them was set up at Beaconsfield, where they were processed and sent home on leave as quickly as possible. The LMS ran 83 special trains carrying 26,592 former POWs between 10 April and 1 June.[142]

Flying bombs

Exactly a week after D-Day, the first V-1 rocket landed on London, hitting the LNER's Grove Road bridge in Stratford at 4.21 am on 13 June 1944. From the night of 15/16 June until the end of August there was hardly a let-up in the onslaught, the SR receiving the brunt of the V-1 'doodlebugs', with 528 landing on its property. The LNER suffered 226 hits, the LMS 126 and the GWR 45. The alerts caused by pilotless aircraft were often of exceptionally long duration, sometimes all night, which caused considerable strain. The only consolation for those on rooftop spotting duty was that the doodlebugs were easily distinguished by their flame.

The SR logbooks documenting every instance of bomb damage had to be brought back into use after the number of conventional bombing incidents had dwindled to the occasional incident. Though the capital was the principal target of rockets, rural damage was caused by RAF planes successfully shooting down flying bombs before they reached the target. On 11 July 1944 'a flying bomb was exploded in the air by gunfire from a plane about a quarter of a mile from Robertsbridge Station on upside, and caused windows to be broken in down side waiting room.' Two days later a flying bomb was shot down by an Allied plane and exploded ¼ mile from Galley Hill Sidings signal box near Bexhill: 'Twelve panes of glass in the box broken and one window frame damaged. Six slates on roof of box loosened.'[143]

Fig 4.34
LNER B12 passes where a flying bomb landed between London Liverpool Street and Stratford. The pale keys in the rail chairs indicate the replaced sections of track.

During July bombs either falling short or shot down caused damage at Hawkhurst, Appledore, Lydd Town, Sandling Junction, Marden and Goudhurst. Even remote Horsted Keynes station had windows broken from a flying bomb, on 8 August 1944, and again the following day when a flying bomb was shot down near the station, which caused broken windows at 1, 3, 5 and 6 Station Cottages and a cracked window in the Pullman car *Calais*.[144]

The most serious railway incident also occurred in rural Kent, on 16 August 1944, when at about 4.50 pm a flying bomb was diverted from its trajectory by a Canadian pilot 'flipping' the missile with the wing tip of his Tempest fighter. He had been chasing the V-1 from the Kent coast and was horrified to see the bomb descend to hit bridge No 181 at Upchurch, between Rainham and Newington, just as King Arthur class locomotive No 806 *Sir Galleron* was approaching with the 3.35 pm Victoria–Ramsgate train of 10 coaches and a van. The bridge collapsed after the locomotive and the first carriage had crossed it. The locomotive ended up on its side across the up line, and the second and third coaches telescoped, hanging over the bridge. Four bogies were ripped from the coaches and fell into the roadway. Fireman D Humphrey received particular praise for heading towards Newington, despite bad cuts, to prevent the up train proceeding. Two doctors and some medical orderlies in the up train halted by the signalman at Newington were soon on the scene. Broken doors were used as improvised stretchers by a warden and policeman who arrived within two minutes, and the stationmaster from Newington was soon in attendance with ambulances. Both the driver, who sustained shock, and the injured fireman were taken to hospital. Of the 400 or so passengers, 7 were killed, as well as lengthman Sub-Ganger Arthur Naylor, who was sheltering under the bridge. Permanent Way Inspector Bishop and 15 passengers were badly injured; 21 passengers had slight injuries. Coincidentally the SR general manager, Sir Eustace Missenden, was on the train, but was uninjured. Steam cranes from Ashford, Redhill and Bricklayers Arms were sent to the scene, and the locomotive was re-railed by 10 am the following day. On the 18th preparations were made to install new bridge girders, and the up and down lines reopened for traffic by noon on the 19th, 66 hours after the incident.

The ability of engineers to effect quick repairs after V-1 explosions was little short of heroic; when the viaducts carrying the District and Piccadilly lines between Hammersmith and Ravenscourt Park were so badly damaged that many expected the lines to be closed for weeks, engineers managed to get trains running the next day, albeit at 5mph.

Between 13 June and 31 August, 54 railway men and women were killed on duty, and 1,282 injured. By 14 September 1944, 12 staff and 35 passengers on the SR had been killed by rockets; 487 electric vehicles had been damaged and 10 destroyed, which represented 15.98 per cent of the SR's total stock; and 242 steam passenger carriages had been damaged and 10 destroyed. On 25 June 1944 the former London Chatham & Dover Railway general offices at Victoria were extensively damaged, and the Royal Waiting Room was destroyed.[145]

Among the long list of purely factual notes on damage and remedial measures in the SR logbook, the compiler felt compelled to add a unique personal note on 29 June 1944:

> As in the days of the Blitz, the conduct of the Southern Railway staff has been beyond praise. In fact, it is probably no exaggeration to say that the sight of ordinary Railwaymen and women steadily and calmly carrying out their day-to-day duties – manning and dispatching trains, collecting tickets, shunting, patrolling the lines – often in exposed places, is a source of inspiration to many thousands of other workers as they set forth to take up their allotted tasks each day.[146]

Thousands of barrage balloons were brought to London from every part of England, as were many heavy guns, including 76 in 5 trainloads from Scotland. Barrage balloon cables were a constant trial in the SR area, causing short circuits or getting entangled in signals and telegraph wires and sometimes necessitating the third-rail power to be shut off to remove them. Anti-aircraft guns also needed repositioning, first to the south-east and then to East Anglia as Allied forces overran the French launch sites and the targets within range of the V-1s changed.

The V-1s caused a second mass evacuation from the capital, which began on 5 July and ended on 8 September, by which time 2,345 extra trains had been run to take women and children to greater safety in the Midlands, the north and the West Country. It was much less orchestrated than the 1939–40 evacuations; with many adults choosing to leave it was therefore harder to plan, and trains often carried three times as many people as seats. This time the London termini were used rather than suburban stations, but there were also many special trains from Kent and Surrey; some routes were undoubtedly without precedent, such as Malling to Torquay, Eynsford to St Austell and Hever to Newton Abbot.

The first V-2 landed in Chiswick on 8 September 1944, but the mobile launch sites were soon moved to the Netherlands. This had the effect of transferring the brunt of the rockets from the SR to the LNER area, including Norwich. By the time the last V-2 rocket had landed on London on 27 March 1945, 91 people had been killed on railway property and 2,815 coaches had been hit, of which 90 were scrapped. The worst loss of life was at a SR block of flats in Deptford which killed 51 railwaymen and their families. The greatest damage was done by a bomb on the east side of Charing Cross Bridge on 18 June 1944, which took three months to repair. As the Germans lost control of land within firing range, the evacuated had to be brought home again. Anti-aircraft gun units were disbanded and the weapons taken to Arrowe Park, Birkenhead, and from there 1,300 guns had to be moved to Sudbury in Derbyshire when Arrowe Park was derequisitioned.[147]

The finale

The end of the war with Germany did not bring an immediate relief from its logistic pressures. Japan had yet to surrender and munitions were still being moved, quite apart from the trains devoted to demobilised troops and the repatriation of POWs. For example, 720 wagons in 18 trains were loaded with bombs at the US depot at Kimbolton in Huntingdonshire for ports in South Wales and dispatch to the Far East before Japan surrendered. The progressive closure of WD depots meant the transfer of stocks to those remaining open or the movement of supplies for return to the US; the depot at Ashchurch dispatched 122 trains of US stores to South Wales ports and Birkenhead Docks for repatriation.[148]

The recovery of services was quick. Restaurant car services were reinstated on 1 October 1945 in a limited way – the LMS resumed services on 40 main line trains on weekdays and 6 on Sundays, but rationing became more severe in the post-war years so the fare was limited – customers could have a slice of bread or potatoes (often a potato substitute) but not both. Yet by New Year's Eve 1945 the GWR managed to put roast pheasant, Brussels sprouts, parsnips julienne and potatoes on its menus, preceded by cream of vegetables and concluded with Christmas pudding and ice cream; price 3/6 plus service.

Pre-war traffics slowly resumed: the first boatload of bananas arrived at Avonmouth docks on 31 December 1945. This required the reconditioning of 1,500 vans with special steam-heating pipes to continue the ripening process.[149]

Evacuated artefacts and ministries had to be returned. The process of sending back about 2,000 pictures to the National Gallery began on 12 June 1945 and was completed on 4 December. Pictures of 'ordinary dimensions' were packed in covered containers, loaded at Blaenau Ffestiniog and conveyed by passenger and parcels trains to Willesden and thence by freight trip to Camden Goods station for carting to the gallery. At the gallery's request only one container a day was sent for 88 days, because of the capacity for its reception. The larger paintings had to be conveyed by well wagons specially fitted with steam brake pipes, screw couplings and longitudinal timber baulks. The Tate's pictures, evacuated to Muncaster Castle in Cumberland, Eastington Hall in Worcestershire and Hellens in Herefordshire in August 1939, were returned by containers in December 1945.[150]

The Inland Revenue had decamped to Rhyl and Llandudno and required 72 containers and 2 wagons for its return to London in August; the Ministry of Food was brought back from Colwyn Bay by 80 containers in December.

The human cost aside, the principal consequence of the wars for the railways was their competitive position vis-à-vis road transport. Both wars

Fig 4.35
Works returning to the Tate from storage in Piccadilly Underground station in 1946. The painting in the foreground is a 1940 work by Edward Burra, of unknown title.

released a flood of surplus lorries bought up with demob pay at a time when the railways had years of maintenance and investment to make up. On the LMS there were 109 instances of broken rails on the main line south of Carlisle over the last three months of 1945, 11 locomotive derailments in the shed yard at Edge Hill during October and November because of the poor state of the track, and 77 track-circuit failures between Euston and Watford over two consecutive days in November.[151]

The SR war damage claim, lodged in November 1947, was £9,710,499, after depreciation on the total cost of making good or value payments of £11,153,692. The largest sums related to Southampton Docks, the General Offices at London Bridge and Waterloo York Road, and the main station building block at Holborn Viaduct.[152]

The achievement of the railways during the war was perhaps best summed up by the journalist Lord Castlerosse: 'England expects the railways to do their duty and the impossible.'[153]

5 | Second World War theatres

The role of railways overseas during the Second World War was very different from the First, and consequently so too were the demands placed on the RE and railway units. In no theatres was there a repetition of the almost stationary attrition of the Western Front, which had created both the need for huge supply depots and the repetitive transport flows to sustain them. Until D-Day most of the work by the RE was inevitably outside Europe; after it, train ferries shuttled locomotives and wagons across the Channel to help with the reconstruction of railways as the armies pushed eastward.

In an echo of the First World War pals battalions, some regiments were formed by railway companies, such as the 84th (London Transport) Heavy Anti-Aircraft Regiment of the Royal Artillery, which saw service in Norway, Libya, Tripolitania and Italy with the 8th Army and in North Africa with the 1st.[1] But there was no repeat of the First World War's patriotic fervour and rush to enlist,

Fig 5.1
A French 0-6-0 draws a diesel-electric ashore from the SR train ferry *Twickenham Ferry*, built by Swan, Hunter & Wigham Richardson in 1934 (below). The vessel was converted to a minesweeper based at Southampton and then the Irish Sea, but by November 1944 had returned to its original function, shuttling locomotives and trains across the Channel to Calais. The gantry crane was designed to lift locomotives up to 84 tons and was fitted by Cammell Laird at Birkenhead. A gantry was also fitted to her two sister ships until removal in 1947.

and the 'reserved occupation' status of the majority of railwaymen in Britain cut the number in national service to about 100,000, almost half the earlier total. Many of the 44,375 LMS staff who joined the services found themselves in the construction companies of the Royal Engineers. British railway units worked in Palestine, Sicily, Italy and Egypt.

Soon after war was declared, GWR Dean Goods 0-6-0s were put through Swindon and Eastleigh Works for service abroad with WD on the tenders. Some of those overhauled had already seen overseas service during the First World War. But the principal locomotive design for overseas service outside Europe was William Stanier's LMS 8F 2-8-0: before the end of 1939, 100 were ordered from North British, 100 from Beyer Peacock and 40 from Vulcan Foundry. It was expected that they would be driven by British crews and were received in the following numbers (some were lost at sea): Egypt, 42; Iran, 143; Iraq, 10 transferred from Iran; Italy, 10 transferred from Egypt; and Turkey, 25 by sale; some found their way to Palestine from Egypt. Desert sand, poor coal and overloaded trains often reduced even such locomotives as Stanier 8Fs to ignominy. In August 1945 the condition of one was so bad that it took 11½ hours to cover the 195km from Kantara to Cairo, albeit with 650 tons.

Railway workshops also turned out wagons for various theatres, as they had in the First World War. Ashford Works made 1,000 open 13-ton wagons to supply the Soviet Union through the Persian Gulf. They were made in under 10 weeks and supplied as 1,792 numbered components, which were put together in three-quarters of an hour once the assemblers got the hang of it.[2]

Overseas theatres

Until D-Day there was no call for railway expertise on the Continent, but railway units had plenty to occupy them before attention turned to the reconstruction of railways in France. The much greater reliance on oil compared with the First World War made Middle East supplies a deciding factor in strategy. The aim of the German *Drang nach Osten* had partly been to capture Russian oilfields at Maikop and Grozny and the Azerbaijan field at Baku; the British and Russian response was to invade Iran in August 1941, in part to protect the oilfields of that country and Iraq. Allied victories in North Africa and Stalingrad more or less ended the Axis threat to these oil supplies.

Towards the end of 1941, British railway units took over operation of the Trans-Persian Railway, which delivered oil to the Gulf, running for about 925km to Tehran, where they handed over to Russian control. Completed in 1938, the single-track Trans-Iranian Railway linked the Caspian Sea at Bandar Shah with the Gulf at Bandar Shahpur, crossing nearly 5,000 bridges and 133 tunnels, and twice reaching an altitude of nearly 7,000ft in the Zagros Mountains of Loristan Province and the Elburz Mountains.[3] There were long stretches of 1 in 36 gradients and spirals reminiscent of Switzerland's Rhätische Bahn. In places the summer heat was appalling, particularly for about 240km from the Persian Gulf until the railway climbed steeply to reach places where it could be minus 20°C. Tenders were painted white to reduce heat from the sun.

The line had a capacity of just two trains a day when the RE took over, with 80 per cent of the locomotives out of service and many wagons in need of repair. New wagons arrived, but they either had no brakes or had inadequate ones for the gradients, which limited train weights. New equipment was supplied, including LMS 2-8-0 locomotives, but the brutal operating and climatic conditions of the railway, coupled with hard water that 'furred' the boilers, made steam locomotives highly unsuitable, and diesel-electric locomotives were introduced by the US Army Transportation Corps, which took over operations from the RE in December 1942. By installing new passing loops and sidings, the RE increased the daily tonnage from 200 to 1,530 tons.[4] The line had to be protected by Indian troops and every train had an armed guard.

In Iraq the RE restored the line from Basra to Baghdad and Mosul, with links to Turkey and Syria.

In Egypt the Western Desert Railway from Alexandria to Mersa Matruh was extended towards Bomba via Capuzzo and Tobruk, principally by the New Zealand Railway Construction Group, which achieved tracklaying at the rate of 3.2km a day. The dearth of water necessitated construction of a parallel pipeline to supply water for the locomotives.

The burdens placed on Indian railways required an increase in staff, and training of new recruits was in the hands of RE transportation officers from Longmoor (*see* p 154) or senior railway officials released from the Indian railway companies. During the first years of the war, before Japan entered the conflict, Indian railways concentrated on supplies to the Middle East. The danger of using the Mediterranean made it safer to rely on supplies through India's west-coast ports. This included track lifted for the purpose, as well as locomotives and rolling stock, together with units of railway operating and construction companies.

A main supply route through India was the critical 'Line of Communication' from Calcutta to Assam to supply the Chinese forces of Chiang Kai-shek fighting the Japanese. Never an easy route to operate with its change of gauge from broad to metre, a train ferry and steep gradients requiring banking locomotives, it became even harder with the coordinated attacks on the railway system in late 1942 by politically inspired agitators intent on disrupting the war effort. They

Fig 5.2
A train in the Persian desert, hauled by a Stanier 8F 2-8-0, in a painting by Norman Wilkinson (1878–1971), who was formally credited with the invention of dazzle camouflage during the First World War.

Fig 5.3
As this photograph at an unrecorded station on the Trans-Iranian Railway shows British and American personnel, it was probably taken around the end of 1942, when operation of the railway passed from British to American units. In 1941 the British 190 Railway Operating Company Royal Engineers was deployed to the railway.

were well planned, focusing first on block instruments and telephone systems, and then removing rails which were hidden in jungle or paddy fields. From 1944 American railway operating troops in the form of the Military Railway Service arrived to bolster staffing on the line, tearing up the rule book and running the railway as they thought fit.[5]

After D-Day there was no reliance on railways comparable with the First World War. The railways were in ruins because of Allied bombing of railway targets (preceded by dropping flares to give French railwaymen the chance to take cover), the destruction of key infrastructure by the French Resistance, and the use by retreating Germans of a large hook that gouged the track and broke up sleepers. The Germans also destroyed some major structures such as the bridge over the Loire at Montlouis on the Paris–Bordeaux line. These factors and the relatively fast progress of Allied forces across France placed a greater reliance on road transport. On D-Day some French cities were completely inaccessible by rail, such as Strasbourg and Rouen. As areas were liberated, French railwaymen were only too eager to assist Army engineers to rebuild structures and reopen lines, in which the US took a lead.

Railway ships

Railway steamers were again commandeered and some retained their peacetime crews. Of the railway fleet of 130 steamers, 92 had been requisitioned by 1944 by the Government for use as hospital carriers, transports, assault ships, minelayers and sweepers, ammunition carriers, ack-ack ships and rescue ships with Atlantic convoys.[6]

The last passenger sailing from France was made by a railway steamer when a ship built for the LSWR in 1911, SS *Hantonia*, left St Malo with passengers and troops and arrived safely at Southampton on 17 June 1940. The last vessel

Fig 5.4

An idea of the terrain through which the Trans-Iranian Railway passed can be gained from this photograph of WD S200 class 2-8-2 No 1066 at an unidentified station. The locomotive was built by Baldwin as part of an order in 1941 by the British Government under the Lend-Lease agreement for 200 locomotives, of which 91 were sent to Iran. Four were lost at sea. They were erected in Iran by British and American engineers at Ahwaz Works. The locomotive became Iranian State Railways No 42450.

to leave France was another railway steamer, the former LYR SS *Hodder* of 1910. It had been sent to assist the evacuation, but arrived to find all troops had left, so she took in tow a disabled Admiralty store vessel laden with petrol and ammunition, and brought it safely to port.[7] The LMS lost one of its vessels at Dunkirk, the TSS *Scotia*, on 1 June, on its second trip to the beaches. A bomb went down the funnel and exploded in the boiler room.

The last sailing from St Peter Port on Guernsey was by the SR SS *Isle of Sark*, which left at 10 pm for Southampton on 28 June 1940 with 647 people on board. While in dock, there had been a one-hour raid earlier in the evening in which the port was strafed and bombed. According to the *Bournemouth Daily Echo*, 'Captain Golding walked along the decks keeping everybody as calm as possible. His presence was felt immediately wherever he went, and in my [the reporter's] judgment he was largely responsible for the steadiness of the crew, the passengers and the people on the quayside.'[8]

Two GWR ships were lost. The *St Patrick* was attacked twice between Fishguard and Rosslare and finally sunk on 13 June 1941, while the *St David* was sunk off Anzio in January 1944 while serving as a hospital carrier.

Empire railway workshops

Railway workshops around the empire contributed matériel. The Angus Shops of the CPR in Montreal made 1,400 Valentine tanks for the Soviet Army. In India the Eastern Bengal Railway workshops at Kanchrapara north of Calcutta were entirely handed over to war production, such as gun platforms, hand grenades, armoured vehicles and heliograph stands. That is until the Japanese overran so much of South East Asia and threatened India – the likelihood of invasion was considered so great that the machinery in the Bengal Assam Railway workshops at Pahartali near Chittagong was moved to a safer place.[9]

6 | In memoriam

The railways already had experience of commemorating staff who had died in war, following the memorials created after the Boer War. A tablet was unveiled in the Great Hall at Euston by Lord Roberts on 23 April 1903 in memory of 99 LNWR men who died in that war, during which £19,000 was paid to the families of the 1,760 men who went to South Africa.[1] Two memorials are known to survive, at Derby and Crewe.

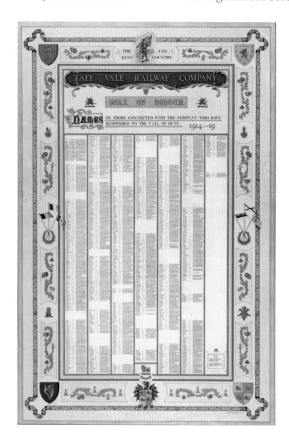

Rolls of honour

During the First World War it became common practice to erect in a prominent place at railway stations rolls of honour listing the fallen or men who had joined the forces. The company with the largest number of surviving rolls is the GWR, which placed them on many of its stations. Some were a plain list with a garlanded border. The framed and glazed LYR's rolls on ornamental card listed the names of the men, their former railway role, and the name of the regiment or ship to which they were attached. They were exhibited at almost every station on the system. The LYR also produced a printed version in October 1915 for 1914–15 with the same information plus the percentages of enlisted men from each department. At the back was a list of those reported missing and POWs and those who had lost their lives.

In the National Railway Museum collection are scrolls that were issued to employees of the Barry Railway and the NSR, which regularly updated its rolls. The Midland Railway produced a souvenir *For King and Country* listing its 7,531 men who had joined the colours up to 18 November 1914, together with the names of those in the casualty lists.

A variation was the LSWR's *Deeds of Valour* poster of 1916, listing seven men and their decorations and a brief description, such as:

> Morgam, A.W. Porter, Stores Dept., Nine Elms. Lance-Corporal, Yorkshire Regiment, awarded Military Medal. On the 5th July 1916, when the Horseshoe Trench [near Contalmaison on the Somme] and its vicinity were being heavily shelled by the enemy after its capture, Lce-Cpl. Morgan laid a telephone wire to Battalion Headquarters under heavy fire in the open and four times went out to repair it during heavy Bombardment. (Afterwards killed in action).[2]

Some were produced after the war had ended, such as that designed by Harry Furniss, who had worked for *Punch* magazine. It featured a border of local buildings and railway scenes, surmounted by a Shakespeare seated on a bardic throne, with the names, regiments and home locations of those who served in the centre. A digital replica by the Railway Heritage Trust of the only known surviving SMJR Roll has been displayed at Stratford-upon-Avon (former GWR) station since 2014. The GWR and LYR are also known to have produced post-war rolls.

Locomotives

As soon as the First World War was declared, various locomotives whose names had Germanic links were hastily renamed, so the GWR renamed Star class *Knight of the Black Eagle* as *Knight of Liège*. Rather oddly the LNWR put a red line through the name *Germanic* and fitted above it a plate reading *Belgic*. The LNWR named locomotives to honour living and dead war heroes, including *General Joffre* and *Edith Cavell*. The latter was used by Rugby shed staff on the first anniversary of her execution to raise funds for the Rugby Prisoners of War Fund, by decorating the Prince of Wales class 4-6-0 with flowers and placing her in a siding beside a road with a collecting box. The LNWR also honoured the

Fig 6.2 (below)
The Stratford-upon-Avon & Midland Junction Railway Roll of Honour. The illustrations emphasise the Shakespeare connections, and show a wounded railwayman returning to duty at the bottom right-hand corner. Enough were produced to hang in every SMJR station.

Fig 6.3 (below right)
Many departments created their own memorials, in addition to the railway company's official commem-oration. An unusual example, in that it includes photographs of six men who had died, was made by the GWR Sheet Department at Worcester.

GER's ship captain, Charles Fryatt (*see* p 65), by naming a 'Claughton' after him, as well as various notable ships which had been sunk, such as the *Lusitania* and its own *Hibernia*. After the war the NBR named locomotives after battles and Allied commanders such as Verdun, Somme, Maude, Petain and Haig, curiously choosing the predominantly goods engine class of J36 0-6-0s on which to bestow the honour.

Three companies chose to commemorate their fallen colleagues by naming a locomotive, either in a collective manner or, uniquely in the case of the LNWR, after individuals who had received the highest decoration, the Victoria Cross. LNWR Claughton class No 1914 was named *Patriot – In Memory of the Fallen L&NWR Employees, 1914–1919* in 1920 and japanned a dull jet black. The background colour of the numberplate was black rather than the usual red, and no LNWR crest was applied. The LMS withdrew the Claughton in July 1934, but the shortened name *Patriot* was given to the first of a new class of 4-6-0, the first two of which used some parts from Claughtons. No 5500 *Patriot* gave its name to the Patriot class of 52 locomotives. At the time of writing, the LMS-Patriot Project is building a replica, to receive the name *The Unknown Warrior*.

The LNWR also named Claughton class locomotives after its three employees who won the VC: *L./Corpl. J.A. Christie, V.C., Private E. Sykes V.C.* and *Private W. Wood V.C.* Lance Corporal John Alexander 'Jock' Christie, who had been a parcels clerk at Euston, won his decoration for using a supply of bombs to halt a counter-attack by the enemy at Fejja in Palestine. Sykes, a platelayer at Micklehurst, was honoured for rescuing wounded men near Arras while under machine-gun fire. Wood, an engine cleaner at Stockport Edgeley shed, won his VC in Italy when, armed with a Lewis gun, he enfiladed an enemy machine-gun nest and in two subsequent actions caused 140 and then 163 of the enemy to surrender.

Christie did not return to railway service, but the LNWR nonetheless named No 1407 after him, but on withdrawal of the Claughtons the name was not

Fig 6.4
LNWR Claughton 4-6-0 No 1407 was named *L./Corp*[l]. *J.A. Christie VC*, one of three Claughtons named after company employees who had won the highest decoration for bravery.

transferred to Patriot class locomotives, unlike those of the other two LNWR VC holders. This omission was rectified in 2014 when a plaque was unveiled inside Euston station by Christie's son, Ken.

In 1920 the GCR named 9P 4-6-0 No 1165 *Valour*. The shield-shaped nameplate was also inscribed 'In memory of GCR employees who gave their lives for their country 1914–1918.'

The LBSCR named the last locomotive built by the company in 1922 before it became part of the SR, 4-6-4 class L tank locomotive No 333, *Remembrance*. It was rebuilt as a class N15X 4-6-0 tender locomotive and renumbered 2333 by the SR and was again renumbered by British Railways as No 32333. It carried rectangular dedicatory brass plaques on the cabside, which were moved to the central wheel splasher after rebuilding. The plates read: 'In grateful remembrance of the 532 men of the L.B. & S.C. Rly who gave their lives for their country 1914–1919.' The name was painted on the tank sides, but later straight brass nameplates (one now in the National Railway Museum) were added, to be replaced after rebuilding by a curved one on the central wheel splasher.

During the Second World War the GWR and SR named or renamed locomotives to honour the services or their equipment. The GWR renamed some of its Castle class 4-6-0 locomotives after fighter and bomber planes, such as *Hurricane*, *Blenheim*, *Defiant* and the American-built *Lockheed Hudson*. Appropriately given its geographical coverage, the SR named most of its Battle of Britain class Pacifics after RAF squadrons, airfields and their planes, with a few celebrating key RAF figures such as Sir Keith Park and Sir Trafford Leigh Mallory.

Memorial locomotives have been created a century after the conflict. The GCR's chosen name has been perpetuated by a GB Railfreight diesel, No 66715, which was first named *Valour* in 2003 to mark the rededication of the GCR war memorial from beneath the Wicker Arch in Sheffield to the square in front of the Royal Victoria Holiday Inn (*see* p 178). On 11 November 2016 Freightliner class 66 No 66418 was unveiled with the nameplate *Patriot In Memory of fallen Railway Employees*, attended by the grandson of Private W Wood, VC.

Company memorials

During the First World War 186,475 railwaymen joined the colours, and of those 18,957 were killed or died of their wounds, though the St Paul's Cathedral order of service has the caveat, 'Omissions from the list of names are occasioned owing to particulars not being available at time of going to press.' It is now accepted that the total was in excess of 21,000.

Railway companies large and small created memorials to the staff who had given their lives for their country. Some also chose to design memorials that honoured those who had fought, as well as the fallen. Though a few memorials had been created following the Boer War, there was uncertainty at some companies as to the most appropriate way to commemorate their staff's sacrifice.

A surviving letter from the LYR secretary, R C Irwin, dated 18 September 1919, suggests that some discussion took place between companies about memorials. Irwin asked the GCR whether a decision had been taken how to commemorate the war dead and, if so, what was proposed: 'We are considering a scheme under which the name of each employee who has lost his life in the War, numbering between 1,100 and 1,200 will be engraved in bronze and the estimated cost of the whole scheme will be about £5,000, which seems to me to be a large sum of money for this purpose.' The reply stated that though a subcommittee had been formed, nothing of a practical nature had been done.[3]

On 13 April 1920 Irwin wrote that they had decided on a cast bronze panel with a marble surround to be placed at Manchester Victoria at an estimated cost of around £5,500. LYR directors had evidently taken a different view of an appropriate cost from Irwin's. Bronze panels bearing the names of 1,465 men and incorporating the arms of Liverpool, Bolton, Preston, Bury, Halifax, Huddersfield and Bradford are flanked by the figures of St Michael and St George. They were cast by George Wragge Ltd at Wardry Works in Salford to a design by the LYR's architect Henry Shelmerdine. The service of dedication was held on 14 February 1922 with addresses by Earl Haig and Edward B Fielden, chairman of the LYR, and the Lord Bishop of Manchester. Music was provided by the Horwich Railway Mechanics' Institute Band.

One of the first memorials to be unveiled was the Metropolitan memorial on the approach to the eastbound Hammersmith & City/Circle line platform at Baker Street, two years after the end of the war, on 11 November 1920. Designed by a member of the company's staff, C W Clark, in white Carrara marble with flanking fluted Ionic columns, the panel of 136 names is surmounted by an allegorical group with a lion subjugating a snake. The inscription is among the more considered:

> The men from the service of the Metropolitan Railway Company whose names are inscribed below were among those who, at the call of King and country, left all that was dear to them, endured hardness, faced danger, and finally passed out of sight of men by the path of duty and self-sacrifice, giving up their own lives that others might live in freedom.
>
> Let those who come after see to it that their names be not forgotten.

Fig 6.5
The GNR and LNER war memorial was first erected at London King's Cross, but after relocation in 1973 only the 11 marble tablets listing the names of the fallen survived. In 2013 they were placed on the concourse at King's Cross with spacing and heights intended to echo John Singer Sargent's 1919 painting *Gassed*.

The unveiling was carried out by the company's vice chairman, Sir Clarendon Hyde. Besides the Baker Street memorial, funds were raised for an athletics ground on 13 acres of Metropolitan Railway land at Wembley, and a club or institute where staff could meet for social, educational and recreational purposes.[4]

Two railways chose to commemorate their fallen with an arch. The NSR created an elliptical arch of Hollington stone, from the quarries of Stanton and Bettany, at the entrance to Stoke-on-Trent station, with two attached bronze tablets listing in raised lettering the names of 146 men (6 others who died were inadvertently omitted, though this was rectified with an additional plate added in 2017). The memorial was unveiled by Lord Anslow, NSR chairman, on 15 August 1922.

The other was the LSWR, which created one of the most elaborate of all railway memorials, at Waterloo station. The Portland stone Victory Arch at Waterloo was designed by the LSWR's chief architectural assistant, James Robb Scott, who became the SR's chief architect. The arch has three groups of sculptural decorations: on the left-hand pylon is Bellona, goddess of war, clad in scaled armour astride the world, dealing death and destruction with naked sword and flaming torch; on the right-hand pylon is Peace with Victory enthroned upon the earth. The panel around the arch lists the countries where LSWR men

Fig 6.6
The LYR war memorial at the entrance to Manchester Victoria station, below a map of the company's network.

fought, while a seated Britannia fills a recess above the cornice. The names of the deceased railwaymen are shown on tablets inside the arch. The monument was commissioned from the architectural sculptors Farmer & Brindley of Lambeth, whose best-known work is decoration for London's Natural History Museum.

The GER chose the booking hall at Liverpool Street as the site for a large marble plaque, another created by Farmer & Brindley, at a cost of £3,326. The list of 1,100 names in 11 columns is surmounted by a segmental pediment with the GER coat of arms and flanked by marble columns. The unveiling on 22 June 1922 was overshadowed by the assassination of Field Marshall Sir Henry Wilson an hour after giving the principal speech. Two London-based members of the IRA shot him as he returned to his home at 36 Eaton Place. A memorial tablet to Sir Henry was placed close to the GER monument. The memorial was moved to the Liverpool Street entrance as part of the rebuilding of the station *c* 1990.

Unusually the LBSCR decided to erect memorials at three places. Bronze tablets designed by the company's architect C D Collins were fixed in decorative stonework and masonry at London Bridge, Victoria and Brighton stations. They were unveiled respectively on 5 October 1921 by the chairman, Charles Macrae, on the 8th, by the deputy chairman, Lord Henry Nevill, and on the 12th, again by the chairman. The text read:

> In honour of Five Thousand Six Hundred and Thirty-five Members of the Staff of the London Brighton and South Coast Railway who joined the Forces of the Crown during the War of 1914–1918, and of whom those whose names appear below gave their lives for victory in that great struggle to secure the Liberty of the World.

> 'Their name Liveth for Evermore.'

The SECR chose Dover as the site for its memorial. Near the seaward end of the train shed at Dover Marine is the memorial to SECR employees who served in the forces. Standing on a granite plinth, a soldier and sailor flank a woman representing 'Victory' and holding aloft the torch of truth. The bronze figures were sculpted by W C H King. The names of the 556 men who died are inscribed on the rear of the wall behind the group. To them were added the 626 SR men who died in the Second World War. The SECR memorial was unveiled on 28 October 1922 by R H Cosmo Bonsor, chairman of the SECR, and the Lord Bishop of Dover. There is also a SECR bronze plaque near the north entrance to Victoria station in London, with an SR addition after the Second World War.

The marble tablet forming the Barry Railway memorial in memory of the 65 employees who fell was sited at the eastern entrance to its headquarters at Barry Docks. The unveiling on 31 October 1922 was performed by the Earl of Plymouth (former chairman), supported by the Bishop of Llandaff, Viscount Churchill and Felix Pole.

The GCR subcommittee, comprising Lord Stuart of Wortley, Lord Kerry and Sir Sam Fay, chose Sheffield Victoria station as the most central location, and tenders were called to construct the design by Messrs Collcutt & Hamp of 20 Red Lion Square, London WC1, who were paid 7 per cent of the cost of the completed work above road level. The design was based on the Arc de Triomphe in the form of a detached screen of four twin Doric columns flanked by stone piers across the approach road. The entablature was made of Stoke Hall stone, and between the columns were nine panels of yellow French Echaillon marble bearing the names of the 1,302 fallen. 'Lord Faringdon particularly emphasised the fact that he wished all work in connection with the Memorial to be well executed, particularly the stonework details, marble panelling and lettering.' G Longdon & Son of Sheffield was awarded the contract and assurances were secured that a 'thoroughly satisfactory job of the Memorial could be made by the Firm for the amount of their tender'.[5]

Trains from all over the GCR network converged on Sheffield for the unveiling of the permanent memorial at the head of Sheffield Victoria station approach, alongside the Royal Victoria Station Hotel, on 9 August 1922. The trains from Manchester and London were hauled by B3 class 4-6-0s *Valour* and *Earl Haig* respectively. About 8,000 people attended the unveiling of the memorial by Earl Haig and listened to the address by the company's chairman, Lord Faringdon. Those who gained any decoration formed a guard of honour, wearing their medals, but the number of invitations had to be limited because of restricted space on Station Approach.[6]

Fig 6.7
The unveiling of the SECR war memorial at Dover Marine on 28 October 1922 by the company's chairman, R H Cosmo Bonsor.

Fig 6.8 (right)
The GCR war memorial
re-erected in 2003 near the
site of the company's Royal
Victoria Station Hotel.

Fig 6.9 (below)
The LNWR memorial outside
London Euston station,
which was in the centre of
Euston Square and on axis
with the demolished Euston
Arch.

However good the workmanship, within two years many of the names had become illegible, so the LNER replaced the marble in 1925 with Kupron bronze plaques with embossed letters. The memorial was moved to the eastern wall of the booking hall when the station was enlarged in 1938. When Victoria station closed in 1970, the memorial was nearly lost, but it was rebuilt under Sir John Fowler's Wicker Arch and rededicated in November 1971. Vandalism and neglect again jeopardised the monument. Thanks to an offer from the Royal Victoria Holiday Inn, formerly the Manchester, Sheffield & Lincolnshire Railway/GCR-owned Royal Victoria Station Hotel, the Great Central Railway Society was able to arrange the plaques' rescue and re-erection in 2003, facing down Victoria Station Approach only yards from their original site.

The HR's memorial on a bronze plaque outside Inverness station was unveiled on 6 August 1921 by General Lord Horne of Stirkoke.

Perhaps the most inexpensive memorial was created by the Furness Railway, at a cost of just £350, possibly because its setting was worked by the railway's own stonemasons. The bronze tablet made by the Birmingham Guild was set in sandstone from Hawcoat Quarry near Barrow. At the head of the tablet with lettering in relief is the FR coat of arms surrounded by a laurel wreath with the text 'This Tablet has been erected by the Directors and employees of the Furness Railway Company, in grateful remembrance of those members of the staff who laid down their lives for their country in the Great War, 1914–1919', followed by 68 names. It was erected in the booking hall of Barrow Central station and unveiled on 16 October 1921 by His Grace the Duke of Devonshire (chairman of the FR, 1908–15, when he became Governor General of Canada, and on the FR board from 1891).

One of the most elaborate memorials was created by the LNWR at Euston. Designed by Reginald Wynn Owen, the 13.7m-high Portland stone obelisk has a cross on each side with four bronze figures with bowed heads and reversed arms at the base representing the Navy, Infantry, Artillery Corps and the Royal Flying Corps. It cost about £12,500, of which the staff contributed about £4,000.[7] The statuary was produced by R L Boulton & Sons of Cheltenham to designs by Ambrose Neale. An album was presented to the nearest relative of all the fallen, listing the names, medals won and a breakdown of men by department, as well as an account of war work done by the LNWR.

The LNWR memorial unveiling on 21 October 1921 was probably the largest gathering for such an occasion. Special trains brought over 8,000 relatives and employees from Leeds, Manchester, Preston, Liverpool, Crewe, Wolverhampton and Northampton. Ernest Sykes, VC, of the Engineering Department at Mossley, held the wreath. A contingent of the company's employees formed a square around the memorial as the company chairman, the Hon Charles Lawrence, spoke and the Archbishop of Canterbury conducted the service. During his unveiling speech, Haig paid tribute to the work of nightly rebuilding narrow-gauge lines destroyed almost daily by German gunfire.

The Caledonian Railway's bronze memorial to its 706 fallen staff at Glasgow Central was unveiled on 15 November 1921, with a collecting box fashioned from shells. A plaque has been added, honouring Second World War casualties.

To commemorate the 2,833 Midland Railway staff who died, the company created a 31ft cenotaph on Midland Road adjacent to the Midland Hotel and station in Derby. Designed by Sir Edwin Lutyens, the cenotaph is surmounted by a catafalque on which lies a soldier, partly covered by a greatcoat, with helmet and bayonet at his feet and a lion's head at each corner. The Midland coat of arms is carved within a wreath. It was built by J Parnell & Son and cost £10,309. The names were originally engraved on the structure but they were replaced by bronze plaques, presumably because of erosion.

A service of dedication was held on 15 December 1921 when the memorial was unveiled by Charles Booth, Midland chairman, and the service was led by the Bishop of Southwell and Nottingham. It would have been impossible to accommodate the families of so many men at the service, so free travel to Derby was offered to parents, widows or children to see the memorial on a subsequent occasion. In common with many other companies, the Midland produced a Book of Remembrance which was sent to the families of all the men listed. The book gave the men's occupation, location on the railway, regiment and rank.

One of the smallest railway workshops in England was chosen as the location for the Somerset & Dorset Joint Railway memorial, at Highbridge, which was unveiled by company director Sir Alan Garrett Anderson and the Midland's CME Sir Henry Fowler. The memorial to the 13 dead and 153 who fought was designed by an apprentice and made at Highbridge Works. When the works closed in 1929, the memorial was moved to the Garden of Remembrance in the town's Southwell Gardens.

Given how many local war memorials chose the figure of a serviceman, usually a 'Tommy', it is surprising that only the GWR adopted this approach for its memorial at London Paddington. Dugald S MacColl, keeper of the Wallace Collection (and previously the Tate), wrote to the GWR's chairman, praising the company's decision to commission a figure from Charles Jagger: 'it is a rare event for a sculptor in this country to have genius and rarer that he should receive commissions'.[8]

Various ideas had been discussed – an arch on the approach to the station, a mural tablet at Paddington or smaller tablets at regional stations, a memorial

Fig 6.10
The Grade II* Midland Railway memorial on Midland Road in Derby.

on the western footbridge with the GWR arms inset into a section of Matthew Digby Wyatt's screen – but the favoured approach was 'a statuary design of an artistic character in some suitable and prominent position on No. 1 platform'.[9]

MacColl advised the GWR on the choice of Jagger's two sketches and models, preferring the 'Letters from Home' concept. The GWR toyed with the idea of a bas relief, but Jagger so disliked the idea that he felt he had best withdraw, whereupon the GWR board had second thoughts and persuaded him to continue with MacColl's recommendation. As part of the scheme, the royal arms and the GWR's coat of arms were carved by Jagger in oak, and the former was placed over the Royal Waiting Room on Platform 1, now the First Class Lounge.

Jagger had served in the Worcestershire Regiment at Gallipoli and on the Western Front, and was awarded the Military Cross during the German offensive of 1918, so it is not surprising that he was able to create such an intensely felt and moving sculpture. The figure wears a sheepskin jerkin, scarf and greatcoat loosely thrown over his shoulders with his head bent over a letter from home. The larger-than-life-size figure was cast at the Thames Ditton Foundry in Surrey, which had been casting ornaments and statues in bronze since 1874. He stands on a plinth of highly polished Aberdeen grey granite with a band of polished black Belgian granite, designed by Thomas S Tait, best known for the pylons of Sydney Harbour Bridge. Beneath the figure, in a hermetically sealed lead box enclosed within a gunmetal casket made at Swindon Works, is a Roll of Names of those who gave their lives. The total cost of the memorial was a relatively modest £4,625, though £5,625 had been authorised.[10]

The fourth anniversary of the end of the war, Saturday 11 November 1922, at 10.45 am, was chosen by the GWR for the unveiling of the memorial at Paddington. An address was given by the Archbishop of Canterbury and the unveiling was performed by the GWR Chairman, the Rt Hon Viscount Churchill. A stage was erected on Platforms 2 and 3, and large well-carriage trucks had been placed between Platforms 1 and 2 on which stepped platforms were constructed. The singing of 'Oh God, our help in ages past' was led by the GWR (London) Musical Society and the Swindon choir. Some 5,000 people attended the service; the nearest relative and another near relative of all who fell were invited, and refreshments were served in the general meeting room after the service.

The NBR war memorial at Edinburgh Waverley was unveiled by the Duke of Buccleuch on 12 March 1923. The 775 names are on a large plaque divided into three sections, with a cartouche of the company arms flanked by shields of the St Andrew's cross and the Scottish lion.

The process of creating memorials was often neither easy nor quick – some companies had vanished in the grouping before their memorials were unveiled – but few could match the difficulties encountered by the NER. The concept of a memorial at York was first discussed in April 1919, when it was agreed that 'the Memorial should be of an ornamental rather than of an utilitarian character'.[11] It was suggested that all members of staff should be invited to contribute to it, but in May the general manager reported that 'the proposal to invite contributions from [the staff] did not meet with general approval'. A subcommittee was appointed to consider the type and cost of a suitable memorial, and at the AGM on 20 February 1920 it was resolved 'to expend a sum not exceeding £20,000 for the erection of a suitable memorial'.[12]

Fig 6.11
The GWR war memorial at London Paddington is one of the most prominently placed of the company memorials, with thousands of passengers a day walking past it on Platform 1, underneath the former boardroom window.

Sir Edwin Lutyens, who was engaged in building New Delhi at the time, was commissioned as architect at a fee of £700 plus travelling and out-of-pocket expenses. However, the choice of a site close to the city walls, coupled with the relationship to the city's own war memorial which was also being designed by Lutyens, led to years of controversy. Even after a construction tender for £11,364 had been accepted in February 1922, further objections from the Ancient Monuments Board of England and the Archbishop of York were received, and were only resolved by a meeting of all parties, including Lutyens, in June. To limit encroachment on the mound beside the walls, he modified the design at the expense of the screen walls and therefore space for names. The tender was trimmed to £11,321 12s 9d and work began, which entailed removing the roof of the old station 'in the rear of the Memorial, so as to improve the view from Lendal Bridge'.[13]

The memorial was made of Portland stone with an obelisk 54ft high and wing walls terminating with large urns. The screen wall has panels with the names of the 2,236 NER men who lost their lives. Behind the Stone of Remembrance, 15 slate panels were added with the names of LNER staff who died in the Second World War. The names faded so badly that a bronze plaque was added in 2011, funded by BRB (Residuary) Ltd.

The York debate made the NER memorial one of the last to be unveiled, on 14 June 1924, at a ceremony conducted by the Archbishop of York, Cosmo Gordon Lang, with a host of mayors and railway officers including Sir Ralph Wedgwood, chief officer of the LNER. The former foreign secretary Edward Grey, 1st Viscount Grey of Fallodon, spoke and pointed out that 'the old North Eastern board and its general manager numbered some twenty persons. Out of those twenty, four lost sons in the war; three lost only sons. There is no reason to suppose that proportion is exceptional.'[14]

Funding was almost invariably provided by the railway company, but the joint lines could prove exceptions. Staff on the Shrewsbury & Hereford Joint (GWR and LNWR) each contributed 2/6, raising £136 15s, to which the Joint Committee added £151 5s to meet the estimated cost of £288 for a memorial at Shrewsbury station to the 42 fallen.

Local memorials

In addition to the company memorials, many railwaymen wanted more local tributes to their fallen colleagues and subscribed to them. With the approach of the centenary of the First World War, efforts were made to catalogue their whereabouts, usually not where they were first unveiled. The work was carried out by the Imperial War Museum and includes all war memorials; the constantly updated register has over 68,000 memorials. This total includes railway memorials, which have been documented by the Railway Heritage Trust and the results passed to the IWM. Not all are accessible to the public.

The majority of local memorials commemorated workshop staff. Staff at the LBSCR's carriage and wagon works at Lancing erected an obelisk of white marble and stone arising from the centre of curving supports, with a central panel bearing in bold letters the inscription: 'To our comrades who fell in the Great War 1914–1918.' Flanking panels of marble bear the names of 76 men of the Carriage and Wagon Department. The design was the result of a combination of suggestions, founded on a sketch by Alfred Gasston, a writer in the department. It stands on a plateau at the south end of the works in Bessborough Terrace, facing the entrance from the road along the seashore.

Mounted on the wall at the north end of Platform 1 at Derby station are brass plaques listing those who had worked at the Midland Railway Locomotive Works Nos 1, 4, 6, 7, 7a, 8, 9, 10, 11, 14, 16, 18, 19a, 19b, 20, 21 and 22 shops and the Chemical Laboratory. The Locomotive Department memorial plates were of standard design, but those for the Carriage and Wagon Department each illustrated the individual skills of the various shops; they are now in the Bombardier Litchurch Lane Works.

One of the most elaborate local memorials was created to commemorate the 21 members of the Midland Accountant's Department at Derby. The memorial tablet was enclosed in a massive frame of fumed oak, while the fallen are depicted in a group of photographs enclosed in a wreath of laurels. The Midland coat of arms surmounts the scroll. A symbolic figure of victory holding a palm guards the heroes, and the Dove of Peace wings its way through clouds above the devastated scene of the battlefields. A sheathed sword at the foot denotes

Fig 6.12
One of the larger local memorials was that created at the LYR's Horwich Works in Lancashire, which bore the names of 121 men who died. It was unveiled by the company's chief mechanical engineer, George Hughes, in August 1921. The sculptor was Paul Fairclough. Restoration of the granite plinth by the town council was funded by the War Memorials Trust in 2010.

the cessation of hostilities. The services were represented by the aeroplane, sea transport and the impedimenta of land forces.

Tablets were created for many of the shops at Swindon, such as Swindon A Erecting Shop, 19B Finishing Shop, Nos 3, 15, 18 and 19D shops in the Carriage and Wagon Department. Some of these can be seen on the walls of STEAM, the Museum of the Great Western Railway at Swindon.

Fig. 6.13 (right)
LNWR memorial at Crewe station dedicated to the men of Crewe North and South steam sheds who died in both wars. It bears the unusual inscription: 'We died in many lands that you may live in this.'

Fig 6.14 (below)
These replicas of locally sponsored GCR memorials in London were recreated by the Railway Heritage Trust and placed on the concourse at Marylebone in 2015.

A local LSWR memorial was created at the Strawberry Hill depot where 142 men had joined the forces and 19 had been killed. Unveiled on Armistice Day 1921, the roll of honour was flanked by a soldier and a sailor, a Urie G16 hump shunting tank and a bull-nose electric unit.[15]

Services of commemoration

Simultaneous services in memory of the almost 19,000 railwaymen of Great Britain and Ireland who died in the service of their country during the war were held at St Paul's and other cathedrals on Wednesday 14 May 1919 at 2.30 pm. The services were organised by the Railway Companies Association, and the back cover of the order of service bore the signature of Lord Bessborough as chairman and Viscount Churchill as deputy chairman. The order of service stated that '186,475 Railwaymen of Great Britain and Ireland, joined His Majesty's Forces, 18,957 of whom were killed in action, died of wounds, etc.' which was followed by a list of all who died, including their decorations, from the Alexandra (Newport & South Wales) Docks and Railway to the Wirral Railway. A separate insert remembered the name of the GER's steamship captain, Charles Fryatt, who was 'foully murdered by the Germans after the capture of his ship the SS *Brussels*', regarded as one of the worst atrocities committed against a serving railwayman.

The St Paul's service was attended by George VI, Queen Alexandra and Princess Victoria, as well as the chairmen of the leading railway companies, and representatives of colonial railways and the NUR and ASLEF. The address was given by the Right Revd the Lord Bishop of Peterborough, and it was the first time women had taken an active part in a service at St Paul's Cathedral, acknowledging the role of women on the railways during the war.[16]

Before the service a selection of appropriate music was played by an orchestra of 150, drawn from various railway companies, supplemented by drummers of the Grenadier Guards, conducted by Colonel W Johnson Galloway, a director of the GER. The *Railway Magazine* recorded that 'women instrumentalists were included – a recognition of the work of their sex upon our railways during the war'.

Concurrently services were held in the cathedrals of Birmingham, Bristol and Llandaff. Railway inspectors and guards in uniform acted as sidesmen.

Neglect and restoration

The record of looking after railway war memorials has been distinctly patchy, ranging from theft, disgraceful neglect and outright vandalism to admirable conservation and sensitivity. The greatest losses have been among those erected by the staff themselves, sometimes because the depot or building ceased to be used by the railway and no one took responsibility for finding a new home for a memorial. In other cases, and most shamefully, railway employees (and others) have profited from their sale as scrap.

But even some major memorials have disappeared, such as the Boer War memorials of the LNWR at Euston and GWR at Paddington, of which not even a photograph is known to exist, and the memorial unveiled in 1920 at Manchester Exchange station.

Station closures and redevelopment have naturally been the greatest threats to the very survival of some memorials. In some instances the negligent attitude to them has reflected badly on those responsible. The Railway Heritage Trust has been instrumental in saving a number of memorials from becoming casualties of neglect. In 1973 the GNR memorial at London King's Cross was dismantled and the panels, shorn of their decorative surround, relocated. During the most recent rebuilding of the station, the panels were placed in a more prominent position. The Trust has also funded replica memorials at Marylebone (GCR) and Manchester Piccadilly (LNWR).

Memorial gazetteer

This gazetteer lists all the British war memorials on the records of the Railway Heritage Trust (RHT), covering the official company memorials, regional company memorials usually subscribed by a department or a section of a workshop, and individual monuments. The UKNIWM (UK National Inventory of War Memorials) numbers were assigned by the project to record over 100,000 war memorials in the United Kingdom from all conflicts, ranging from a small plaque on the wall to a large town memorial. It has been renamed the UK War Memorials Register.

Town/city	Railway	Location	Memorial type/honouree(s)	UKNIWM reference
Aberdeen	GNSR	Passage from station to shopping arcade	Fallen GNSR employees	13431
Abergavenny, Monmouthshire	LNWR	Abergavenny Town Hall	Abergavenny locomotive depot	3625
Alrewas, Staffordshire	Various	National Memorial Arboretum	LNWR Audit Office	61164
			LYR Audit Account Office	61278
			LMS Chief Accountants Department (Audit Section), London	61280
			LBSCR Accountants Office staff	61088
Ashford, Kent	SECR	Library	Chief Mechanical Engineers Department	48023
			Staff who served	49022
Attenborough, Nottinghamshire	Midland Railway	Station	Replica of original memorial to station staff	65280
Attleborough, Norfolk		Station	Memorial to men of 452 Bomber Group (Second World War)	Not yet registered
Ayr (originally at Glasgow St Enoch)	GSWR	Station	Fallen GSWR staff	13354
Bangor, Gwynedd	LNWR	St David's Church	Railway Institute Boys' Corps (First World War)	51511
Barrow-in-Furness, Cumbria	Furness Railway	Barrow Central station	Fallen Furness Railway staff	4095
Barry, Glamorgan	Barry Railway	Barry Docks Offices	Plaque to Fallen	6635
			1915 Roll of Honour	61369
Belfast	Belfast & County Down Railway	Belfast Central station	Fallen BCDR staff	6226
Belfast	Great Northern Railway (Ireland)	Central station		6225
Belfast	Midland Railway (Northern Counties Committee)	Translink Railway workshops, Northern Ireland Railways		6188
Bere Ferrers, Devon		St Andrew's Church	NZ Expeditionary Force – railway accident at station (First World War). Plaque unveiled 2001	25998
Birkenhead, Merseyside	GWR	Station	Memorial to N Tunna, GC (Second World War)	61024
Birkenhead, Merseyside	GWR	Woodside Ferry Terminal	Memorial to N Tunna, GC (Second World War)	1952
Birmingham, West Midlands	GWR	Moor Street station	Roll of Honour	61044

Town/city	Railway	Location	Memorial type/honouree(s)	UKNIWM reference
Birmingham, West Midlands	Midland Railway	Saltley Train Crew Depot	Locomotive Depot memorial	68491
Birmingham, West Midlands	Network Rail	New Street station approach	Modern memorial listing names of those who fell from LNWR Goods Department; replica of original plaques too fragile to display	Not yet registered; original plaques 17327 and 61085
Brighton, Sussex	LBSCR and SR	Station	LBSCR staff who fell in the First World War, plus plaque to commemorate SR staff who fell in the Second World War	40145, 40146
Bristol	GWR	Bristol & Exeter House	Roll of Honour	68495
Bristol	GWR	Temple Meads station	Roll of Honour	3161
Bristol	Midland Railway	Temple Meads station	Roll of Honour for Bristol St Phillips Goods depot	Replica of 61242. Not yet registered
Bristol	Midland Railway	Bristol Reference Library	Roll of Honour for Bristol St Phillips Goods depot	Replica of 61242. Not yet registered
Bury, Lancashire	East Lancashire Railway	Bolton Street Station & Museum	Local plaque for Oldham staff of LYR Carriage & Wagon Department	61514
Cambridge	GNR	Cambridge county archives	GNR Roll of Honour for Platelayer T Mead	68496
Cardiff	Arriva Trains Wales	Central station	Modern memorial to Cardiff railwaymen who fell in the First World War	68497
Cardiff Queen Street	Taff Vale Railway	Station	Roll of Honour (replica of 6669), funded by RHT, 2014	Not yet registered
Carnforth, Lancashire	LMS	Railway Station Visitor Centre	LMS Accounts Office staff plaques to commemorate fallen colleagues in both world wars	61058, 61059
Chester	GWR	Station	Roll of Honour	21195
Chester	LNWR	Station	LNWR Locomotive Department	20337
Coatbridge Sunnyside, Glasgow	NBR	Shimla Cottage Restaurant (former British Railways Staff Association)	Kipps Locomotive Shed memorial	61190
Crewe, Cheshire	LNWR	Council Offices	2nd Cheshire RE (Railway Volunteers), Boer War	18290
			Mechanics Institute (First World War)	20421
			Memorial to Villiers Russell twins	57119
Crewe, Cheshire	LNWR, LMS	Christ Church	Tranship shed staff of both world wars	2667
Crewe, Cheshire	LNWR	Crewe Railway Works buildings	Memorials of various LNWR departments	4066, 18343–5 57673/6, 61033/4

Town/city	Railway	Location	Memorial type/honouree(s)	UKNIWM reference
Crewe, Cheshire	LNWR	Queens Park	Memorial to reservists who served in Boer War	2781
Crewe, Cheshire	LNWR, LMS	Virgin First-Class Lounge, Crewe station	Crewe North and South Sheds staff (First World War and Second World War additional plaque)	18346
Crewe, Cheshire	LNWR	Weston Lane car park	Weston Lane Office staff	57705
Darlington, Co Durham	NER		Chief Mechanical Engineers Dept, Mileage Office	52155
Darlington, Co Durham	Robert Stephenson & Co	North Road Station Museum	To staff of the Robert Stephenson & Co works who fell in the First World War	41908
Derby	Midland Railway	Carriage and Wagon Works	Various Carriage and Wagon plaques	18916–20, 68498/9
Derby	Midland Railway	John Ellis House	Engineers and Estate Agents, Accounts, and Mines and Minerals department plaques	14201/56, 18905, 64009
Derby	Midland Railway	Midland Road	Midland Railway memorial for 2,833 staff who fell in First World War. Designed by Sir Edwin Lutyens	893
Derby	Midland Railway	Platform 1, Derby station	Various department memorials	891, 19064/79/115, 57634–48, 60921
			Boer War	892
			RHT memorial to Jacob Rivers, VC, erected 2017	Not yet registered
Derby	Midland Railway (incl North Counties Committee)	Silk Mill museum	First World War memorials and Rolls of Honour	18934, 60115, 68500
Didcot, Berkshire	GWR	Railway Museum	Rolls of Honour (2)	59985, 68503
			Reading Signal & Telegraph Department	68501
Dingwall, Highlands	Glasgow, Barrhead & Kilmarnock Joint Railway	Station frontage	Memorial to Sergeant J Meikle, VC. Relocated from Nitshill station due to vandalism.	13465
Dingwall, Highlands	HR	Station	Tea Stall during First World War	61031
Dover, Kent	SECR and SR	Marine station	Main SECR First World War memorial, plus SR plaque to fallen of the Second	1588
Dovercourt, Essex	GER	All Saints churchyard	Grave of Captain Fryatt and monument to him	22718
Dowlais, Mid-Glamorgan	GWR	Library	Roll of Honour, ex Merthyr Tydfil station (First World War)	60431
Dumbarton, Dunbartonshire	Dumbarton & Balloch Joint Railway	Central station booking office	Plaque to the fallen of this small joint line company	13357
Eastleigh, Hampshire		Museum	Eastleigh Works memorials	40441, 61064/5

Town/city	Railway	Location	Memorial type/honouree(s)	UKNIWM reference
Edinburgh	Caledonian	Princes Street Hotel	Roll of Honour for Station Staff, rediscovered 2017	Not yet registered
Edinburgh	NBR	Waverley station	Main NBR memorial	44630
Edinburgh	Railtrack/ Railway Mission	Waverley station	Railway men and women who served in the Second World War	61062
Exeter, Devon	GWR	Station	Roll of Honour	46043
Fawley Hill, Buckinghamshire	British Railways (Eastern Region)	Private museum	Commemoration plaque to GNR and LNER fallen ex Kings Cross station, erected 1970s at King's Cross and moved to Fawley Hill, 2013	60608
Fulbeck, Lincolnshire	RCH	St Nicholas' Church	Corporal H H Else, Boer War	54208
Gateshead, Newcastle	NER	Raven House, off Askew Road	Roll of Honour in glazed case, formerly in Forth Banks Office, for various NER engineers' staff	48358
Glasgow	Caledonian, Network Rail	Central station	Main Caledonian memorial plus modern plaque to those who served and fell in the Second World War	13356, 61029
Glasgow	North British Locomotive Company	Springburn Works Administration Building (now North Glasgow College)	First World War memorial window	5998
			First World War memorial	61075
			Second World War memorial	61076
Goole, Yorkshire	LYR	Museum	LYR Goole Steam Shipping (2)	34648/9
Gretna Green, Dumfries and Galloway	Western Front Association	Visitor centre	1995 plaque to commemorate those who died in Quintinshill collision, 1915	44218
Guildford, Surrey	LSWR and SR	Station	Memorial to those station staff who fell in the First World War, plus SR plaque to those who fell in the Second	23284
Heaton, Tyne and Wear	NER	Virgin East Coast Admin Block at Heaton Junction	Roll of Honour for fallen locomen of Heaton Junction Depot	34507
Highbridge, Somerset	Somerset & Dorset Joint Railway	Garden of Remembrance	Ex-Locomotive Works	24739
Highley, Hereford and Worcester	Severn Valley Railway	Engine House	Roll of Honour, Royal Engineers Transportation Units, Second World War	61307
Holyhead, Gwynedd	LMS	Holyhead Maritime Museum	Holyhead Goods & Traffic departments (Second World War)	37037
Horwich, Greater Manchester	LYR	Chorley New Road Gardens	Memorial to fallen staff from Horwich locomotive works, both world wars	3276
Hull, Yorkshire	HBR	Beverley Road Signal & Telegraph	Roll of Honour for HBR Signal & Telegraph staff	35347
Hull, Yorkshire	HBR	Street Life Museum	Company memorial	35561
Inverness	HR	Station Square	Main HR memorial	44152
Keswick, Cumbria	Cockermouth, Keswick & Penrith Railway	County Square, rear face of Town memorial (formerly at the station)	Main CKPR memorial	3996
Kidderminster, Worcestershire	GWR	Kidderminster Railway Museum	Roll of Honour	Not yet registered

Town/city	Railway	Location	Memorial type/honouree(s)	UKNIWM reference
Kidderminster, Worcestershire	GWR	Kidderminster Severn Valley Railway station booking hall	Roll of Honour	32358
Kidderminster, Worcestershire	LNWR	Kidderminster Railway Museum	Birmingham Goods Department	61086
Lancing, Sussex	LBSCR	Lancing Park	Carriage & Wagon Works	16574
Lancing, Sussex	LBSCR	St Michael's Church	Carriage & Wagon Works staff (First World War) and SR memorial for those who fell in the Second World War	16573
Larbert, Falkirk	Caledonian	Station	Quintinshill accident memorial	13438
Leamington Spa, Warwickshire	GWR	Station	Roll of Honour	61043
Leconfield, Yorkshire	Various	St Martin's Church	Memorials to GWR, LMS, LNER and SR, Canadian National Railway, CPR, RE, Royal Corps of Transport, US Army units	35158–62 35164/67 35170–72
Leith, Edinburgh	Memorial Fund	Rosebank cemetery	To commemorate the 214 troops who died in the Quintinshill accident	53610
Lichfield, Staffordshire	Royal British Legion	Station	Private W Davies, killed on station, Northern Ireland Troubles	61167
Lincoln	Midland Railway	Central station (formerly at St Marks station)	Midland Railway Goods, Passenger and Locomotive Department staff at Lincoln	889
Liverpool	Network Rail	Lime Street station	Pals memorial (2014 memorial) unveiled by HRH Duke of Cambridge	67303
			Railway men and women of Liverpool (2012 memorial)	61028
Liverpool	Mersey Railway	James Street station	Plaque for fallen in both world wars	2370
London	GCR	Marylebone Chiltern Boardroom (moved from concourse when replica memorials were erected)	Employees in both world wars	39776
London	GER	Liverpool Street station	Main GER First World War memorial	11787
			Memorial to Captain C Fryatt (First World War)	11789
London	GNR and Network Rail*	King's Cross station	Main GNR memorial list of First World War names incorporated into new memorial for GNR and LNER (Second World War) fallen, 2013	2776
London	GWR	Paddington station	First World War GWR memorial to the fallen, with additional plaque to those of the Second	11358
London	LBSCR and SR	London Bridge station concourse	Original LBSCR First World War memorial to the fallen, with SR plaque to those who fell in the Second World War. Present site since 2016	61089, 12575
London	LBSCR, SECR and SR	Victoria station	LBSCR First World War memorial and SR Second World War plaque	9538
			SECR First World War memorial and SR Second World War plaque	11377
			Plaque commemorating arrival of the Unknown Warrior	11609

Town/city	Railway	Location	Memorial type/honouree(s)	UKNIWM reference
London	LNWR and LMS	Euston Grove	Main LNWR First World War memorial plus later LMS dedication to the fallen of the Second World War	2087
London	LSWR	Waterloo station	Free buffet for soldiers and sailors, First World War	56668
London	LSWR and SR	Waterloo station	Nine Elms Motive Power Depot LSWR First World War memorial plaque and SR Second World War plaque	12179
			Victory Arch (LSWR, First World War) with SR Second World War dedication included	12182, 12188
London	LT	Balham Underground station	Memorial to Second World War bombing raid	60963
London	LT	Bethnal Green Underground station	Memorial to 173 civilians who died during Second World War bombing raid	12606
London	LT	Bounds Green Underground Station	Memorial to those killed in Second World War bombing raid	11968
London	LT	Covent Garden Museum	Memorial to Second World War Balham bombing raid	52421
London	NLR	Hoxton station	NLR First World War memorial, originally Broad Street, then Richmond	3089
London	Metropolitan Railway	Baker Street station	Main memorial, First World War	3090
London	Railtrack	Waterloo station	Railwaymen who died on D-Day. Unveiled 2004	56667
London	Docklands Light Railway*	East India station	RHT memorial plaque to C Robertson, VC, erected 2016	Not yet registered
London	*	Marylebone station	Three replicas of GCR First World War plaques that had been lost: UKNIWM 60752, 53497 and 53501	74796 (replica of 53497); others not yet registered
London	Network Rail*	Euston station concourse	Memorial to Lance Corporal J A Christie, VC, erected 2014	65946
London	Underground Electric Railways	Acton, Museum depot	UER Audit Office staff	58848
London	Underground Electric Railways	Petty France	Main memorial, First World War	39043
London Bridge	*	Stainer Street	Plaque to commemorate bombing of 17 February 1942	68559
Londonderry	Great Northern Railway (Ireland)	In store	To the fallen of the GNR(I), both world wars	61106
Manchester	LNWR and LMS	Longsight North West Trains cleaning depot	Longsight Locomotive Depot (First World War) and Repair Depot (Second)	44844, 44849
Manchester Piccadilly	LNWR and LMS	Platform 10	Modern replacement of lost First World War memorial to London Road Goods Depot (UKNIWM 10743)	70645
		Fairfield Street concourse	Central station staff, Second World War	16037

Town/city	Railway	Location	Memorial type/honouree(s)	UKNIWM reference
Manchester Victoria	LYR and Network Rail	Station	LYR main First World War memorial	13093
			LYR Chief Goods Manager office staff, First World War	43964
			Soldiers Gate, First World War	68555
March, Cambridgeshire	British Railways	Museum	Nameplates form Class 47 locomotives named after B Gimbert and J W Nightall, Second World War	61153, 61154
March, Cambridgeshire	LNER	Station booking hall	Roll of Honour to B Gimbert and J W Nightall for their heroism at Soham, Second World War	3542
Maryport, Cumbria	Maryport & Carlisle Railway	Memorial Gardens	Company memorial to fallen of MCR, First World War	4053
Melton Constable, Norfolk	M&GNJR	Main Street	Company memorial to fallen of M&GNJR, First World War, and plaque for Second World War	20137
Mexborough, Yorkshire	GCR	Station platform face	Memorial to GCR staff who worked at Mexborough	28095
	Northern*	Waiting room	RHT memorial to T N Jackson, VC, dedicated September 2017	Not yet registered
Middlesbrough, North Yorkshire	Railtrack	Station	Memorial to those killed in bombing raid, Second World War	61174
Moor Row, Cumbria	LNWR and Furness	Working Men's Institute	Roll of Honour and fallen of LNWR and Furness First World War staff	2221
Mossley, Greater Manchester	Northern*	Station building	RHT memorial to E Sykes, VC, dedicated 9 April 2017	Not yet registered
Newcastle	NER and LNER	Co-operative Nursery (formerly British Transport Police office)	Accounts Office plaques, both world wars	48365/6
Newton Abbot, Devon	GWR	Station	Roll of Honour	45949
Nitshill, Glasgow (ex Glasgow, Barrhead & Kilmarnock Joint Railway)	Scotrail*	Station	RHT memorial to J Meikle, VC, dedicated 18 October 2016. Original memorial (63890) now located at Dingwall station	75264
Norchard, Gloucestershire	GWR	Dean Forest Railway station	Roll of Honour, ex Severn Tunnel Junction	63686
Norwich	LNER	Station	Station staff (Second World War), unveiled 1998	54349
Nottingham	Midland Railway	Station porte cochère	Goods Station staff	60947
Oswestry, Shropshire	Cambrian Railways	Cae Glas Park	Main Cambrian Railways memorial	3088
Oswestry, Shropshire	Cambrian Railways	Station building (now Museum)	Cambrian Railways Roll of Honour	70865
Perth	Caledonian, HR, NBR	Station	Station staff	13321
Plymouth, Devon		Station booking office	Memorial to Falklands conflict	25698

Town/city	Railway	Location	Memorial type/honouree(s)	UKNIWM reference
Porthmadog, Gwynedd	Ffestiniog Railway	Harbour station	Memorial to No 2 Dutch Troop, Commandos Second World War	60689
Preston, Lancashire	Network Rail/ Virgin	Station	Memorials to station free buffet and pals battalion	61063, 61290/1, 68556
Ramsgate, Kent	Railtrack/ South Eastern Railway	Station	Memorial to 2 staff killed on duty by enemy air action. Unveiled 2001	62342
Retford, Nottinghamshire	British Railways	Station	Plaque to WRVS free buffet	68557
Rotherham, South Yorkshire	Midland Railway, LMS	Steel Terminal, Midland Road	Memorial to staff who fell in both world wars, plus civilian casualties in Second World War	64010
Rugby, Warwickshire	LNWR and LMS	Rugby Shed 8, in the former electric depot, now owned by Colas	Plaque to the fallen locomen, both world wars	19480
			LMS locomotive *Patriot* nameplate	50567
			Rugby Steam Shed Roll of Honour, both world wars	61305
Salehurst, Kent	Kent & East Sussex Railway	Church	Plaque commemorating the single member of the KESR to fall, Private Henry Osborne, Battle of Loos, 1915	17076
Shackerstone, Leicestershire	Midland Railway	Station (Battlefield line)	Roll of Honour, Engineers' Department, Burton, First World War	58482
Sheffield	GCR	Royal Victoria Holiday Inn	Relocated from Sheffield Victoria Station after closure	27674
			GCR Roll of Honour inside hotel, 2006	61157
Shenfield, Essex	GER	Station	Station staff	2247
Shildon, Co Durham	NER	NER Institute	Names of Fallen	10319
Shrewsbury, Shropshire	Shrewsbury & Hereford Joint (GWR & LNWR)	Platform 3	Station staff Roll of Honour (First World War)	13876
	GWR	Station offices	GWR Roll of Honour (First World War)	68558
	LNWR	Station offices	LNWR Locomotive Department Roll of Honour (First World War)	14043
	GWR Staff Association	Staff Association	Plaque to seven fallen (Second World War)	38089
Soham, Cambridgeshire	LNER	Soham Village Museum	Plaque originally placed at Soham station honouring B Gimbert & J W Nightall	3449
		St Andrew's Church	Stone tablet, as above	46611
		Red Lion Square	Monument, as above. Unveiled 2007 by Duke of Kent	61169
Southampton, Hampshire	LSWR and SR	NatWest Bank, Canute Street	Memorials to LSWR Docks & Marine Department (First World War)	21601
			SR Docks & Marine (Second World War)	21602
Southampton, Hampshire	†	Dock gate 8, Herbert Walker Avenue	Plaque presented to SR to honour the troops of the United Nations who sailed from the port (Second World War)	21625
Stockport, Cheshire	Virgin*	Platform 2	RHT memorial to W Wood, VC, unveiled October 2017	Not yet registered

Town/city	Railway	Location	Memorial type/honouree(s)	UKNIWM reference
Stoke-on-Trent, Staffordshire	NSR	Station	Main NSR memorial, with additional names, 2017	13561
Stratford-upon-Avon, Warwickshire	SMJR	Station	RHT replica Roll of Honour, installed 2014 (original in private ownership)	68562
Swindon, Wiltshire	GWR	STEAM Museum of the Great Western Railway	Swindon workshops plaques	24171–93
			Roll of Honour	61045
Swinton, South Yorkshire	GCR	St Margaret's Church	Memorials to T N Jackson, VC	46648
		Public library	Memorials to T N Jackson, VC	46842
Taunton, Somerset	GWR	Station	Roll of Honour	25176
Tongham, Surrey	SR	The Street, junction with Poyle Road	Plaque to commemorate heroism of Keen and Leech, Second World War. Unveiled 1996	41574
Wakes Colne, Essex	Colne Valley & Halstead Railway, GER	East Anglian Railway Museum	CVHR memorial	61160
			GER Stores Athletic Club	46010
			GER London Division Commercial Superintendent's Office	51121
Warrington, Lancashire	LNWR	DB Cargo building	Locomotive Department, Warrington	42926
Wolverhampton, West Midlands	LNWR	Station	Goods Department, Wolverhampton District	1418
Worcester Shrub Hill	GWR	Platform 2 waiting room	Memorial to those who served and died from GWR Sheet Depot, Worcester (copy of 60754, held in the NRM)	Not yet registered
York	NER	Rougier Street	Main NER war memorial, designed by Sir Edwin Lutyens	30905
York	Various	National Railway Museum	Some 40 assorted memorials, rolls of honour and war-associated nameplates can be found in the museum	York

Table footnotes: * (Co-)sponsored by the RHT; † Provided by the 14th Major Port US Army.

Notes

Introduction

1   Simmons and Biddle 1997.
2   Overy, R 1995 *Why the Allies Won*. London: Jonathan Cape.
3   Crump 1947.
4   Wolmar 2010; Pratt, E A 1915 *The Rise of Rail-Power in War and Conquest, 1833–1914*. London: P S King.

Chapter 1

1   Cited in Simmons 1991, 365.
2   Quoted in Edwards, C 1898 *Railway Nationalisation*. London: Methuen.
3   Mitchell 2000, 81.
4   *The London Gazette*, no 27459, 4835–6, 29 July 1902.
5   Quoted in Richards and MacKenzie 1986.
6   French 2005, 13.
7   Hamilton 1967.
8   'Engineer and Logistic Staff Corps', https://en.wikipedia.org/wiki/ Engineer_and_Logistic_Staff_ Corps [accessed 26 March 2018].
9   Darroch 1920, 11–12. G R S Darroch was assistant to the LNWR's CME and won the Croix de Guerre.
10 Findlay, G 1889 *The Working and Management of an English Railway*. London: Whittaker.
11 Pratt 1922.
12 White 1992.

Chapter 2

1   University of Warwick (UW), MSS.127/NU/4/1/2, *The Railway Review*, 1914.
2   *Railway Magazine*, November 1919.
3   Ibid, December 1914.
4   Ibid, November 1919.
5   TNA, ZPER 9/32, Railway Gazette Special War Number, 21 September 1920.
6   TNA, AN 1/1, REC Minutes, 1914.
7   TNA, ZLIB 10/38, Records of Railway Interests in the War, published by the Railway News.
8   York, National Railway Museum (NRM), B4-7/244, The Railway Gazette Special War Transportation Number, 1920.
9   TNA, AN 1/1, REC Minutes, 1914.
10 Pratt 1922.
11 *Railway Magazine*, April 1915.
12 TNA, RAIL 250/446, GWR War Reports.
13 Ibid.
14 Faulkner and Williams 1988.
15 TNA, AN 1/1, REC Minutes, 1914.
16 Ibid.
17 Ibid.
18 Hamilton 1967.
19 TNA, RAIL 250/446, GWR War Reports.
20 TNA, RAIL 1080/147, REC Minutes of Superintendents' Meetings.
21 *The Times*, 26 August 1914.
22 UW, MSS.127/NU/4/1/2, *The Railway Review*, 1914.
23 TNA, AN 1/1, REC Minutes, 1914.
24 Hamilton 1967.
25 TNA, RAIL 250/446, GWR War Reports.
26 UW, MSS.127/NU/4/1/2, *The Railway Review*, 1914.
27 UW, MSS.127/NU/4/1/4, *The Railway Review*, 1916.
28 TNA, RAIL 227/506, War-time Instructions, GER.
29 TNA, AN 1/20, RCH set of REC Instructions.
30 TNA, RAIL 236/595, War-time Notices, GNR.
31 TNA, RAIL 250/446, GWR War Reports.
32 Pratt 1922.
33 TNA, RAIL 411/458.
34 'What you must not do', http:// merthyrww1.llgc.org.uk/en/items/ show/121 [accessed 19 February 2018].
35 TNA, WO 33/862, Summary of Railway Arrangements in Connection with Home Defence, dated 14 March 1917 (closed until 1969).
36 *Railway Magazine*, November 1914.
37 Ibid, October 1919.
38 Pratt 1921.
39 TNA, MUN 7/205, Ministry of Munitions.
40 Ibid.
41 Ibid.
42 TNA, MUN 4/6381, Railway War Manufactures Sub-Committee.
43 *Railway Magazine*, April 1920.
44 Ibid 1920.
45 *GWR Magazine*, December 1917.
46 TNA, RAIL 1080/148, REC Minutes of Superintendents' Meetings.
47 *Railway Magazine*, April 1916.
48 *Furness Railway Magazine*, October 1923.
49 *Railway Magazine*, March 1920.
50 TNA, RAIL 312/42, Hull & Barnsley Railway Minutes, 1918–19.
51 Pratt 1922.
52 Ibid.
53 Reed 1996.
54 TNA, RAIL 312/42, Hull & Barnsley Railway Minutes, 1918–19.
55 TNA, RAIL 411/888.
56 TNA, RAIL 250/51, GWR Board Minutes.
57 *Railway Magazine*, November 1919.
58 UW, MSS.127/NU/4/1/4, *The Railway Review*, 1916.
59 *Railway Magazine*, August 1919.
60 TNA, RAIL 250/446, GWR War Reports.
61 TNA, AN 1/20, RCH set of REC Instructions.
62 TNA, RAIL 226/596, GCR papers.
63 TNA, AN 1/1, REC Minutes, 1914.
64 TNA, MT 6/3477, Railway Executive Committee: Minutes 292-500.

65 TNA, RAIL 250/446, GWR War Reports.
66 UW, MSS.127/NU/4/1/3, *The Railway Review*, 1915.
67 Ibid.
68 TNA, AN 1/1, REC Minutes, 1914.
69 TNA, AN 1/20, RCH set of REC Instructions.
70 Quoted in McKillop 1950.
71 UW, MSS.127/NU/4/1/5, *The Railway Review*, 1917.
72 TNA, AN 1/20, RCH set of REC Instructions.
73 Ibid.
74 TNA, ZLIB 10/38, Records of Railway Interests in the War, published by the Railway News.
75 TNA, RAIL 150/761, REC Circular Letters, 1915.
76 UW, MSS.127/NU/4/1/3, *The Railway Review*, 1915.
77 TNA, RAIL 250/51, GWR Board Minutes.
78 TNA, RAIL 250/446, GWR War Reports.
79 TNA, RAIL 250/51, GWR Board Minutes.
80 TNA, RAIL 250/446, GWR War Reports.
81 Ibid.
82 TNA, AN 1/57, Minutes of Meetings of Committee on Recruiting and Substitution of Railwaymen.
83 Ibid.
84 Ibid.
85 Quoted in Wojtczak 2005.
86 *Great Central Railway Magazine*, July 1916.
87 UW, MSS.127/NU/4/1/3, *The Railway Review*, 1915.
88 UW, MSS.127/NU/4/1/5, *The Railway Review*, 1917.
89 TNA, ZLIB 10/38, Records of Railway Interests in the War published by the Railway News.
90 *Great Central Railway Magazine*, October 1916.
91 TNA, RAIL 250/51, GWR Board Minutes.
92 Wojtczak 2005.
93 UW, MSS.127/NU/4/1/3, *The Railway Review*, 1915.
94 TNA, ZLIB 10/38, Records of Railway Interests in the War, published by the Railway News.

95 TNA, RAIL 250/51, GWR Board Minutes.
96 UW, MSS.127/NU/4/1/4, *The Railway Review*, 1916.
97 Ibid.
98 Ibid.
99 UW, MSS.127/NU/4/1/5, *The Railway Review*, 1917.
100 TNA, RAIL 312/42, Hull & Barnsley Railway Minutes, 1918–19.
101 TNA, ZLIB 10/38, Records of Railway Interests in the War, published by the Railway News.
102 Ibid.
103 UW, MSS.127/NU/4/1/5, *The Railway Review*, 1917.
104 Ibid.
105 TNA, ZPER 7/103, Records of Railway Interest in the War, published by the Railway News.
106 Pratt 1922.
107 TNA, MT 6/2509/3, Board of Trade – Tramway Employment.
108 UW, MSS.127/NU/4/1/5, *The Railway Review*, 1917.
109 TNA, MT 6/2509/3, Board of Trade – Tramway Employment.
110 UW, MSS.127/NU/4/1/4, *The Railway Review*, 1916.
111 Ibid.
112 UW, MSS.127/NU/4/1/5, *The Railway Review*, 1917.
113 Ibid.
114 Ibid.
115 Ibid, 24 August 1917.
116 UW, MSS.379/G/4/2.
117 TNA, RAIL 250/446, GWR War Reports.
118 *The Locomotive Journal*, February 1918.
119 Circular on display in former Royal Station Hotel, York.
120 *Railway Magazine*, January 1917.
121 Hamilton 1967.
122 *GWR Magazine*, January 1916.
123 Hamilton 1967.
124 *Railway Magazine*, April 1916.
125 TNA, ZLIB 10/38, Records of Railway Interests in the War, published by the Railway News.
126 *Railway Magazine*, January 1917.
127 TNA, RAIL 250/446, GWR War Reports.

128 TNA, RAIL 1080/147, REC, Minutes of Superintendents' Meetings.
129 Ibid.
130 TNA, RAIL 1080/249, RCH Minutes.
131 TNA, ZLIB 10/38, Records of Railway Interests in the War, published by the Railway News.
132 *Railway Magazine*, February 1917.
133 Faulkner and Williams 1988.
134 Ibid.
135 TNA, CAB 42/26, Minutes of War Committee, 10 Downing Street.
136 Ibid.
137 TNA, CAB 23/1/3, War Cabinet Minutes.
138 TNA, RAIL 1080/147, REC, Minutes of Superintendents' Meetings.
139 Ibid.
140 UW, MSS.127/NU/4/1/3, *The Railway Review*, 1915.
141 UW, MSS.127/NU/4/1/4, *The Railway Review*, 1916.
142 Pratt 1921.
143 TNA, AN 1/1, REC Minutes, 1914.
144 Hamilton 1967.
145 Ibid.
146 TNA, RAIL 250/761, REC Circular Letters.
147 NRM, B4-7/244, The Railway Gazette Special War Transportation Number 1920.
148 TNA, ZLIB 10/38, Records of Railway Interests in the War, published by the Railway News.
149 TNA, MT 49/35, MoT/REC.
150 TNA, RAIL 250/446, GWR War Reports.
151 TNA, MT 49/35, MoT/REC.
152 *Railway Magazine*, April 1915.
153 Pratt 1922.
154 *Railway Magazine*, September 1915.
155 TNA, RAIL 250/446, GWR War Reports.
156 *Railway Magazine*, September 1915.
157 *The Locomotive Journal*, May 1918
158 Hamilton 1967.
159 TNA, RAIL 250/446, GWR War Reports.
160 TNA, AN 1/1, REC Minutes, 1914.
161 TNA, RAIL 250/446, GWR War Reports.

162 TNA, MT 6/3477, Railway Executive Committee: Minutes 292-500.
163 TNA, MUN 4/6381, Railway War Manufactures Sub-Committee.
164 *Great Central Railway Magazine*, November 1915.
165 *Railway Magazine*, September 1915.
166 Pratt 1922.
167 Larkin and Larkin 1988.
168 Ibid.
169 TNA, RAIL 250/446, GWR War Reports.
170 TNA, RAIL 250/52, GWR Board Minutes.
171 *GWR Magazine*, November 1918.
172 TNA, CAB 40/59, War Priorities Committee – Loco and Wagon Shortage.
173 Ibid.
174 Ibid.
175 TNA, RAIL 250/51, GWR Board Minutes.
176 Ibid.
177 UW, MSS.127/NU/4/1/4, *The Railway Review*, 1916.
178 *Great Central Railway Magazine*, July 1915.
179 TNA, MT 6/2443/23, Labour Situation on British Railways, Board of Trade paper.
180 UW, MSS.127/NU/4/1/4, *The Railway Review*, 1916.
181 TNA, MT 6/2443/23, Labour Situation on British Railways, Board of Trade paper.
182 Ibid.
183 Ibid.
184 TNA, MT 6/2430/10, Ministry of Transport.
185 TNA, MT 6/2447/2, Ministry of Transport and successors, Railway Divisions: Stoppage of War Bonus for Bad Timekeeping.
186 TNA, MT 6/2447/2, Ministry of Transport.
187 UW, MSS.127/NU/4/1/5, *The Railway Review*, 1917.
188 TNA, RAIL 250/51, GWR Board Minutes.
189 UW, MSS.127/NU/4/1/5, *The Railway Review*, 1917.
190 *The Locomotive Journal*, September 1917.

191 TNA, RAIL 250/52, GWR Board Minutes.
192 Ibid.
193 TNA, RAIL 250/761, REC Circular Letters.
194 TNA, RAIL 250/446, GWR War Reports.
195 Pratt 1922.
196 *Railway Magazine*, August 1917.
197 *Great Eastern Railway Society Journal*, October 1982, no 32.
198 TNA, AN 1/1, REC Minutes, 1914.
199 Hamilton 1967.
200 TNA, RAIL 421/9, The Operating Department of the LMS Railway during the Second World War, 1939–1945.
201 *Railway Magazine*, June 1915.
202 TNA, RAIL 250/446, GWR War Reports.
203 Pratt 1922.
204 Hamilton 1967.
205 Ibid.
206 TNA, RAIL 1080/246, RCH Goods Managers' Committee Minutes.
207 Hamilton 1967.
208 TNA, MT 6/3477, Railway Executive Committee: Minutes 292-500.
209 TNA, ZLIB 10/38, Records of Railway Interests in the War published by the Railway News.
210 Ibid. Also *Railway Magazine* July 1916.
211 TNA, RAIL 250/761, REC Circular Letters.
212 Pratt 1921.
213 *Railway Magazine*, December 1919.
214 TNA, AN 1/1, REC Minutes, 1914.
215 Hamilton 1967.
216 *Railway Magazine*, November 1919.
217 Pratt 1921.
218 *Railway Magazine*, January 1920.
219 Pratt 1921.
220 *Railway Magazine*, April 1920.
221 TNA, ZLIB 10/38, Records of Railway Interests in the War published by the Railway News.
222 Hamilton 1967.
223 Ibid.
224 Pratt 1921.
225 TNA, ZLIB 10/38, Records of Railway Interests in the War published by the *Railway News*.

226 NER Magazine, November 1918, vol 8 no 95.
227 'Private Arthur Vincent Wood', www.peterboroughww1.co.uk/ soldiers/av-wood/ [accessed 2 March 2018].
228 TNA, CAB 24/3/34, Report by Adjutant-General, 1916.
229 Clwyd-Powys Archaeological Trust 2016 'First World War Prisoner of War Camps', Report No 1385.
230 Reed 1996.
231 Pratt 1922.
232 Richards and MacKenzie 1986.
233 Larkin and Larkin 1988.
234 *GWR Magazine*, January 1920.

Chapter 3

1 Shakespear 1926.
2 Grieves 1989.
3 Many of the points in the first part of this chapter are indebted to C Phillips, 'Sir Eric Geddes and the BEF's Transportation Network, 1916–18', www. academia.edu/5298960/ Sir_Eric_Geddes_and_the_BEFs_ Transportation_Network_1916-18 [accessed 21 April 2017].
4 Phillips, C 2013 'A railwayman goes to war: Francis Dent and the challenge of total war', http://ww1 centenary.oucs.ox.ac.uk/?p=2854 [accessed 22 February 2018].
5 Anon, 'Footplate work with the R.O.D. in France', *Railway Magazine*, vol 73, July 1933, 29.
6 NRM, B4-7/244, The Railway Gazette Special War Transportation Number 1920.
7 'Granet, Sir (William) Guy', *Oxford Dictionary of National Biography*, https://doi.org/10.1093/ref:odnb/ 33513 [accessed 21 August 2018].
8 NRM, B4-7/244, The Railway Gazette Special War Transportation Number 1920.
9 Ibid.
10 Ibid.
11 Ibid.
12 Ibid.
13 Hamilton 1967.
14 NRM, B4-7/244 The Railway Gazette Special War Transportation Number 1920.

15 Ibid.

16 *The Locomotive Journal*, January 1918.

17 TNA, RAIL 250/446, GWR War Reports.

18 *The Locomotive Journal*, September 1917.

19 TNA, RAIL 491/1259, Book of Remembrance.

20 Shakespear 1926.

21 Ibid.

22 Ibid.

23 Ibid.

24 *Railway Magazine*, September 1915.

25 *GWR Magazine*, August 1919.

26 Much of this description is taken from the *GWR Magazine*, August 1919.

27 *GWR Magazine*, July 1916.

28 *GWR Magazine*, November 1920.

29 NRM, B4-7/244, The Railway Gazette Special War Transportation Number 1920.

30 TNA, WO 95/4389, Director of Railway Transport GHQ report, November 1915 – May 1918.

31 *Locomotive News and Railway Notes*, January 1921.

32 *Railway Magazine*, March 1917.

Chapter 4

1 NRM, B4-7/64P, Sir Charles H Newton, *British Railways during the War* (published paper presented to the Fifth Pan-American Railway Congress, Buenos Aires, 1946).

2 NRM, B4-7/143L, Railway Clearing House, History of Railways during the War, September 1939–15 August 1945. Papers prepared by Operating Superintendents, Amersham, Bucks, January 1946.

3 NRM, B4-7/64P, Newton, *British Railways during the War*. Bradshaw's timetable covered Britain.

4 NRM, B4-7/143L, Railway Clearing House, History of Railways during the War.

5 Ibid.

6 TNA, RAIL 421/9, The Operating Department of the LMS Railway during the Second World War, 1939–1945.

7 Holder, G 'Evacuating Glasgow wartime kids' *Evening Times* 27 May 2013, www.eveningtimes.co.uk/news/13256851. Evacuating_Glasgow_wartime_kids/ [accessed 26 February 2018].

8 *Views: War and Peace*, National Trust, No 51, 68.

9 Darwin 1946.

10 TNA, RAIL 421/9, The Operating Department of the LMS Railway during the Second World War, 1939–1945.

11 Ibid.

12 Ibid.

13 Wragg 2006.

14 TNA, RAIL 648/101, REC Instructions.

15 Nash 1946.

16 TNA, RAIL 421/9, The Operating Department of the LMS Railway during the Second World War, 1939–1945.

17 John [1947].

18 Tatlow 2010.

19 John [1947].

20 Darwin 1946.

21 John [1947].

22 https://en.wikipedia.org/wiki/Charles_Howard,_20th_Earl_of_Suffolk [accessed 11 March 2018]

23 John [1947].

24 NRM, B4-7/143L, Railway Clearing House, History of Railways during the War.

25 Ibid.

26 Darwin 1946.

27 John [1947].

28 Balfour 1981.

29 Ibid.

30 Ibid.

31 Snell 1983.

32 Crump 1947.

33 TNA, ZLIB 15/45/7, Speeches by the Rt Hon Lord Ashfield at the Staff Reunion Victory Dinners, 5 and 10 July 1946, at the Connaught Rooms.

34 TNA, RAIL 648/114, SR Air Raid Log Book No 13, Commenced 11 July 1944.

35 TNA, RAIL 648/19, Eastleigh Air Raid Precautions.

36 NRM, B4-7/64P, Newton, *British Railways during the War*.

37 John [1947].

38 Ibid.

39 Ibid.

40 Nash 1946.

41 John [1947].

42 TNA, RAIL 648/94, REC Instructions.

43 TNA, RAIL 421/206, LMS War Journal kept for G Royde-Smith, Assistant, then Secretary of the LMS.

44 TNA, RAIL 421/9, The Operating Department of the LMS Railway during the Second World War, 1939–1945.

45 Nash 1946.

46 Wragg 2006.

47 Ibid.

48 John [1947].

49 Nash 1946.

50 TNA, RAIL 648/90, SR War Damage File.

51 TNA, RAIL 648/87, War Damage.

52 TNA, RAIL 421/157, Log Book of Fire Watcher, Broad Street.

53 TNA, RAIL 421/206, LMS War Journal kept for Royde-Smith.

54 TNA, RAIL 648/92, SR Damage Reports.

55 TNA, RAIL 648/90, SR War Damage File.

56 Ibid.

57 Wragg 2006.

58 TNA, RAIL 648/90 SR War Damage File.

59 Ibid.

60 TNA, RAIL 648/92, SR Damage Reports.

61 Ministry of Information on behalf of Ministry of War Transport 1942.

62 Wragg 2006.

63 NRM, B4-7/143L, Railway Clearing House, History of Railways during the War.

64 TNA, RAIL 421/9, The Operating Department of the LMS Railway during the Second World War, 1939–1945.

65 TNA, RAIL 648/89, Southern Bomb Damage, 1945.

66 John [1947].

67 Quoted in Wragg 2006.

68 Crump 1947.

69 NRM, B4-7/143L, Railway Clearing House, History of Railways during the War.

70 Crump 1947.
71 NRM, B4-7/143L, Railway Clearing House, History of Railways during the War.
72 British Railways Press Office, 1943.
73 TNA, RAIL 648/94, REC Instructions.
74 British Railways Press Office, 1943.
75 TNA, RAIL 648/94, REC Instructions.
76 TNA, RAIL 421/9, The Operating Department of the LMS Railway during the Second World War, 1939–1945.
77 Wragg 2006.
78 NRM, B4-7/143L, Railway Clearing House, History of Railways during the War.
79 TNA, RAIL 421/9, The Operating Department of the LMS Railway during the Second World War, 1939–1945.
80 TNA, RAIL 421/206, LMS War Journal kept for Royde-Smith.
81 Wooler 1987.
82 Bell 1946.
83 TNA, RAIL 421/9, The Operating Department of the LMS Railway during the Second World War 1939–1945.
84 Nash 1946.
85 TNA, RAIL 421/206, LMS War Journal kept for Royde-Smith.
86 Quoted in Wojtczak 2005.
87 TNA, RAIL 421/207, War Journal, Vol 2, LMS HQ, Watford.
88 TNA, RAIL 421/9, The Operating Department of the LMS Railway during the Second World War, 1939–1945.
89 Ibid.
90 Ibid.
91 Nock 1967.
92 TNA, RAIL 421/206, LMS War Journal kept for Royde-Smith.
93 TNA, ZLIB 10/3, British Railways in Peace and War, 1944.
94 TNA, RAIL 421/207, War Journal, Vol 2, LMS HQ, Watford.
95 TNA, RAIL 421/206, LMS War Journal kept for Royde-Smith.
96 John [1947].
97 Darwin 1946.

98 Wojtczak 2005.
99 NRM, B4-7/143L Railway Clearing House, History of Railways during the War.
100 Ministry of War Transport 1946 *Summary Table of Statistical Returns of Railways of Great Britain, 1938 to 1944* HMSO (UW, MSS.379/R/14/12).
101 Ministry of Information on behalf of Ministry of War Transport 1942.
102 Nash 1946.
103 *Railway Magazine*, January/February 1947.
104 TNA, WO 199/2698, Historical Sketch of Movement Control in Scottish Command from the Outbreak of War to 'D' Day.
105 Watson, N 2008 *WRVS in Scotland: Seventy Years of Service*. Edinburgh: Black & White.
106 TNA, WO 199/2698, Historical Sketch of Movement Control in Scottish Command from the Outbreak of War to 'D' Day.
107 Gilbert 1983, 1154.
108 TNA, WO 199/2698, Historical Sketch of Movement Control in Scottish Command from the Outbreak of War to 'D' Day.
109 TNA, RAIL 421/88, Report on the Working of Trains over the Highland Section, 23 November 1942.
110 *Highland Railway Journal* **7**, No 104, 16.
111 TNA, RAIL 421/88, Report on the Working of Trains over the Highland Section, 23 November 1942.
112 *Highland Railway Journal* **3**, No 40, 16.
113 NRM, B4-7/143L, Railway Clearing House, History of Railways during the War.
114 Crump 1947.
115 TNA, RAIL 421/207, War Journal, Vol 2, LMS HQ, Watford.
116 Ibid.
117 John [1947].
118 Nash 1946.
119 John [1947].
120 *Railway Magazine*, March/April 1943.
121 Wragg 2006.

122 https://en.wikipedia.org/wiki/Aldenham_Works [accessed 11 March 2018].
123 NRM, BA-7/20, *Beyer Peacock & Co. Ltd and Associated Companies* (privately published, 1945).
124 Ibid.
125 Subterranea Britannica, Ridge Quarry site record, www.subbrit.org.uk/sb-sites/sites/r/ridge_quarry/index.shtml [accessed 26 February 2018].
126 Historic England, 'MoD Corsham: Tunnel Quarry', https://historicengland.org.uk/listing/the-list/list-entry/1409857 [accessed 26 February 2018].
127 NRM, B4-7/143L, Railway Clearing House, History of Railways during the War.
128 NRM, PS 5/26, Pearce Higgins collection, War Diary Shropshire & Montgomeryshire Railway, written at Kinnerley, 18 April 1943.
129 TNA, RAIL 421/9, The Operating Department of the LMS Railway during the Second World War, 1939–1945.
130 Ibid.
131 NRM, B4-7/143L Railway Clearing House, History of Railways during the War.
132 Ibid.
133 TNA, RAIL 421/9, The Operating Department of the LMS Railway during the Second World War, 1939–1945.
134 NRM, B4-7/143L Railway Clearing House, History of Railways during the War.
135 Crump 1947.
136 UW, MSS.379/R/14/2, Address by ASLEF President of the Executive Committee, Mr D F Sharman, Southport conference, 1944.
137 TNA, RAIL 421/9, The Operating Department of the LMS Railway during the Second World War, 1939–1945.
138 Nash 1946.
139 John [1947].
140 Wragg 2006.
141 'RLY ambulance trains', www.bbc.co.uk/history/ww2peopleswar/stories/26/a4682126.shtml [accessed 2 March 2018]. This

is part of the WW2 People's War online archive of wartime memories contributed by members of the public and gathered by the BBC, available at www.bbc.co.uk/ ww2peopleswar/.

142 TNA, RAIL 421/9, The Operating Department of the LMS Railway during the Second World War, 1939–1945.

143 TNA, RAIL 648/114, SR Air Raid Log Book No 13, Commenced 11 July 1944.

144 Ibid.

145 TNA, RAIL 648/89, Southern Bomb Damage, 1945.

146 Ibid.

147 TNA, RAIL 421/9, The Operating Department of the LMS Railway during the Second World War, 1939–1945.

148 Ibid.

149 Ibid.

150 Ibid.

151 Ibid.

152 TNA, RAIL 648/101, SR Claims.

153 Nash 1946.

Chapter 5

1 TNA, ZLIB 15/45/7, Speeches by the Rt Hon Lord Ashfield at the Staff Reunion Victory Dinners, 5 and 10 July 1946, at the Connaught Rooms.

2 John [1947].

3 Hughes 1981.

4 Ibid.

5 Thomas 1947.

6 TNA, RAIL 421/207, War Journal, vol 2, LMS HQ, Watford.

7 TNA, ZLIB 10/3, British Railways in Peace and War, 1944.

8 'The story of an evacuation hero', http://news.bbc. co.uk/local/guernsey/hi/ people_and_places/history/ newsid_8379000/8379301.stm [accessed 27 February 2018].

9 Thomas 1947.

Chapter 6

1 TNA, ZPER 7/103, Records of Railway Interests in the War.

2 *Railway Magazine*, March 1917.

3 TNA, RAIL 226/621, GCR War Memorial.

4 *Railway Magazine*, July 1919.

5 TNA, RAIL 226/621, GCR War Memorial.

6 Ibid.

7 Pratt 1922.

8 TNA, RAIL 258/447, GWR War Memorial.

9 Ibid.

10 Ibid.

11 TNA, RAIL 390/1565, LNER: Minutes and Reports.

12 Ibid.

13 Ibid.

14 Skelton, T and Giddon, G 2008 *Lutyens and the Great War*. London: Frances Lincoln.

15 Faulkner and Williams 1988.

16 *GWR Magazine*, June 1919.

Picture credits

The author and publisher have made every effort to identify and contact copyright holders. We will happily correct, in subsequent editions, any error or omissions that are brought to our attention.

Courtesy of John Alsop Collection: Fig 2.26

American Railway Association 1922 Locomotive Cyclopedia of American Practice. New York: Simmons-Boardman: Fig 3.5

Bentley Archive/Popperfoto/Getty Images:
Fig 4.16 (80748062)

Central Press/Hulton Archive/Getty Images:
Fig 4.3 (80693223)

Paul Childs: Fig 6.11

Chronicle/Alamy Stock Photo: Figs 2.3 (G3AK7Y), 3.1 (DRHHM0)

Corbis Historical/Getty Images: Fig 1.2 (615314282)

Crecy Publishing: Figs 4.6, 4.14, 4.15, 4.17, 4.18, 4.19, 4.20, 4.21, 4.32, 5.1

Daily Herald Archive/Science & Society Picture Library:
Fig 4.13 (10682716)

Granger Historical Picture Archive/Alamy Stock Photo:
Fig 2.18 (FG767A)

Harry Todd/Fox Photos/Hulton Archive/Getty Images:
Fig 4.11 (671693979)

J B Helsby/Topical Press Agency/Getty Images:
Fig 2.22 (3137807)

Hulton-Deutsch Collection/Corbis Historical/Getty Images:
Fig 4.25 (646298768)

© Imperial War Museum: Frontispiece (Art.IWM PST 15258), Figs 2.13 (Q 031019), 2.14 (Q 028150), 2.28 (Q 069062), 4.2 (PST 003362), 4.4 (LN 006194), 4.7 (Art.IWM PST 3458), 4.10 (H 001632), 4.12 (H 003043), 4.27 (H 006089), 4.28 (H 006123), 4.35 (HU 036134)

Library of Congress/Nick Parrino: Figs 5.3, 5.4

© McCord Museum: Fig 1.3 (II-129700)

© National Museum of Wales: Fig 6.1

National Portrait Gallery, London: Figs 1.5 (x44475), 2.6 (x167776)

NRM Pictorial Collection/Science & Society Picture Library:
Front cover (10283086), Figs 4.22 (10175047), 5.2 (10283043)

National Railway Museum/Science & Society Picture Library:
Figs 2.4 (10660934), 2.7 (10623937), 2.8 (10442434), 2.11 (10660947), 2.12 (10461799), 2.15 (10669188), 2.17 (10689897), 2.25 (10689431), 2.27 (10319620), 3.2 (10660930), 4.1 (10449204), 4.26 (10623876), 4.30 (10652987), 6.7 (10662237)

Pictorial Press Ltd/Alamy Stock Photo: Fig 4.5 (B3N8XF)

Planet Pix Ltd – Planet News/Science & Society Picture Library: Figs 4.24 (10553642), 4.33 (10555280)

Popperfoto/Getty Images: p xii (79655791), Figs 2.23 (455245586), 2.24 (455245654)

Railway Heritage Trust/Paul Childs: Figs 6.1, 6.2, 6.3, 6.5, 6.6, 6.8, 6.9, 6.10, 6.13, 6.14

Courtesy of RCL Publications: Figs 3.3, 3.4, 3.6, 3.7, 3.8, 3.9, 3.10

Reproduced with the kind permission of Colonel David Ronald: Figs 2.19, 2.20, 2.21

Royal Photographic Society/Science & Society Picture Library: Fig 1.4 (10648785)

Science Museum Archive/Science & Society Picture Library:
Fig 2.5 (10326064)

Science & Society Picture Library: Figs 2.16, 2.29, 4.34, 6.4, 6.12

Science & Society Picture Library/Getty Images:
Fig 4.9 (90748110)

Smith Art Gallery and Museum: Figs 2.9, 2.10

The late Major Taylorson Collection via John Townsend:
Fig 4.31

Trinity Mirror/Mirrorpix/Alamy Stock Photo:
Fig 4.8 (B3P3RK)

Universal History Archive/UIG/Bridgeman Images:
Fig 1.1 (UIG539131)

Bibliography

Aves, W 2009 *R-O-D: The Railway Operating Division on the Western Front*. Donnington: Shaun Tyas

Aves, W 2016 *The Lines behind the Front*. Lydney, Glos: Lightmoor

Balfour, G 1981 *The Armoured Train*. London: Batsford

Barries, D S M 1980 *A Regional History of the Railways of Great Britain*. Vol 12: *South Wales*. Newton Abbot: David & Charles

Baughan, P E 1966 *North of Leeds: the Leeds-Settle-Carlisle line and its branches*. Hatch End: Roundhouse

Bell, R 1946 *History of the British Railways during the War, 1939–45*. London: Railway Gazette

Berridge, P S A 1969 *Couplings to the Khyber*. Newton Abbot: David & Charles

Bonavia, M R 1980 *The Four Great Railways*. Newton Abbot: David & Charles

British Railways Press Office 1943 *Facts about British Railways in Wartime*. [London]: British Railways Press Office

Bulleid, H A V 1967 *The Aspinall Era*. London: Ian Allan

Carter, E F 1964 *Railways in Wartime*. London: Frederick Muller

Christiansen, R and Miller, R W nd *The Cambrian Railways, 1889–1968*. Newton Abbot: David & Charles

Crump, N 1947 *By Rail to Victory*. [London]: London and North Eastern Railway

Darroch, G R S 1920 *Deeds of a Great Railway*. London: John Murray

Darwin, B 1946 *War on the Line*. London: Southern Railway

Dow, A 2006 *Dow's Dictionary of Railway Quotations*. Baltimore, Md: Johns Hopkins University Press

Dow, G 1965 *Great Central*. London: Ian Allan

Faulkner, J N and Williams, R A 1988 *The London & South Western Railway in the 20th Century*. Newton Abbot: David & Charles

French, D 2005 *Military Identities: The Regimental System, the British Army, and the British People, c.1870–2000*. Oxford: Oxford University Press

Gilbert, M 1983 *Winston S. Churchill*. Vol. 6: *Finest Hour, 1939–1941*. London: Heinemann

Grieves, K 1989 *Sir Eric Geddes*. Manchester: Manchester University Press

Hadrill, J 1999 *Rails to the Sea*. Penryn: Atlantic

Hamilton E C 1955 *The North British Railway*. London: Ian Allan

Hamilton, J A B 1967 *Britain's Railways in World War I*. London: George Allen & Unwin

Holmes, A nd *Railways at War*. National Railway Museum [York, NRM, B4-7/219P]

Hughes, H 1981 *Middle East Railways*. Harrow: Continental Railway Circle

Hughes, H 1994 *Indian Locomotives, Part 3: Narrow Gauge, 1863–1940*. Harrow: Continental Railway Circle

Joby, R S 1984 *The Railwaymen*. Newton Abbot: David & Charles

John, E [1947] *Time Table for Victory*. London: British Railways

Larkin, E 1992 *An Illustrated History of British Railways' Workshops*. Sparkford: Oxford

Larkin, E J and Larkin, J G 1988 *The Railway Workshops of Britain, 1823–1986*. London: Macmillan

Lloyd, R 1953 *Railwaymen's Gallery*. London: George Allen & Unwin

MacDermot, E T 1964 *History of the Great Western Railway*. Vol 2: *1863–1921*. London: Ian Allan

McKillop, N 1950 *The Lighted Flame*. London: Nelson

Ministry of Information on behalf of Ministry of War Transport 1942 *Transport Goes to War*. London: HMSO

Mitchell, A 2000 *The Great Train Race: Railways and the Franco-German Rivalry*. New York: Berghahn

Nash, G C 1946 *The LMS at War*. London: L M S Railway

Nock, O S 1960 *The London & North Western Railway*. London: Ian Allan

Nock, O S 1967 *History of the Great Western Railway*. Vol 3: *1923–1947*. London: Ian Allan

Pratt, E A 1921 *British Railways and the Great War*. London: Selwyn & Blount

Pratt, E A 1922 *War Record of the London & North Western Railway*. London: Selwyn & Blount

Reed, M C 1996 *The London & North Western Railway*. Penryn: Atlantic Transport Publishers

Reid, W 2006 *Douglas Haig*. Edinburgh: Birlinn

Richards, J and MacKenzie, J M 1986 *The Railway Station*. Oxford: Oxford University Press

Ronald, D W and Carter, R J 1974 *The Longmoor Military Railway*. Newton Abbot: David & Charles

Shakespear, Lt Col 1926 *A Record of the 17th and 32nd Service Battalions Northumberland Fusiliers, N.E.R. Pioneers, 1914–1919*. Newcastle upon Tyne: Northumberland

Simmons, J 1991 *The Victorian Railway*. London: Thames and Hudson

Simmons, J and Biddle, G (eds) 1997 *The Oxford Companion to British Railway History*. Oxford: Oxford University Press

Smith, W H 2008 *The Hereford, Hay and Brecon Branch*. Kidderminster: Kidderminster Railway Museum

Snell, J B 1983 *One Man's Railway*. Newton Abbot: David & Charles

Tatlow, P 2010 *Railways from Dunkirk*. Usk: Oakwood

Thomas, J 1947 *Line of Communication*. London: Locomotive

Thomas, J 1966 *The Callander & Oban Railway*. Newton Abbot: David & Charles

Thomas, J 1977 *The Skye Railway*. Newton Abbot: David & Charles

White, H P 1992 *A Regional History of the Railways of Great Britain*. Vol 2: *Southern England*. 5 edn. Newton Abbot: David & Charles

Wojtczak, H 2005 *Railwaywomen*. Hastings: Hastings

Wolmar, C 2010 *Engines of War*. London: Atlantic

Wooler, N 1987 *Dinner in the Diner*. Newton Abbot: David & Charles

Woolliscroft, D J and Fell, M G 2015 *Gone to War: The North Stafford's Fallen Railwaymen*. Lydney, Glos: Lightmoor

Wragg, D 2006 *Wartime on the Railways*. Stroud: Sutton

Wrottesley, A J 1970 *The Midland & Great Northern Joint Railway*. Newton Abbot: David & Charles

Periodicals and society journals

Furness Railway Magazine

Great Central Railway Magazine

Great Eastern Railway Society Journal

Highland Railway Journal

Industrial Archaeology News

Locomotive Journal

North Eastern Railway Magazine

Railway Archive

Railway Magazine

The Railway Review

Transport and Travel Monthly

Index

Page numbers in **bold** refer to figures and tables.

2nd Cheshire Engineers (Railway) Volunteers 5
17th Northumberland Fusiliers (NER) Pioneers 91–4
84th Heavy Anti-Aircraft Regiment of the Royal Artillery 165
96th Light Railway Operating Company 97
98th Light Railway Train Crew Company 97
115th Railway Company Royal Engineers (RE) 94, 97
116th Railway Construction Company Royal Engineers (RE) 94, 97
265th Railway Construction Company 97
266th Railway Construction Company 97
275th Company Royal Engineers Railway Troops 94–5
565th Wilts Army Troop Company RE(T) 95–6

A

Abbey Mills Junction (London) **118**
Aberdeen 70
Abergavenny (Monmouthshire) 46, 132
Aberystwyth (Ceredigion) 6, 9
accidents, railway 11–12, 20, 36, 106–7, 107–8, 134
Acheux (France) 93
Achnasheen (Highland) 68, 145, 146
Achnashellach (Highland) 146
Ack Ack Command 113
acts of courage 20, 64, 128–9, 141, 153–4
Addison Road station (London) **111**, 147
Admiralty
  Boer War 3
  First World War 20, 44, 45, 52, 63, **63**, 64, 66–9, **67**
  gauge change concerns 1
  preferential treatment law 1

Second World War 99, 125, 146, 148
Agadir crisis (1911) 6
Air Ministry 106, 127
air-raid precautions (ARP) 101, 106–9, **107**, **108**, **109**, 117–20
aircraft and parts manufacture 53, 54, 115, 148, 149
airfields 145, 150, 152–3, 154
Aldenham (Herts) 149
Aldershot (Hants) 6, 10, 41, 109, 159
Alexandra, Queen 185
Alleyn Park Road (West Dulwich) 123
Alness (Highland) 43, 145
Alnmouth (Northd) 115
ambulance stretchers 52
ambulance trains
  First World War 11, 45–9, **45**, **46**, 76, **83**
  Second World War 102, 109, 119, 156–7, 159
America *see* United States
American Locomotive Company (ALCO) 85–6, **85**
Amiral Ganteaume liner 64
Anderson, Sir Alan 100, 126–7, 179
Anglia, SS 64
Anslow, Tonman Mosley, Baron 175
anti-aircraft camps 113, 152
anti-aircraft guns 61, 112, 126–7, 144–5, 162
Antwerp (Belgium) 12, 46
Arborfield (Berks) 22
Ardeer (Ayrshire) 18
armoured trains **4**, 13, 16, 53, 98, 112, 113–15, **114**, 141–2
Armstrong Whitworth (Sir W G) & Co Ltd **3**, 18–19, **81**, 82–3, **143**
Arras (France) **81**, 85, 172
Arrowe Park (Birkenhead) 162
Ashbury Railway Carriage & Iron company 53
Ashchurch (Gloucs) 162
Ashford (Kent) 109, 113, 114, 115, 148–9, 166
Aspinall, John A F 7, 79
Associated Society of Locomotive Engineers and Firemen (ASLEF) 26–7,

32, 36–8, 48, 55, 56, 58, 185
Audruicq (France) 87, 90
Australian troops 51, 73–4, 78
Austria 2–3
Austro-Prussian War 2–3
Avonmouth (Bristol) 19, 22, 23, 47, 99, 132, 163
Avonside Engine Co **51**
awards for bravery 91, 129, 141, 154, 170, 180
Ayr 75

B

Baedeker raids 122
Baghdad Railway 97–8
Bain, David 38
Baker Street station (London) 174–5
Balaclava, Sebastopol (Russia) **1**, 2
Baldwin Locomotive Works (USA) 85–6, **85**, **86**, **169**
Baluchistan Chrome Mines Company (Pakistan) 98
Banbury (Oxon) 67, 71, 130
Bank of England evacuation 104
Barassie (Ayrshire) 148
Barnham (Suffolk) 150
Barnstaple (Devon) 57, 115, 126
Barrow-in-Furness (Cumbria) 20, 178
Barry Railway (Glamorgan) 170, 176
Basingstoke & Alton Light Railway 42
Bassett-Lowke manufacturers 50
Bassin Loubet operation (France) 78
Beatty, Lady Ethel 72
Beauly (Highland) 145, 146
Bedale (Yorks) 46
Beenham Grange, Aldermaston (Berks) 101
Belgian refugees 12–13, **13**, 28, 46, 64, 65, **110**
Belgium 12–13, **13**, 64, 78, 79, 81–2, **84**, **88**, 93, 95
Bellamy, Albert 56
Bentley (Hants) 6
Bentley, Nellie 141

Bentley (Suffolk) 60
Bere Ferrers (Devon) 11–12
Bessborough, Edward Ponsonby, 8th Earl 185
Betts, Edward **1**
Beyer Peacock & Co Ltd **50**, 53, 149–50, 166
Bicester Military Railway 154
Bideford, Westward Ho! & Appledore Railway 42
'Big Four' railways 99
Birkenhead (Merseyside) 67, 129, 157, 162, **165**
Birmingham
  Bordesley Junction 128
  First World War **9**, 58, 76
  New Street station **9**, 118, 121–2
  Second World War **103**, 118, 121–2, 128, 147
  service of commemoration 185
  Snow Hill station 76
  Sutton Park goods depot 147
  Tyseley works 58
Birmingham Railway Carriage & Wagon company 53
Black Hall (Montgomeryshire) 73
blackout adaptations 15, **33**, 60, 101, 106–9, **107**, **108**
Blaydon (Tyne and Wear) 16, 94
Blenheim locomotive 173
Bletchley (Bucks) 106–7
Blyth (Northd) 115
Board of Trade 7, 36, 37–8, 41–2, 43, 52, 55, 57, 58
Boer War 3, **4**, 5, 50, 170, 185–6
bogie vehicles 46, 53, 119, 127, 131, 148
bomb types
  delayed-action 124
  high-explosive 120, 121, 123–4
  incendiary 120, 124–5, 128, 129
  parachute mines 120, 123
  unexploded (UXBs) 124, 130
  V-1 and V-2 rockets 129, 159–62, **160**
bombing and damage, home front
  First World War 15, 60–2, **61**, **62**

Second World War 117,
118, **119**, 120–8, **121**,
122, **123**, **124**, **125**, **128**,
129, 159–62, **160**
bombing, recovery from 118,
130–1, 161, 162–3
Bonsor, R H Cosmo 176, **177**
Booth, Charles 179
Bordon (Hants) 41, 50, 154
Bordon Light Railway 6
Boston (Lincs) 47
Boulton (R L) & Sons, sculptors
179
Bourne Park Tunnel (Kent) 142
Bournemouth Daily Echo 169
Bournemouth (Dorset) 112,
147
Bow Street station (London) 6,
61, 118
Bowen-Cooke, C J 52
Boxer Uprising (China) 5–6
boys, employment of 36, 38,
56, 137, 149
Bradford Moor (Yorks) 72
Bradford (Yorks) **103**
brake vans 44, 87, 119
Bramley (Surrey) 141
Brassey, Lady 71
Brassey, Thomas **1**
Bratton Court (Somerset) 23
Brest (France) 73, 111
Bricklayers Arms goods depot
(London) 33
Bridgend (Glamorgan) 150–1,
151
bridges 14, 90, 93, 95, 96, 115,
118, 119, 123–4, **124**,
161, 162
Brigg (Lincs) 16
Brighton (Sussex) 141, 147,
148–9, 162
British Expeditionary Force
(BEF)
First World War
demobilisation 74–6, **76**
mobilisation 9–13, **9**
supplying 17–23, **17**,
18, **22**, 77–82, 84
Second World War 99, 109,
132–3
Bromley, John 37
Brookwood–Bisley Camp
Tramway 73
Broompark, SS 112
Brownlow, Adelbert Brownlow-
Cust, 3rd Earl 51
Bruges (Belgium) 65
Brussels, SS 65, **65**, 185
Buccleuch, John Scott, 7th
Duke 180
Bulford (Wilts) 11–12, 41
Burgin, Dr Leslie 101
Burntisland (Fife) 67
Burscough Junction station
(Lancs) 23

Burton & Ashby Light Railway
38, 42
Burton Common Crossing
(Dorset) 129
Bury, SS 64
Butterworth, Sir Alexander
Kaye 7, 19, 38, 77

C

Cairnryan (Dumfries and
Galloway) 143
Calais (France) 74, 75, 82, **83**,
165
Caledonian Railway
memorials 179
movement of troops 10
service reductions 40
serving the fleet 66, 68
staff issues 30, 33, 57
supplying the front 18
vessels 64
works and equipment 53,
90
Calthrop, Guy 29, 38
Cambrai, Battle of 21, 87
Cambrian Railways 9
Camden goods shed (London)
104, 108, 163
camouflage, dazzle painting
iv, **167**
Canada 80, 112, 169
Canadian Pacific Railway
(CPR) 3, 169
Canadian railwaymen 3, **3**,
27–8, 82, 87
Canadian troops 11, 23, 69,
73, 75, 132, 147, 154,
156, 161
Canterbury (Kent) 114, 142
Canterbury, Randall Davidson,
Archbishop of 179, 180
Cardiff 58, 68, 157, **170**
Carey, Robert 64
cartridge cases 53
Castlerosse, Valentine Browne,
Viscount 164
Castletown (Highland) 145
Casualty Evacuation Trains
(CETs) 119–20; *see also*
ambulance trains
Caterham (Surrey) 104
Catterick Bridge (Yorks) 51,
92, 144
Catterick (Yorks) **50**, 51, 75,
142, **143**
Chalk Farm (London) 33
Channel Islands 111
Charfield (Gloucs) 20
Charing Cross Bridge (London)
162
Charing Cross station (London)
8, 65, 120
Chatham (Kent) 5, 45, 67

chemical works/chemicals 21,
183
Cheshire Royal Engineers
(Railway Battalion) 5
Chiddingfold (Surrey) 22
Chieveley (South Africa) **4**
Chilwell (Notts) 20
China 5–6, 82, **153**, 167–8
Chinese workers 80, **89**
Chiseldon (Wilts) 11
Chislehurst Caves (Bromley)
129
Chiswick (London) 162
Chorley (Lancs) 151
Christie, Lance Corporal John
Alexander 'Jock,' VC 172–
3, **172**
Church Fenton (Yorks) 71
Churchill, Victor Spencer, 1st
Viscount 71, 176, 180, 185
Churchill, Winston 3, **3**, **4**, 55,
74–5, 131, 145
Cirencester (Gloucs) 52
City of Bradford, SS 63
City of Leeds, SS 63–4
Clacton-on-Sea (Essex) 104
Clark, C W 174
Claughton, Sir Gilbert 65
Clipstone (Notts) 16, 51, 75
Clyde River (Glasgow) 63, 83,
132, 155, 156, 157, 159
Clydebank evacuations **103**
coal quality 86, 135
coal, transport of 14, 41, 44,
66–8, **67**, 70, 80, 110,
142, 144
Codford (Wilts) 11, 51
Colchester (Essex) 16
Colchester, SS 64
Collcutt & Hamp architects 176
Collins, C D 176
Cologne (Germany) 65, 90
Commands 15–16
commemoration services 185
Committee on Recruiting and
Substitution of
Railwaymen 29–30, 37
communication lines 117–18
compensation to railways 8,
52, 63
conscription *see* enlistment/
conscription of railwaymen
cordite paste 18, **18**, 20
Corsham (Wilts) 20, 152
Coventry Trades Council 34, 36
Craig, Ernest 53
Cranwell (Lincs) 51
Crewe (Cheshire) 26, 52–3,
69, 80, **84**, 108, 148, 155,
170, **184**
Crimean War **1**, 2
Croft Spa (Yorks) 75
Cromarty (Highland) 69, 146
Cubitt, B B 26
Culzean Castle (Ayrshire) 103

Cunard White Star 127
Cunninghame Graham, R B 22
Cupar (Fife) 22, 75

D

D-Day 130–1, 136, 144, 145,
156, 157–9, 168
Dalcross (Highland) 145
Dalmally (Argyll and Bute) 152
Dalmore (Highland) 42, 68, 70
damage from enemy action *see*
bombing and damage,
home front; strafing
Darbyshire, G L 133–4
Darlington (Co Durham)
18–19, 55, 71
Davington Light Railway 18
deaths in railway
First World War 11–12, 15,
18, 26, 62, 75
Second World War 106–7,
115, 117, 120–1, **122**,
123, **125**, 129, 141, 144,
153–4, 161–2
Decauville, Paul 84, 86
Deepdene (Surrey) 101
defence, home front 13–16,
14, 53, 95, 112–16, **113**,
114, **116**, 127–8, 144–5
Defence of the Realm Act
(1914) 15, 38, 43
Defiant locomotive 173
demobilisation 74–6, **76**, 96,
162
demurrage 42–3
Dent, C H 7, 29, 52
Dent, Francis H 7, 12–13, 36,
47, 78
Deptford (London) 162
Derby
First World War 53
memorials 170, 179, **179**,
183–4
Second World War 102,
113, 148, 162
Derby, Edward Stanley, 17th
Earl 28, 74
Derby Scheme 28
Devizes (Wilts) 155
Devonport (Devon) 47, 67,
125–6
Devonshire, Victor Cavendish,
9th Duke 178
Didcot (Berks) 20
'Dig for Victory' campaign 106,
106
Dingwall (Highland) 69
dining cars 40, 101, 134–5,
162–3; *see also* refresh-
ments for passengers
Dinton (Wilts) 41, 51
disabled staff, war- 39, 58
diversionary routes 130, 131

docks, railway 17, 62–3, 69, 121, 143, 158, 164, 176
dogs 109
Donaldson, Sir Frederick 52
Doncaster (Yorks) 26, 28, 75, 102, **140**, 148, 157
Dornoch (Sutherland) 73
Dover, Harold Bilbrough, Bishop of 176
Dover (Kent) 12, 60, 65, 99, 109, 110, 129, 147, 159, 176, **177**
Dovercourt (Essex) 65
Down Street Underground station (London) 100
Draycott (Wilts) 11
Dudley (West Midlands) 61
Duke of York, TSS 111
Dunbridge (Hants) 144, 158
Dundee **103**
Dunkirk (France) 82, 95, 109–12, **110**, **111**, 169
Durham 16

E

Ealing Broadway station (London) 104
Earl Haig locomotive 177
East & West Yorkshire Union Railway 12
East Africa 98
East Croydon (London) 30, 141
Eastleigh (Hants) 26, 41, 102, 106, 117, 138, 148, 166
Ebbw Junction, Newport (Gwent) 157
Eden, Anthony 109, 112
Edinburgh 71, 72, 75, **103**, 117, 180
Edinburgh, Leith & Granton Railway 117
Edith Cavell locomotive 171
Egypt 44, 64–5, 94, 96, 166, 167
Egyptian Expeditionary Force (EEF) 96–7
Eisenhower, Gen Dwight D 141–2
El Ferdan (Egypt) 94
El Kantara (Egypt) 94, 96
Elswick (Tyne and Wear) **3**, **81**, 82–3, **143**
Empress, HMS 64
Engadine, HMS 64
Engineer and Railway Volunteer Staff Corps 4–5
enlistment/conscription of railwaymen
  First World War 12, 23, **24**, 25–30, 31, 38, 91
  Second World War 133, 136–7, 165–6

Epsom (Surrey) 75
equipment *see* workshops, railway
Euston station (London) 68, 101, 112, 137, 145, 170, 173, 178–9, **178**, 185–6
evacuations from cities 101, 103–4, **103**, **104**, **105**, 129, 162
evacuations from continent 64, 109–12, **110**, **111**
Evanton (Highland) 145
Evesham Abbey locomotive **102**
Ewell (Surrey) 104
Exeter (Devon) 104, 122, 131
export trade 40

F

Fairclough, Paul **183**
Fairfield Shipbuilding 82–3
Falmouth (Cornwall) 112
Faringdon, Harold Henderson, Baron 177
Farmer & Brindley sculptors 176
Farnborough (Hants) 41
Faslane (Argyll and Bute) 143
Fay, Sir Sam 5, 7, 25, 32, 38, 79, 176
Felixstowe (Suffolk) 104
Fenay Bridge and Lepton (Yorks) 21
ferries, cross-Channel train 82–3, **83**, 165, **165**
Fielden, Edward B 174
Findlay, Sir George 5
fire-watchers 125
First World War
  in Britain
    ambulance trains 45–9, **45**, **46**
    American troops 73–4, **74**
    BEF, mobilising 9–13, **9**
    blackout adaptations 15
    compensation to railways 8
    damage from enemy action 60–2, **61**, **62**
    demobilisation 74–6, **76**
    doing more with less 42–5, **44**
    horses 21–3, **22**
    management of railways 7–8
    military railways 49–51, **49**, **50**, **51**
    prisoners of war 72–3
    protecting railways 13–16, **14**

railway docks and vessels 62–5, **63**, **65**
railway hotels 73
railway land, use of 59–60, **59**
railway works and war equipment 52–5
REC *see* Railway Executive Committee (REC), First World War
refugees 12–13, **13**
service reductions 39–42
serving the fleet 66–71, **67**
staff shortages 23, **24**, 25–30
supplying fronts 17–23, **17**, **18**, **22**
sustenance for servicemen 71–2, **72**
wages 55–9
women, employment of **28**, 30–9, **31**, **33**, **35**
commemoration services 185
memorials
  Captain Fryatt **65**
  company 173–82, **174**, **175**, **177**, **178**, **179**, **180**, **181**
  local 182–5, **183**, **184**
  locomotives, naming of 171–3, **172**
  neglect and restoration 185–6
  rolls of honour 170–1, **170**, **171**
  overseas
    cross-Channel train ferry service **83**, 98
    India 98
    light railways 83–6, **83**, **85**, **86**
    Mesopotamia 97–8
    military ports 82–3, **83**
    Palestine 96–7
    rail-mounted guns **81**
    railway battalions 91–5
    railwaymen in France 86–7, **88**, **89**, 90
    railwaymen on the front 90–6, **92**
    theatres of war 77–82
fleet *see* Admiralty
Flying Scotsman locomotive 126
Flying Scotsman Spitfire 129
Folkestone (Kent) 12, 13, 74, 75, **76**, 109, 129, 159
food and drink see refreshments for passengers

food supplies 21, 59–60, **59**, 104, 106, **106**, 146, 159
Fort George (Highland) 72
Foster (William) & Co Ltd 20–1
Fovant Military Railway **50**, 51
Fowler (John) & Co 53
Fowler, Sir Henry 38, 179
France
  British foreign policy regarding 6
  First World War
    ambulance trains **46**, 47
    Bassin Loubet operation 78
    Battle of Cambrai 21, 87
    Battle of the Somme 29, 47–8, 79, 92–3, 95, 170
    British locomotives and wagons 78–9, 80, 82, 87, 90
    Chinese workers 80, **89**
    demobilisation 75
    inland water transport system 82
    light railways 81, 83–6, **84**, **85**, **86**, **88**, **89**, **92**
    management of BEF railways 77–81
    military ports 82–3, **83**
    movement of supplies to 17
    movement of troops to 9–12, **9**, 17
    pals battalions 91–6
    rail-mounted guns **81**
    railwaymen on the front 90–6, **92**
    Royal Engineers (RE) 77, 80
    tracks, new 79, 80–1, 82, 90–1, 93
    wagons 79, 80, 82, 83, **88**
    working conditions 86–7, 90
    workshops 80, 82, 87, 93
  Franco-Prussian War 2, 3
  Second Italian War of Independence 2
  Second World War 166, 168–9
Free Polish Army 127
French, Sir John 77–8
Frith Hill (Surrey) 73
Fryatt, Captain Charles 13, 65, **65**, 171–2, 185
fuel rationing 99
Fulham (London) 39
Furness Railway 20, 39, 178
Furniss, Harry 171

G

Gainsborough (Lincs) 30
Galloway, Col W Johnson 185
gas masks 21, 101, **102**
Gasston, Alfred 182–3
gauge changes 1, 2
Geddes, Brigadier General
    Auckland 29
Geddes, Sir Eric Campbell 19,
    19, 38, 41, 77, 78, 79, 81,
    84, 85
General Joffre locomotive 171
George VI 185
German Central Military
    Railway (East Africa) 98
Germany 2, 6, 63, 84, 96, 99,
    152, 162
Gimbert, Ben 153–4
Girouard, Sir Eduoard Percy
    Cranwill 3, **3**, 77–8
Glascoed (Monmouthshire)
    151
Glasgow
    Central station 179
    First World War 12, 36, 57,
      67, 71, 75
    memorials 179
    Queen Street station 71
    Second World War 99, 103,
      103, 131, 157
    St Rollox station 57
    Wallneuk Junction 36
Glasgow & Paisley Joint
    Railway 36
Glasgow & South Western
    Railway (GSWR) 18, 52,
    64, 66, 73, 148
Globe Road/Devonshire Street
    goods yard (London)
    124–5
Gloucester Railway Carriage &
    Wagon company 53
Godwin, G H 56–7
Goodmans Yard (London) **118**
goods traffic 28, 39, 40, 43,
    144–5, 146, **149**, 150, **153**;
    see also coal, transport of;
    munitions
Gordon, Sir James Willoughby
    1
Gorton (Manchester) 52, 82, 141
Goschen, Sir Edward 8
Gosport (Hants) 67, **103**, 155
Govan (Glasgow) 82–3
Granet, Sir Guy 7, 38, **38**, 44,
    79, 82
Grangemouth (Falkirk) 66, 68
Grantham (Lincs) 16, 75, 135
Great Central Railway (GCR)
    ambulance trains 46, 47
    BEF, mobilising 11
    docks and vessels 62–3,
      63–4, **63**
    Hotel Great Central 73

locomotives sent overseas
    44, 82
memorials 173–4, 176–7,
    178, **178**, **184**, 186
new links 21
service reductions 40
serving the fleet 67
signal boxes **109**
staff shortages 25
warehouse shelter 62
women, employment of 30,
    32, 33, **33**, **35**, **109**
Great Eastern Railway (GER)
    ambulance trains 46, 47
    BEF, mobilising 11
    bombing and damage 60,
      61, 62
    docks and vessels 62, **63**,
      65, **65**, 83
    hotels 73
    memorials 176, 185
    Poultry Demonstration Train
      60
    protecting railways 15, 113
    railwaymen POWs 39
    service reductions 40
    supplying the front 20
    women, employment of 33,
      33
Great North of Scotland Railway
    (GNSR) 10, 33, 70
Great Northern Railway (GNR)
    ambulance trains 46
    memorials **174**, 186
    military railways 51
    protecting railways 15
    redundancy worries 12
    service reductions 39, 40
    supplying the front 20–1
    working hours 26
    works and equipment 52, 53
Great Western Railway (GWR)
    acts of courage 128, 129,
      141
    ambulance trains 45, 46, 47,
      101
    BEF, mobilising 11
    bombing and damage 61,
      122, 124, 129, 159
    D-Day 157, 158
    demobilisation 75, 76
    docks and vessels **63**, 64,
      169
    evacuations from cities 101,
      102
    evacuations from continent
      109, 111
    factories and airfields,
      building/supplying 150–
      1, **153**
    flying bombs 159
    funding hospital beds 48
    land, use of 59
    locomotives sent overseas
      43–4, 82, 87, 90, 138, 166

memorials 147, 170, 171,
    171, 173, 179–80, **180**,
    181, 182, 184, 185
military railways **50**, 51
parcels to serving
    railwaymen 38–9
post-war recovery 162–3
protecting railways 14, 15
railwaymen on the front 90,
    94–6
refreshments for passengers
    71
refugees 13
resilience 130, 131
service reductions 39, 40,
    41, 101
serving the fleet 66, 68
special trains 8, 141
staff shortages **24**, 25, 26,
    28, 29, 37, 38
supplying the front 19, 20,
    22
theft of goods 23, 147
traffic pressures 133, 134,
    135, 136
volunteer paid labour 137–8
wages 55, 58
wagon shortage 43
war-disabled staff 57–8
women, employment of 30,
    31, 32, 33
working hours 26, 36
works and equipment 52,
    53–4, 147, 148
greatcoats 75
Gresley, Sir Nigel 113
Gretna/Eastriggs cordite
    factory 18, **18**
Grey, Edward, 1st Viscount
    Grey of Falloden 182
Grimsby Docks (Lincs) 62–3
Grimsby Telegraph 30–1
Grove, Brigadier General
    Edward 14
Grove, The (Watford) 101
gun carriages 52
gun trucks 53
Guston Tunnel (Kent) 142
GWR Magazine 23, 30, 95

H

Haig, Sir Douglas, 1st Earl 43,
    53, 77, 79, 80, 81, 174,
    177, 179
Haldane, Richard, 1st Viscount
    5
Hamburg (Germany) 63
Hamilton, Lord Claud 27, 39,
    64, 65
Hampshire, HMS 78
Hantonia, SS 168
Harrowby (Lincs) 51
Hartlepool (Co Durham) 60, 91

Harwich (Essex) 73, 83, 99,
    109, 159
Hayes (Avonmouth) 19
Headcorn (Kent) 110
Healing (Lincs) 16
heating 135
heavy water 112
Henbury (Bristol) 19
Hercules locomotive 115
herring 146
Heywood, Sir Arthur 84
Hibernia, SS 64–5, 172
Highbridge (Somerset) 179
Highland Railway (HR)
    ambulance trains 48
    hotels 69, 73
    memorials 178
    protecting railways 14
    service reductions 42
    serving the fleet 66, 69–71
    special trains 145
    staff shortages 30, 38
    sustaining war effort 145
    traffic pressures 43, 146
    working hours 36–7
Highlands Special Military Area
    66, 144–7
Hockley (Essex) 76
Hodder, SS 169
Hollingdale, Harold 23
Holyhead (Gwynedd) 65, 67
Holzminden internment camp
    (Germany) 65
Home Ambulance Trains
    (HATs) 102
Home Guard 112, 113, 115,
    116, 148, 149
Home Guard locomotive 112
Hoo, The, Hitchin (Herts) 101
Horne, General Henry, Baron
    178
Hornsey (London) **124**
horse races 135
horses 6, 10, 11, 21–3, **22**, 60,
    74, 75–6, 108
Horsham (Sussex) 72
hospital ships 64, 159
hospitals 46, 48, 73, 102, 120
Hotel Great Central
    (Marylebone) 73
hotels, railway 13, 38, 73
Hudswell, Clarke and Company
    51
Hughes, George **183**
Hull & Barnsley Railway (HBR)
    12, 21, 26, 33, 91
Hull (Yorks)
    First World War 16, 33, 47,
      67, 75, 91–2
    Paragon station 16, 128, 129
    Second World War **103**,
      120, 128, 129, 157
    Southcoates station 16
Humphrey, D 161
Hunslet Engineering 53, **88**

Hurricane locomotive 173
Hurst, Nelson and Company, Ltd 53
Hurstbourne Park (Hants) 104
Hyde, Sir Clarendon 175
hydrogen gas 143
Hythe (Kent) 142
Hythe, SS 64

I

Ibex, TSS 64
Immingham (Lincs) 63, 67, 75
Imperial War Museum 182
India 19, 98, 167–8, 169
Indian troops 97–8, 167
influenza 75, 137
Invergordon (Highland) 42, 66, 69, 70–1, 144, 145
Inverness 42, 43, 66, 68, 69, 70, 114, 146, 178
Invershin (Highland) 146
Invicta Spitfire 129
Ipswich (Suffolk) 16, 104, 114
Iran 148, 166–7, **167**, **168**, **169**
Iraq 166, 167
Irwin, R C 173–4
Isle of Sark, SS 111, 169
Isle of Wight Central Railway 36
Italy 2, 101, 166, 172

J

Jagger, Charles 179–80, **180**, **181**
Japan 138, 162, 167, 169
Jellicoe, Admiral John, 1st Earl 66
Jellicoe specials 66–8, **67**, 145
Jerusalem 97
Jutland, Battle of 64

K

Kempton Park (Surrey) 146, 155
Kerry, Lord 176
Kerry Tramway (Monmouthshire) 73
Keymer, Revd B W 26
Killingworth (Tyne and Wear) 16
Kilmister, Mr 20
Kilnhurst (Yorks) 30
Kimbolton (Hunts) 162
King Lynn's (Norfolk) 61
King, W C H 176
King's Cross Station (London) **116**, **122**, 131, 136, **174**, 186

Kinloss (Highland) 145
Kinmel Park (Flintshire) 11
Kirkcudbright (Dumfries and Galloway) 152
Kirkpatrick, R C 94
Kitchener, Herbert, 1st Earl 3, 13, 27, 77, 78
Knight, Laura 138
Knight of Liège locomotive 171
Knott End Railway 37
Kowarski, Lew 112
Kretschmer, Otto 145
Kyle of Lochalsh (Highland) 70, 144, 145–6, 155

L

L./ Corp[l]. J.A. Christie VC locomotive 172, **172**
Lake, E 94
Lambeth (London) **62**
Lancashire & Yorkshire Railway (LYR)
  ambulance trains **45**, 46–7, **83**
  Horwich Works **17**, **28**, 148, **183**
  memorials 170, 171, 173–4, **175**, **183**
  railwaymen POWs 39
  redundancy worries 12
  service reductions 40
  supplying the front **17**, 22–3
  theft of goods 23
  vessels **63**, 169
  wagon shortage 43
  women, employment of **28**, 30
  works and equipment 52
Lancaster 72
Lancing (Sussex) 102, 141, 148, 182–3
land, use of railway 59–60, **59**, 106
Langemarck, Battle of **84**
Lathom Park (Lancs) 22, **22**
lavatories 40
Lawrence, Captain 64
Lawrence, Charles 179
Le Roy-Lewis, Colonel 77
Lee, Mrs 111
Leeds (Yorks) 34, 71, **103**
Leicester 21
Leith (Edinburgh) 67, 131
letters 11, 48, 147
Lewis, Henry Gethin 68
Lidster, Miss 30
light railways
  in Britain 6, 18, 51, 146
  on Continent 79, 80–2, 83–6, **84**, **85**, **86**, **88**, **89**, **92**, 93
Lighting Committee 106

Limerick, Lady 71
Lincoln 20–1, 33
Liphook (Hants) 41
Liss (Hants) 154
Littlehampton (Sussex) 17, 158
Liverpool
  1830s troubles 1
  First World War 12, 21, 22, 47, 73–4, **74**
  Knotty Ash & Stanley station **74**
  Riverside station 22, 159
  Second World War 104, 121, 129, 156
Liverpool & Manchester Railway 1
Liverpool Street station (London) 8, 33, 47, 60, 62, 65, **65**, **105**, **125**, 176
Llandaff , Joshua Hughes, Bishop of 176
Llanidloes (Powys) 9
Llantrisant (Glamorgan) 58
Lloyd George, David 19, 38, 41, 53, 55, 78, 79
Lloyd, Sir Charles 4
Local Defence Volunteers 112, **113**
Loch Ewe (Wester Ross) 145
Lockheed Hudson locomotive 173
Locomotive Journal 36–7
locomotives
  First World War
    0-4-0s 49, 86
    0-4-4s 86
    0-6-0s 43–4, 51, **51**, 78, 86, 87, 90, 98
    0-6-2s 53
    0-8-0s 44, **44**, **67**, 84, 86, 87
    2-4-2s **45**
    2-6-0s 44, 87
    2-6-2s 86
    2-8-0s 39, 44, 82
    4-4-0s 11, **35**
    4-4-2s **50**
    4-6-0s 8, 85, **85**, **88**
    American 85–6, **85**
    Belgian 78, 80
    captured by Germans 87
    construction 43, 45, 51, **51**, 52, 82, 85–6, **85**, **86**, **88**
    Péchot-Bourdon 86, **86**
    repairs 12, 30, 44, 51, 53, 54, 80
    requisitioned for overseas service 43–4, **44**, 80, 82, 87, 94, 98
    returned from overseas 45

named in honour 171–3, **172**, 177
Second World War
  0-4-4s 127, **128**
  0-6-0s 126, 127, 154, 157, **165**, 166
  0-6-2s **113**
  0-8-0s 131
  2-4-2s 113–15, **114**
  2-6-0s 138
  2-6-2s 126
  2-8-0s 146, **149**, 150, 155, 157, 166, 167, **167**
  2-8-2s **169**
  2-10-0s 150
  4-4-2s 131
  4-6-0s **102**, 112, 156
  4-8-2s 115
  American 157
  construction 130–1, 133, **149**, 150
  Dean Goods 138, **153**
  pug shunters **152**
  repairs 126, 131, 134, 161
  requisitioned for overseas service 138, 166, 167
London
  First World War
    bombing and damage 61–2, **61**, **62**
    food supplies 59–60, **59**
    horses, stabling of 22
    leave trains 41
    REC offices 8
    refreshments for passengers 71, **72**
    refugees 12
    memorials **174**, 176, 178–9, **178**, 179–80, **180**, **181**, **184**, 186
  Second World War
    acts of courage 128
    barrage balloon cables 162
    blackout adaptations 108
    bombing and damage 118, **118**, **119**, 120–1, **121**, **122**, 123–4, 124–5, 159–60, **160**, 161–2
    Casualty Evacuation Trains (CETs) 120
    evacuations 103, **103**, 104, **105**, 129, 162
    railway pair-horse van **139**
    refreshments for passengers **111**
    Royal Family 136
    service restoration planning 118–19

see also named railways; named stations

London & North Eastern Railway (LNER)
allied troops 156–7
ambulance trains 102, 156–7
blackout adaptations **107**
bombing and damage **118**, **124**, **125**, 129, 159, **160**, 162
Dodnash Priory Farm 60
evacuations from cities 104
evacuations from continent 109, **110**, 111
factories and airfields, building/supplying 151, 152–3
flying bombs 159, **160**, 162
Local Defence Volunteers **113**
memorials **174**, 178, 182
protecting railways 115
refreshments for passengers 135
resilience 131
service reductions 101
special trains 141–2
Spitfire 129
supplying liberated areas 159
sustaining war effort 144, 147
theft of goods 147
traffic pressures 136
training exercises 132
vessels 143
women, employment of **140**
works and equipment 147, 148, 149

London & North Western Railway (LNWR)
allied troops 74
ambulance trains 45, 46, 47
Crewe tractors **84**
Crewe Works *see* Crewe (Cheshire)
damage, war 61, 122
demobilisation 75
foreign lines, control of 78
homes for war-disabled staff 39
land, use of 59
locomotives sent overseas 44
memorials 170, 171–3, **172**, 178–9, **178**, 182, **184**, 185, 186
mobilisation timetables 6
movement of troops **9**, 10
protecting railway 15
railway vessels **63**, 64–5
railwaymen on the front 90, 94
railwaymen regiments 5, 94
secretarial responsibilities 6
service reductions 40

serving the fleet 66, 69
staff shortages 27, 29, 38
supplying fronts 21
wages 39
wagon shortage 43
women, employment of 30, 33, 34
works and equipment 52, 53, 80

London & South Western Railway (LSWR)
allied troops 74
ambulance trains 47
blackout adaptations 15
docks and vessels 62, **63**, 64, 168
horses 21–2
land, use of 59, **59**
locomotives sent overseas 94, 98
memorials 170, 175–6, 185
military railways 50, **50**, 51
movement of troops 3, 6, 10, 11–12, 17
prisoners of war 73
serving the fleet 70
special trains 41
supplying the front 17
women, employment of 33
working hours 26

London Bridge station **31**, 71, 128, 176

London Brighton & South Coast Railway (LBSCR) 20, 30, 38, **63**, 64, 173, 176, 182–3

London Midland & Scottish Railway (LMS)
acts of courage 141
air-raid precautions (ARP) 117, 119
allied troops 156, 157
ambulance trains 102
blackout adaptations 108
bombing and damage 118, 120, 121, 123, 124, 125–6, 129, 159, 169
British POWs 159
D-Day 158
evacuations from continent 109, 111
factories and airfields, building/supplying 154
flying bombs 159
locomotives sent overseas 167
memorials 172
military railways 154
post-war recovery 162, 164
prisoners of war 155
railwaymen on the front 166
railwaymen POWs 138
resilience 130
service reductions 101, 134
special trains 141, 144

staff shortages 136, 137
sustaining war effort 145
theft of goods 147
traffic pressures 133, 135, 136
vessels 169
women, employment of 141
working hours 133, 134
works and equipment 147–9, 150

London Tilbury & Southend Railway 60–1
London Transport (LT) 115, 121, 138, 149, 165
London Underground 101, 103, 120–1, **163**
Longdon (G) & Son 177
Longmoor (Hants) **49**, 50–1, **51**, 94
Longmoor Military Railway (LMR) 6, 50–1, **50**, **51**, 154
lorries 79, **83**, 84, 91, 163–4
Louth (Lincs) 16, 115
Lovegrove (Ceredigion) 9
Low Fell (Gateshead) 16
Lowestoft (Suffolk) 61, 67
Lubbock, General G 97
Ludgershall–to–Tidworth military railway 50
Ludgershall (Wilts) 11
Lundie, Captain 63
Lutyens, Sir Edwin 179, **179**, 182
Lynton & Barnstaple Railway 57
Lynx, TSS 64

M

McAlpine (Sir Robert) & Sons engineering and construction 100
Macauley, Sir George 96
MacColl, Dugald S 179–80
Machen (Monmouthshire) 52
McIntosh, J F 80
Mackay, F E **67**
Macrae, Charles 176
Maginot Line (France) 83
Maida Vale station (London) 30
Malcolm, Lieutenant Colonel 11
management of railways 7–8, 77–81
Manby, Charles 4
Manchester
Ardwick No 2 signal box 33
Exchange station 186
First World War 12, 30, 33, 47, 52, 82
Gorton works 52, 82, 141
Horwich Works **17**, **28**,

148, **183**
Irlam o' the Heights station, Salford 30
memorials 174, **175**, 186
Newton Heath Carriage Works 47
Piccadilly station 186
Second World War **103**, 108, 117, 121, 141, 147, 155, 157, 159, 174, **175**, 186
Victoria station 159, 174, **175**
Victoria West Junction signalbox 108
Manchester Guardian 99
Manchester, William Temple, Bishop of 174
Marchbank, John 134
Margate (Kent) 109, **110**
Market Weighton (Yorks) 115
Marriott, William 53
Martin, Annie Eva 33
Marylebone (London) 33, 62, 73, **184**, 186
Maryport & Carlisle Railway 42
Matheson, Donald A 7
Mathwin (Wm) & Son, coal merchants 66
meals *see* refreshments for passengers
Medway Towns (Kent) **103**
Melbourne Military Railway 154
Melton Constable (Norfolk) 53, 114, 147
Melton Mowbray (Leics) 22
memorials
Captain Fryatt 65, **65**
company memorials 173–82, **174**, **175**, **177**, **178**, **179**, **180**, **181**
local memorials 182–5, **183**, **184**
locomotives named in honour 171–3, **172**
neglect and restoration 185–6
rolls of honour 170–1, **170**, **171**
Merseyside **103**, 132, 154, 155, 156, 157, 159; *see also* Birkenhead (Merseyside); Liverpool
Mesopotamia 97–8
Metropolitan Carriage, Wagon, and Finance Company 21, 83
Metropolitan Railway 59–60, 174–5
Metropolitan Railway Carriage & Wagon company 53
Middle East 96–7, 132, 150, 166–7
Middlesbrough (Yorks) 16, 34, 120, **123**

Midland & Great Northern
    Joint Railway (M&GNJR)
    53, 61, 152
Midland & South Western
    Junction Railway
    (MSWJR) 11, 50
Midland Railway
    ambulance trains 46
    bombing and damage 62
    factories and airfields,
        building/supplying 153
    locomotives sent overseas 87
    memorials 170, 171, **171**,
        179, **179**, 183–4
    military railways 154
    movement of troops 10
    railwaymen on the front 91
    resilience 130
    service reductions 39, 40
    staff shortages 38
    supplying the front 20
    sustaining war effort 144
    vessels **63**
    wagon shortage 43, 44
    war-disabled staff 58
    working hours 26
    works and equipment 52, 53
Milestones Living History
    Museum (Hants) **51**
military camps
    pre-First World War 6, 9
    First World War 9, 10, 11,
        23, 49–51, **49**, **51**, 69, 70,
        94, 95
    Second World War 113,
        115, 132, 144, 152
military railways 22, 49–51,
    49, **50**, **51**, 154–5
Military Services Act (1916) 29
milk 146
Milne, Sir James 100, 135–6
minelaying 64, 70
mines, naval 125
minesweepers 63, 64, **165**
Ministry of Food 104, 137,
    159, 163
Ministry of Labour 58, 137,
    149
Ministry of Munitions 18, 19,
    43, 44, 52, 53–4, 55, 78,
    82
Ministry of Supply 131, 146,
    150
Ministry of Transport 76, 106,
    137
Ministry of War Transport
    127, 135, 136
Missenden, Sir Eustace 126–7,
    161
Mobile Advanced Headquarters
    Train 53
Moltke, Helmuth von 3
Monk Fryston (Yorks) 71
Montgomery, General Bernard
    145

Montreuil-sur-Mer (France)
    84
Moore-Brabazon, Lieutenant
    Colonel J T C 101
Moreton (Dorset) 129
Moreton-in-Marsh (Gloucs)
    155
Morgan, Lance Corporal A W
    170
Morpeth (Northd) 115
motor vehicle bans 99
Mount, Sir Alan 131
movement of troops
    pre-First World War 1–2, 3,
        6
    First World War 9–13, **9**, 17
    Second World War 99, 131–
        3, 158
mules 21–3, 132
munitions
    First World War
        accidents 18, 20
        for Admiralty 68
        delivery problems in
            France 79
        manufacture **17**,
            18–19, **18**, 52–3,
            54–5
        storage 20, 49, 52, 87
        transport 17–18, 20, 21,
            43, 83–4, **84**, 85, **89**
    Second World War
        accidents 153–4
        manufacture 148,
            150–1, **151**
        storage 144, 152
        transport 152, 162
Munitions Act (1915) 37

N

National Defence Act (1888) 5
National Gallery 163
National Railway Museum
    (NRM) **51**, 170, 173
National Shell Filling Factory
    No 6, Chilwell (Notts) 20
National Union of Railwaymen
    (NUR)
    redundancy worries 12
    St Paul's commemoration
        service 185
    staff shortages 36
    wages 55–6, 56–7, 58, 138
    women, employment of 31,
        32–3
    women, membership of 32
    working hours 36, 37, 134
Naylor, Arthur 161
Neale, Ambrose 179
Netley (Hants) 47, 48
Nevill, Henry, Marquess of
    Abergavenny 176
Neville Hill (Leeds) 34

New Zealand Railway
    Construction Group 167
New Zealand troops 11–12
New Zealand Tunnelling
    Company RE 96
Newbury (Kent) 21
Newbury Racecourse (Berks)
    157
Newcastle upon Tyne 16,
    32–3, 66, 67, 71, 75
Newhaven (Sussex) 17, 120,
    149, 155, 158
Newton Abbot (Devon) 115,
    147
Newton, Sir Charles H 99,
    100
Nicholls, Horace W **4**
Nigg (Highland) 69
Nightall, James W 153–4
Nine Elms goods depot
    (London) 33, 59
Nine Elms Stable Yard
    (London) 22
Nobel Explosives factory
    (Ayrshire) 18
North Africa 64–5, 132, 143,
    155, 165, 166; see also
    Egypt
North British Locomotive Co
    53, 147, 150
North British Railway (NBR)
    10, 12, 22, 33, 40, 53, 64,
    69, 166, 172, 180
*North Eastern Railway
    Magazine* 72
North Eastern Railway (NER)
    locomotives sent overseas
        44, 87
    memorials 180, 182
    military railways 51
    pals battalion 91–3
    refreshments for passengers
        71, 72
    service reductions 40
    staff shortages 38
    supplying the front 18–19,
        21
    timetables 11
    wagon shortage 43
    women, employment of 33,
        34
    works and equipment 52, 55
North London Railway (NLR)
    61
North Pembrokeshire &
    Fishguard Railway 155
North Staffordshire Railway
    (NSR) 94, 170, 175
North Western Railway (India)
    98
Northampton 21
Northampton & Lamport
    Railway 51
Northern Barrage 70
Northern Ireland 112

Northumberland Fusiliers
    (NER) Pioneers, 17th
    91–3
Norway 112, 113, 131, 165
Norwich 14, 16, 114, 162
Nottingham Victoria station
    147

O

oil supplies 166
Oldbury (Worcs) 83
Oldham (Manchester) 155
Olympia POW camp (London)
    72
Order of the White Feather
    26–7
Ormskirk (Lancs) 22, **22**, 23
Ostend (Belgium) 46, 64
Overseas Ambulance Trains
    (OATs) 102
Owen, Elizabeth May 141
Owen, Reginald Wynn 178,
    178
Owen, Sir Charles 7

P

Paddington station (London)
    8, **24**, 59, 71, **72**, 135–6,
    179–80, **180**, **181**, 185–6
paintings, evacuation and
    return 104, 163, **163**
Palestine 94, 96–7, 166, 172
Palmers Green station
    (London) **113**
pals battalions 91–6, 165–6
parcels to serving railwaymen
    38–9, 47, 138
Paris, HMHS 111
Parker, Madeline 33
Parkeston Quay (Essex) 62,
    149
Parnell (J) & Son **179**
Passchendaele, Battle of 81–2,
    93
passenger traffic 41, 43, 133,
    135–6, **136**, 146
passing loops, new 6, 9, 21,
    167
Patriot locomotive 172, 173
Peascliffe–to–Belton Park
    military railway 51
Péchot, Captain Prosper 84–5,
    86
Pembrey (Carmarthenshire)
    19
Péronne–Marcoing railway 87
Pershing, General John J 73
Perth 68, 69, 71, 72, 145, 146
Peterborough (Cambs) 72, 135
Peterborough, Frank Wood,
    Bishop of 185

Peterson, Mr 146
Peto, Samuel Moreton **1**
Pick, Frank 100
pipelines 154, 158, 167
pit-props 69, 146
Plymouth (Devon) 9, 11, 74,
    111, 112, 115, 125–6,
    129, 158
Plymouth, Ivor Windsor-Cline,
    2nd Earl 176
Pole, Felix 29, 176
policewomen 33
Pontypool Road station
    (Monmouthshire) 66
Portland (Dorset) 95, 155
Portmadoc (Gwynedd) 9
ports, military 82–3, **83**
ports, railway 62–3, 67, 69,
    143; see also Southampton
    (Hants)
Portsmouth (Hants) 94, 99,
    103, 152
postal service 38–9, 147
Potter, Frank 7, 15, 29, 36
Poultry Demonstration Train 60
Poundbury (Dorset) 72
Powell, Cyril 159
Pownall, Lt Gen Sir Henry 112
Princess Mary locomotive 8
Princess Maud, TSS 111
prisoners of war
    British 39, 47, 63–4, 138,
        159, 162
    enemy 49, 69, 72–3, 80,
        145–6, 155–6, **156**
Private E. Sykes V.C.
    locomotive 172
Private W. Wood V.C.
    locomotive 172
Prussia 2–3
Purfleet (Essex) 155

Q

Quaker's Yard, Merthyr Tydfil
    (Glamorgan) 66
quality of service, decline in 13,
    40, 134–5
Quartermaine, Allan S 94
Queen, The, SS 64
Queensferry (Flintshire) 19,
    21, 72
Quintinshill disaster (Gretna
    Green) 11

R

rail-mounted guns **81**, 142,
    142, **143**
rails, requisitioning of 42
Railway Advisory Committee
    76

Railway Clearing House (RCH)
    8, 40, 43, 100, 133
Railway Conciliation Board 12
Railway Conciliation Scheme
    55
Railway Construction Corps
    50, 90
Railway Executive Committee
    (REC)
    First World War
        ambulance trains 47
        BEF, mobilising 12, 13
        control of railways 7
        demobilisation 75
        demurrage 42–3
        enlistment/conscription
            of railwaymen 25,
            26, 27, 29
        formation 6
        lights, extinguishing of
            60
        maintenance and
            repairs 44
        managers 7
        meetings 8
        protecting railways
            14–15, 16
        railway docks and
            vessels 63
        railway land, use of 59
        routes and timetables
            16
        service reductions
            39–40, 41, 42
        serving the fleet 70
        wages 55–6
        women, employment of
            31
        working hours 36–7,
            58
        works and equipment
            52
    Second World War
        armed trains 126–7
        Casualty Evacuation
            Trains (CETs) 119–
            20
        formation 99
        location 100
        managers 100
        objectives 100
        railway workshops 148
        staff shortages 137
        traffic pressures 133,
            136
Railway Heritage Trust (RHT)
    65, **170**, 171, **184**, 186
Railway Magazine 17, 34, 185
Railway Operating Corps 94
Railway Operating Division
    (ROD)
    founding 78
    locomotives returned to
        Britain 90
    Longmoor Depot 50

railwaymen on the front 90
railways in Europe 50, 78,
    80, 87
railways in Middle East 94
requisition of locomotives
    44, 82, 138
staff shortages 50
Railway Review, The 14, 15,
    32, 34, 42
Railway Transport
    Establishments 50, 90
Railway War Manufacturers'
    Sub-committee 52
Railwaymen's Convalescent
    Home, Herne Bay (Kent)
    73
Ramsgate (Kent) 60, 109, 129
Raven, Vincent 19
Ravenglass & Eskdale Railway
    115
Reading (Berks) **139**
Redbridge (Hants) 138
Redhill (Surrey) 20, 104, 109,
    110
Redman, Major A 29
redundancy worries 12
refreshments for passengers
    39, 40, 69, 71–2, **72**, 76,
    110, **111**, 134–5, 162–3
refugees 12–13, **13**, 28, 64,
    65, 70–1
Regulation of the Forces Act
    (1871) 5, 6, 7
Reith, Sir John 101
Remembrance locomotive
    173
reserved occupations 28–9, 38,
    166
Reservists 5–6, 12, 14–15, 25,
    136
resilience of railways 130–1
Rhayader (Powys) 9
Rhondda Valley (Glamorgan)
    66
Rhyl (Flintshire) 11, **13**, 75,
    163
Richborough (Kent) 82, **83**,
    111
Ricketts, Mrs 129
Riddles, Robert 150
Ridge Quarry, Corsham (Wilts)
    20
Ripon (Yorks) 51, 75
River War, The (Churchill) 3
Riviera, HMS 64
Roberts, Frederick, 1st Earl
    170
rolls of honour 170–1, **170**,
    171, 185
Romney, Hythe & Dymchurch
    Railway 115
Romsey (Hants) 22, 23
Roosevelt, Franklin D 145
Ross and Cromarty 69, 146
Rosyth (Fife) 68, 69, **103**

roundhouses 49
Royal Armoured Corps (RAC)
    113–14
Royal Army Medical Corps 45,
    46
Royal Arsenal Railway 49; see
    also Woolwich (London)
Royal Engineer Railway reserve
    5
Royal Engineers (RE)
    2nd Cheshire Engineers
        (Railway) Volunteers 5
    First World War 77, 80, 82,
        84, 93, 94, 95, 96–7
    founding 4
    Second World War 113,
        165, 166–7, **167**, **168**
    see also Railway Operating
        Division (ROD)
royal family 136
Royal Oak, HMS 144, 145
Royle, T W 100
Runciman, Walter 36, 41, 43,
    52, 57
Runcorn (Cheshire) 21, **103**
Runge, Mrs J J, OBE 71
Russell, Alfred Pope 49
Russia 2, 6, 36, 70–1, 123,
    133, 166

S

St Andrew, TrSS 64
Saint Boswells (Scottish
    Borders) 22, 75
St Budeaux (Devon) 126, 158
St David, TrSS 64, 169
St Etienne-du-Rouvray
    (France) 80
St Helier, TSS 111
St Malo (France) 111, 168
St Omer (France) **44**, 95
St Pancras station (London)
    62, 120, **121**
St Patrick, TrSS 64, 141, 169
St Paul's commemoration
    service 173, 185
St Petersburg, SS 8
St Valery-en-Caux (France)
    111
Salisbury Plain 10, 11, 92, 109
Salisbury Plain–Southampton
    line 14
Saxmundham (Suffolk) 114,
    114
Scapa Flow (Orkneys) 43, 64,
    66, 69, 144–5
Scarborough (Yorks) 60, 115
Schleger, Hans **108**
Schlieffen, Alfred Graf von 3
scientists, evacuation of 112
Scotia, TSS 169
Scott, James Robb 175
Seaford (Sussex) 23, 74

Second Schleswig War 2
Second World War
  in Britain
    acts of courage 128–9
    air-raid precautions
      (ARP) 101, **109**,
      117–20
    allied troops 156–7
    ambulance trains 102
    BEF, mobilising 99
    blackout adaptations
      106–9, **107**, **108**
    bombing and damage
      118, **119**, 120–8,
      121, **122**, **123**, **124**,
      128, 159–62, **160**
    D-Day 157–9
    after the end of war
      162–4, **163**
    evacuations from cities
      101, 103–4, **103**,
      104, **105**
    evacuations from
      continent 109–12,
      110, **111**
    factories and airfields,
      building/supplying
      150–4, **151**, **152**, **153**
    food supplies 104, 106,
      106
    fuel rationing 99
    gas-attack precautions
      102
    home defence 112–16,
      113, **114**, **116**
    military railways 154–5
    motor vehicle bans 99
    movement of troops
      131–3
    post-war recovery 162–4
    prisoners of war 155–6,
      156
    rail-mounted guns 142,
      142, **143**
    railway equipment,
      requisitioning of 138
    railwaymen POWs 138
    REC see Railway
      Executive Committee
      (REC), Second World
      War
    requirements and
      problems 100–1
    resilience of railways
      130–1
    service reductions 101
    special trains 141–2
    staff shortages 136–8
    state control 99
    Stores Shipment
      Programme 132–3
    sustaining war effort
      142–7
    traffic pressures 133–6,
      136

wages 138
women, employment of
  138, **139**, **140**, 141
workshops 147–50
memorial locomotives 173
memorials 176, 179, 182
overseas
  cross-Channel train
    ferry service **165**
  after D-Day 168
  Egypt 167
  gauge changes at
    borders 2
  German invasion of
    Russia 2
  India 167–8
  Iran 166–7, **167**, **168**,
    169
  Iraq 167
  locomotives
    requisitioned 166
  new tracks 167
  railway battalions
    165–6
  railway vessels 168–9
  railway workshops
    across empire 169
  roles of railways 165
Secretary Railway Companies
  15–16
Selborne, William Palmer, 2nd
  Earl 27
Select Committee on Transport
  7–8, 71
service reductions 13, 29,
  39–42, 79, 101, 134–5,
  136
Shawford (Hants) 41
Sheerness (Kent) 109
Sheffield (Yorks) 30, 31, 36,
  75, **103**, 173, 176–8,
  178
shell crisis (1915) 18, 77
Shelmerdine, Henry 174
shelters for railway staff 108,
  117
Shepherdswell (Kent) 142
ships see vessels, railway
Shirehampton (Bristol) 22, 23
Shoeburyness (Essex) 114,
  120, 159
Shrewsbury & Hereford Joint
  Railway 66, 182
Shropshire & Montgomeryshire
  Railway 155
sidings, new 21, 42, 66, 69, 94,
  146, 152, 158, 167
signal-box work 33, **33**, 141
signal boxes **33**, **61**, 66, 106,
  108, **109**, 118, 120, 125–
  6, 154
Sikh Pioneers 96, 97
Simpson, William **1**
Sinai Military Railway
  (Palestine) 96–7

Sir Ralph Wedgwood
  locomotive 128
Slieve Bloom, TSS 64
Smith, F G 70
Smith, G Murray 58
Soham (Cambs) 20, 153–4
Somerset & Dorset Joint
  Railway 179
Somme, Battle of the 29, 47–8,
  79, 92–3, 95, 170
South Africa 3, **4**, 5, 50, 53,
  170
South Eastern & Chatham
  Railway (SECR)
  air-raid precautions (ARP)
    60–1
  ambulance trains 45, 46, 47
  Bassin Loubet operation 78
  docks and vessels **63**, 64, 82
  Fryatt's coffin 65
  memorials 176, **177**
  refugees 12
  serving the fleet 70
  staff shortages 36
Southampton (Hants)
  Boer War 3, 5
  First World War 9–10,
    10–11, 17, 23, 47–8, 62,
    67, 75, **83**
  Second World War 99, **103**,
    117, 149, 155, 158, 159,
    164
Southern Railway (SR)
  air-raid precautions (ARP)
    117, 118–19
  allied troops 157
  ambulance trains 102
  barrage balloon cables 162
  bombing and damage 116,
    120, 123–4, 125–6, 127,
    128, 129, 159–60, 161,
    162
  D-Day 158
  evacuations from cities **104**
  evacuations from continent
    109, 111
  flying bombs 159–60, 161,
    162
  food supplies 104, 106
  memorials 173, 176
  military railways 154
  protecting railways 112
  resilience 131
  service reductions 101
  traffic pressures 136
  vessels **165**, 169
  war damage claim 164
  women, employment of
    141
  works and equipment
    148–9
Southwell and Nottingham,
  Edwyn Hoskyns, Bishop
  of 179
Southwold Railway 57

Southwold (Suffolk) 61
Spanish Civil War 103
Special Railway Reserve 6
Special Railway Volunteer
  Companies of the
  Volunteer Force 16
special trains
  First World War
    ambassadors 8
    coal 14, 41, 44, 66–8,
      67, 70, 80
    demobilisation 75–6
    guns and tanks 20–1
    horses 22–3, **22**
    leave trains 41
    Mobile Advanced
      Headquarters Train
      53
    munitions and
      munitions workers
      17–20
    Naval specials 68–9
    nurses 11
    Poultry Demonstration
      Train 60
    POWs 73
    refugees 12–13, **13**
    supplying the front 17
    troops 9–13, **9**, 74, **74**
  Second World War
    airfield personnel 153
    Casualty Evacuation
      Trains (CETs)
      118–19
    coal 110, 142, 144
    D-Day 145, 158
    evacuations from cities
      101, 103–4, **103**,
      104, **105**, 129, 162
    evacuations from
      continent 109–12,
      110, **111**
    food supplies 159
    Highland trains 145
    hydrogen gas 143
    key individuals 141–2,
      145
    leave trains 145, 159
    munitions and
      munitions workers
      150–1, **151**, 153
    Nuremberg witnesses
      156
    prisoners of war 145–6,
      155, **156**
    supplying the front
      158–9
    troops 99, 131–3, 156–
      7, 158
spies 13, 15, 66, 109
Spitfire funds 129
Spon Lane (Staffs) 21
staff shortages 23, **24**, 25–30,
  36–7, 38, 136–8
Stamer, Arthur C 19

Stamfordham, Arthur Bigge,
  Baron 65
Stamp, Sir Josiah 123, 134
Stanley, Sir Albert 37, 58
state control of railways 4–5,
  7, 99
Steel, J 129
Steenwerck (Flanders) 90–1, 95
Stirling **24**, 114
Stobs (Borders) 72–3
Stocks, George 29
Stockton (Co Durham) 16
Stockton, USS 64
Stoke-on-Trent (Staffs) 175
Stone, Eugenia 30–1
Stores Shipment Programme
  132–3
Stourton, John 147
strafing 126–8, **128**
Stratford-upon-Avon &
  Midland Junction Railway
  (SMJR) 171, **171**
Stratford works (London) 60,
  113
Strathpeffer (Highland) 48, 73,
  145
Strawberry Hill depot (London)
  185
Strevett, Miss 30
strike action 36–7, 55, 56, 58,
  59, 134
Sudan Military Railway 3, 96
Suez Canal 94, 96
Suffolk, Charles Howard, 20th
  Earl 112
Sunday Express 130
Sunderland (Tyne and Wear) 33
supplying fronts 17–23, **17**,
  18, **22**, 132–3, 158–9
Surrey Commercial Docks
  (London) 75
Sutton Veny (Wilts) 51
Swan, Hunter & Wigham
  Richardson **165**
Swansea 26, 120
Swaythling (Hants) 11, 22, 23
Swindon (Wilts)
  First World War 29, 45–6,
    50, 53–4, 56, 58
  memorials 180, 184
  Second World War 95–6,
    102, 138, 148, 166
Sykes, Private Ernest, VC 172,
  179
Szlumper, Gilbert 100

T

Taff Vale Railway **170**
Tain (Highland) 145
Tait, Thomas S 180
Tanfield (Yorks) 144
tanks (military) 20–1, 83, 113,
  143, 148

Tara, HMS 64–5
Tate Gallery 163, **163**
Tatlow, F 29
Teesside evacuations **103**
Temple Mills yard (London)
  128
temporary employees 26, 28
Territorial Army 6, 9, 12, 25,
  50, 72–3, 99, 136
Thames Ditton Foundry 180
Thames estuary ports 67
theft of goods 23, 147
Thomas, Bert **136**
Thomas, J H 36, 37, 58
Thornhill (Yorks) 23
Thornton, Henry Worth 38
Thorp Arch (Yorks) 151
Thurso (Caithness) 68, 69,
  145, 155
Tidworth (Wilts) 11, 41, 50
Tilbury (Essex) 75, 155, 159
timber, supply and transport of
  69, 73, 146
Times, The 13, 48
timetables 6, 75, 101, 157
Tonbridge (Kent) 16, 110
tracks, new
  First World War 21, 79,
    80–1, 82, 90–1, 93
  Second World War 117,
    130, 143, 146, 154, 158,
    167
traffic pressures 20–1, 39–41,
  42, 133–6, **136**
train ferries 82–3, **83**, 111,
  165, **165**
Train Ferry No 1 82–3
Train Ferry No 2 82–3, 111
Train Ferry No 3 82–3, 111
tramway workers 34
Trans-Iranian Railway 166–7,
  167, **168**, **169**
Trelewis Halt (Glamorgan) 30
Troedyrhiw Halt (Glamorgan)
  30
troop trains 9–13, **9**, 74, **74**,
  99, 131–3, 158
Tunbridge Wells (Kent) 104
Tunna, Norman 129
tunnels
  accidents in 20
  aircraft train-busting shoots
    155
  bomb damage 120, 123
  protecting 14, **14**, **116**, 142
  sanctuaries 128, 136
  stabling use 158
Turkey 166
Turnberry Hotel (Ayrshire) 73
Turnbull, Sir Robert 7, 79
Turnchapel (Devon) 126
Twickenham Ferry **165**
Twining, Brig Gen Philip 84
Tyne Dock (South Shields) 129
Tynside evacuations **103**

U

Uganda Railway 98
uniforms 42
United States
  Civil War 2, **2**
  First World War 27–8, 49,
    70, 73–4, **74**, 80, 85–6, **85**
  Second World War 141,
    147, **153**, 156–7, 158–9,
    162, 167, 168, **168**
Unknown Warrior, The
  locomotive 172
Upchurch (Kent) 161
Usambara Railway (East
  Africa) 98

V

Vale of Rheidol Railway
  (Ceredigion) 9
Valour locomotive 173, 177
van Halban, Hans 112
Vauxhall station (London) 125
vessels, railway 63–5, **63**, 111,
  143, 168–9
Vickers Shipbuilding &
  Engineering 20
Victoria, Princess 185
Victoria station (London) 161,
  176
Voi Lake Railway (East Africa)
  98
volunteer paid labour 60,
  137–8
volunteers in armed forces 4–5
volunteers, non-military 59,
  71–2, **72**
Vulcan Foundry 53, 150, 166

W

Wadebridge (Cornwall) 115
wages
  First World War 32, 37, 42,
    53, 55–9, 90, 91
  Second World War 138
wagons
  First World War
    in Britain 20, 21, 41,
      42–3, 54, 67, 68, 69
    overseas 44, 45, 52, 79,
      80, 82
  Second World War
    in Britain 107, 108,
      113, 133, 143–4,
      146, 150, 153, 154
    overseas 148–9, 166–7
Walker, Sir Herbert Ashcombe
  6, **6**, 7, 21–2, 27, 30, 36,
  71
Wallace, Capt. Euan 101
Walsden (Yorks) 141

Walton (Suffolk) 104
War Bonus 55–6, 57, 58
War Committee 41, 43
War Department (WD) *see*
  War Office
War Office
  Boer War 3
  pre-First World War 1
  First World War
    ambulance trains 45,
      47, 49
    Bassin Loubet operation
      78
    civilian help unwanted
      77
    demobilisation 75
    enlistment/conscription
      of railwaymen 25,
      26, 29, 36, 50
    faith in railway
      companies 13
    lorries 84
    military railways 50, 51
    protecting railways 12,
      14, 16
    Railway Corps 6
    railwaymen on the front
      90, 94
    state control on railways
      7
    timetables 6
    wagon misuse 43
    works and equipment
      52
  Second World War
    ambulance trains 119
    armoured trains 112,
      114
    BEF, mobilisation of 99
    Casualty Evacuation
      Trains (CETs) 119,
      120
    Dunkirk evacuation 109
    locomotives
      requisitioned for
      overseas service 138,
      150, **153**
    military railways 154,
      155
    supplying the front 159
    works and equipment
      147–8, 150
War Priorities Committee 54–5
War Railway Council 5–6
Warcop (Cumbria) 152
Ward, Lt Col V M Barrington
  87
Wareham (Dorset) 18
warehouses 63
Warrington (Lancs) 21
Waterloo station (London) 41,
  61, 71, 120, 125, 175–6
Watt, Henry 36
Watten (Caithness) 145
Waverley, PS 111

Waverley station (Edinburgh) 71, 117, 180
Wearside evacuations **103**
weather problems 146–7
Wedgwood, Sir Ralph 100, 182
Wellington, Arthur Wellesley, 1st Duke 1
West Grinstead (Sussex) 127
Westminster, Hugh Grosvenor, 2nd Duke 65
Westonhoek (Belgium) **88**
Weybourne (Norfolk) 113, 152
Weymouth (Dorset) 95, 109
Whippingham, PS 111
Whitby (Yorks) 60
White, Colonel W A 29
Whitelaw, William 70
Wick (Caithness) 120, 131, 145
Widnes (Cheshire) 21, **103**
Wilkinson, Norman **167**
Willesden Junction (London) 30
Williams, J E 32, 57
Willoughby (Lincs) 16
Wilson, Field Marshall Sir Henry 176
Wilson, Woodrow 73
Windermere (Cumbria) 155, 156

Windsor Castle 112
Wisdom, Violet 141
Wolverhampton (West Midlands) 58
Wolverton (Bucks) 34, 45, 53, 102, 148
women
  First World War
    munitions factory workers 18, **18**, 52–3, 55
    planting vegetables 60
    prisoners of war 63–4, 65
    railway workers **28**, 29, 30–7, **31**, **33**, **35**, 56, 60
    refreshments volunteers 71–2, **72**
    tramway workers 34, 36
    War Bonus 56
  Second World War
    railway workers 117, 138, **139**, **140**, 141, 148, 149, 161
    refreshments volunteers 110, 145
  St Paul's commemoration service 185
Wood, Private W V 72, 172, 173

Wood, Sir William 100
Woodbridge (Suffolk) 104
Woodford Halse (Northants) 67, 130
Woodhouse, J 87
Wool (Dorset) 21, 129
Woolmer Instructional Military Railway 6, 50
Woolmer locomotive **51**
Woolwich (London) **3**, 19, 22, 42, 49, **152**
Worcester 131, 147, 157
working hours
  First World War 25–6, 36–8, 58, 71, 86
  Second World War 110, 133–4, 137, 148–9
workshops, railway
  First World War
    ambulance trains 45–7, **45**
    munitions production **17**, 18, 19, 53
    staff shortages 27–8, 29
    war equipment production 20–1, 52–5, **84**
    women, employment of **28**
    working hours 26

Second World War
  ambulance trains 102
  armoured trains 113, 115
  empire workshops 169
  war equipment production 147–50, 166
  women, employment of **140**, 141
Wortley, Charles Stuart-Wortley, Baron 176
wounded staff, return of 57–8, **171**
Wragge (George) Ltd 174

Y

York 71–2, 102, **107**, 128, 134, 148, 180, 182
York, Cosmo Gordon Lang, Archbishop of 182
Yorkshire Evening Press 71
Young, Mrs Millie **139**

Z

Zeppelin raids 60–1